Sailing ships

SAILING SHIPS

Prints by the Dutch Masters from the Sixteenth to the Nineteenth Century

Edited by IRENE DE GROOT and ROBERT VORSTMAN

Published in cooperation with the printroom of the Rijksmuseum, Amsterdam

A STUDIO BOOK   THE VIKING PRESS   NEW YORK

Translated from the Dutch by Michael Hoyle
Jacket designed by The Viking Press
Designed by Alje Olthof
Lithography by Litho de Lang en Co., Zwanenburg, The Netherlands
Printed by Drukkerij Nauta, Zutphen, The Netherlands
Bound by Wöhrmann Boekbinders, Zutphen, The Netherlands

First published in 1980 by Gary Schwartz, Maarssen, The Netherlands, and The Viking Press,
625 Madison Avenue, New York, N.Y. 10022

Published simultaneously in Canada by Penguin Books Canada Limited

Library of Congress Cataloging in Publication Data

Groot, I. M. de.
   Sailing ships.
   (A Studio book)
   Bibliography: p.
   Includes index.
   1. Sailing ships in art. 2. Prints, Dutch.
I. Vorstman, Robert, joint author.   II. Title.
NE957.3.N4G76   769'.437'09492   80-5362

ISBN 0-670-61527-7

Printed in The Netherlands

Contents

INTRODUCTIONS

The prints *by* Irene de Groot *p.* 7

The ships *by* Robert Vorstman 17

ILLUSTRATIONS

Frans Huys *after* Pieter Bruegel: *nrs.* 1-5

Pieter van der Borcht IV [?]: 6

Hendrick Goltzius [?] *after* Cornelis Claesz. van Wieringen [?]: 7-8

Hans Collaert *after* Johannes Stradanus: 9

Theodoor Galle *after* Johannes Stradanus: 10

Robert de Baudous *after his own design and designs of* Hendrik Vroom *and* Cornelis Claesz. van Wieringen: 11-16

Simon Frisius: 17

Cornelis Liefrinck II: 18

Pieter Bast: 19

Pieter Serwouter *after* Pieter Sibrantsz: 21

Claes Jansz. Visscher *after his own design and designs of* Jan Porcellis: 20, 22-24, 30-35

Claes Jansz. Visscher [?] *after* Jan Porcellis: 25-29

Anonymous [ca. 1600]: 36-40

Anonymous *after* Cornelis Claesz. van Wieringen: 41-44

Hercules Segers: 45

Jan van de Velde *after his own design and designs of* Cornelis Claesz. van Wieringen: 46-51

Anonymous [ca. 1640]: 52-56

Crispijn de Passe II: 57

Monogrammist AB: 58-59

Matthijs van Plattenberg: 60-61

Willem Basse: 62

Rembrandt: 63

Bonaventura Peeters: 64-68

Dirck de Bray [?]: 69-70

Reinier Nooms: 71-94

Michiel Mousijn *after* Jan Lievens *and* Herman van Aldewerelt *and* Reinier Nooms: 95

Monogrammist ABk: 96-97

Joost van Geel: 98-101

Abraham Casembrot: 102-106

Cornelis Bol IV: 107-109

Ludolf Backhuizen: 110-115

Richard Adam: 116-118

Jan Luyken: 119-120

Jan van Almeloveen *after* Herman Saftleven: 121-132

Johan van den Aveele: 133-134

Caspar Luyken: 135

Pieter Bout: 136

Isaak van de Vinne: 137

Sieuwert van der Meulen: 138-153

Adam Silo: 154-156

Adolf van der Laan *after* Sieuwert van der Meulen: 157-163

Jan Caspar Philips: 164

Simon Fokke *after* L. Loosjes: 165

Simon Fokke: 166

Isaac Lodewijk la Fargue van Nieuwland: 167

Paulus Constantijn la Fargue: 168

Carel Frederik Bendorp: 169-173

Noach van der Meer: 174

Noach van der Meer *after* Hendrik Kobell: 175

Jan Punt *after* Hendrik Kobell: 176

Hermanus Schoute[n]: 177

Matthias de Sallieth *after* Hendrik Kobell: 178-180

Matthias de Sallieth *after* Dirk de Jong: 181-182

Dirk de Jong: 183

Hendrik Kobell: 184-190

Gerrit Groenewegen: 191-213

Jan Kobell: 214-215

Johannes Christiaan Schotel: 216

Andreas Schelfhout: 217-218

Pieter le Comte: 219-229

Antonie Waldorp: 230-231

Petrus Johannes Schotel: 232

Petrus Paulus Schiedges: 233-234

Frans Arnold Breuhaus de Groot: 235-236

Johan Conrad Greive: 237-243

Johan Barthold Jongkind: 244-250

SUPPLEMENT

Biographies *p.* 272

Literature 277

Glossary 279

Index 281

Unless otherwise stated, all the prints reproduced in this book are from the printroom of the Rijksmuseum, Amsterdam. The 220 numbered prints for which no dimensions are given are reproduced in true size. All the 250 illustrations forming the body of the book have been reproduced directly from the original prints. The illustrations in the introductions and the supplementary illustrations in the body of the work have been reproduced from photographs. Illustrations 18–31 of the introduction were photographed by Thijs Quispel of Amsterdam. The other photographs were made by the photographic departments of the various owners.

As far as possible, the prints have been ordered chronologically by the date of birth of the artists. Biographies of the artists and publishers of the prints will be found on pp. 272–76.

The publisher and authors are indebted to the staff of the printroom of the Rijksmuseum and to its Director, Dr. J. W. Niemeijer, for their unstinting help in the preparation of this book.

Almost all the information on flags was provided by the Foundation for Banneristics and Heraldry, Muiderberg.

The translations of Latin inscriptions are based on the translations into Dutch by S. Bremer.

ILL. I

The prints *by Irene de Groot*

INTRODUCTION The prints chosen for this book cover approximately the period from 1560 to 1870. The earliest examples are the series of ship prints engraved by Frans Huys after designs by Pieter Bruegel the Elder. At the other end of the scale we find ourselves in the second half of the nineteenth century, when mechanization was beginning to sweep all before it. Sail was giving way to steam in the navies and merchant fleets of the world, and new modes of transport, such as the train, were gradually taking over inland freight carriage from the sailing ship. The print, too, was being elbowed aside by photographic reproduction and new printing processes. This book does not cover the development of the sailing ship after ca. 1870, when it was often used solely as a pleasure craft.

The first prints in the book were published in the southern Netherlands – present-day Belgium. In Antwerp, the leading art center in the second half of the sixteenth century, printmaking was leading a flourishing existence. Initially artists had made their own prints, but before long printers and publishers were offering the advantages of larger editions and wider distribution, often throughout the whole of Europe. Prominent publishing houses included the 'Aux quatre Vents' of Hieronymus Cock (whose output included the prints after Bruegel, nrs. 1-5), and those of Christopher Plantin, the Wierix brothers, and Philips Galle (see nrs. 9 and 10).

The Spanish suppression of the revolt in the southern Netherlands towards the end of the sixteenth century disrupted this flourishing artistic activity. In 1585 Antwerp fell to the Spanish forces under the Duke of Parma. The subsequent religious persecution and the decline in trade brought about by the Dutch blockade of the River Scheldt forced many to flee the south. Among them were numerous artists, who made their new home in the northern Netherlands, bringing with them an artistic impetus that raised painting, drawing and printmaking to unprecedented heights in towns like Amsterdam and Haarlem. In a part of the world where water played such a vital role in everyday life it is hardly surprising that ships were such a popular subject for artists. The Dutch depended on the sea for their overseas trade and for defense in time of war, and on their rivers and waterways for the inland movement of goods and passengers.

The sailing ship appears in prints by the leading Dutch graphic artists from the beginning of the sixteenth century, although at that stage it had not yet become a theme in its own right. One of these early prints is *The ship of St. Stony-broke (St. Reynuut)*, an allegorical scene of about 1520 which for a long time was attributed to Lucas van Leyden (ill. 1). The numerous ships in the port and on the stocks in Cornelis Anthonisz.'s *Bird's-eye view of Amsterdam* (1544, ill. 2) testify to the importance of shipping and shipbuilding in the life of Amsterdam. The ships in the large seventeenth-century prospect of Amsterdam by Claes Jansz. Visscher (nr. 20) serve a similar function, symbolizing the thriv-

ILL. 2

Ill. 1 Anonymous, The ship of St. Stony-broke (St. Reynuut), ca. 1520. Woodcut, 74 x 116 cm.

Ill. 2 Cornelis Anthonisz., Bird's-eye view of Amsterdam, 1544. Woodcut, 107.5 x 109 cm.

ILL. 3

ing mercantile life of the city. Visscher, graphic artist and publisher, was active in a period when artists were becoming increasingly aware of their surroundings. No longer did they set out to create fanciful and allusive compositions, but to depict the world around them as freshly and naturally as possible using only a handful of elements. It was therefore only to be expected that a group of artists should abandon engraving in favor of the swifter and more sensitive technique of etching. Apart from Visscher, this is illustrated in the prints of Simon Frisius (nr. 17), Cornelis Claesz. van Wieringen (nrs. 41-44) and Jan van de Velde (nrs. 46-51). Around 1630 there was a transition from a linear to a more painterly style, and this set the stage for the greatest flowering of the Dutch print, the period 1645-65, when Rembrandt ruled supreme. The sailing ship, however, failed to excite Rembrandt's interest. The great master of the ship print at this time was Reinier Nooms, who called himself 'Zeeman' (Seaman), significantly enough, and who specialized in seascapes, ship types and topography. He made only a few prints of naval battles, despite the abundant opportunities presented by the Anglo-Dutch wars of the second half of the seventeenth century. It is extraordinary how few prints there are of sea battles from this period. The great masters in this field, the two Willem van de Veldes, were draftsmen and painters only. The quality of the battle prints we found was too poor to warrant their inclusion in this book. Moreover, the scenes are often so stereotype that they could be used, with only minor alterations, for any of a number of engagements.

Towards the end of the seventeenth century the economic and artistic vitality of the Dutch Republic began to decline. It is true that the old traditions were carried on, but the truly creative impulse and the desire to break new ground were lacking. However, the eighteenth century did produce a large number of interesting documentary print series, among them the *Navigiorum aedificatio* of Sieuwert van der Meulen (nrs. 138-153), and *The great fishery* of Adolf van der Laan (nrs. 161-163). The publication of topographical works also came into its own, perhaps the best-known example being the *Atlas* of Pierre Fouquet (see nrs. 166, 177). Harbor scenes, townscapes with ships, etc. make up a large proportion of popular publications of this nature.

The most specialized artist in the field at the end of the eighteenth century was Gerrit Groenewegen, with his views of the port of Rotterdam and his series of eighty-four ship types, which was published in instalments. True to the traditions of the eighteenth century, he depicted his subjects accurately, but with little liveliness of touch.

The emphasis in the nineteenth century is on rather romantically-tinged marine and river views, the majority of which served as illustrations in albums and similar publications. At this time the print was regarded primarily as a means of illustration and reproduction, and the newly-invented technique of lithography was ideal for this purpose.

Towards the middle of the century the print regained its place as a work of art in its own right, but by then the era of the sailing ship was already drawing to a close. The etchings of Johan Barthold Jongkind, which anticipated Impressionism, the art of the new age, therefore mark a fitting end to the art of printmaking and to the age of sail.

Ill. 3   Monogrammist WA, 'Carrack,' ca. 1470. Engraving, ca. 20 x 16 cm (after a reproduction).

Ill. 4   Wenzel Hollar, Dutch flutes, 1647. Etching, 14.3 x 23.4 cm.

Ill. 5   David Kleyne, 'A gaff boat,' ca. 1700. Etching, colored, 20.5 x 14.7 cm.

Ill. 6   Anonymous, 'Navire Royale,' 1626. Etching, 36.8 x 52.8 cm.

Ill. 7   Johan Conrad Greive, 'Cutter De Sperwer,' ca. 1860. Colored lithograph, 36 x 52 cm.

Ill. 8   Frans Huys after Pieter Bruegel, Battle in the Strait of Messina, 1561. Engraving, 42.5 x 71.5 cm.

THE FUNCTION OF SHIP PRINTS A number of questions which might be prompted by a close study of the prints in this book are answered in the Introduction on 'The ships' (pp. 17-23), by Robert Vorstman, and in the commentaries on the individual prints. What they do not explain, though, is the purpose or function of the prints. The majority of them are straightforwardly 'documentary,' depicting a particular type of ship or providing a record of an historical event or geographical location. Some of the other prints are allegories. Although a print may appear at first sight to be nothing more than a pleasant prospect of a river or the sea, there is very often an allusion or hidden meaning which is not always immediately apparent.

The prints are arranged in approximate chronological order. The majority fall thematically into one of five categories: ship portraits, history prints, topographical prints, prints with an allegorical significance, and marine and river views. This classification is, of course, artificial, nor is it elaborate enough to really accommodate all prints of sailing ships. However, it does provide a framework for demonstrating the variety of functions served by ship prints, or prints with a ship in them. The few prints in this book which do not fall into one of the above categories are unique in their sort, and have been chosen because they fall outside the established pattern.

SHIP PORTRAITS This group comprises, first and foremost, prints portraying a particular ship type or a specific ship. Secondly, there are the scenes of shipbuilding and illustrations of the special use of ships, such as the ferry, peat boat, shrimper and herring buss.

Prints are ideal for this purpose. They are easily published in the form of series, complete with inscriptions or explanatory text, and they can even be included in books or pamphlets. Each century produced one or more well-known and representative series of ship portraits. It is noteworthy that the closer we come to the present day the more documentary the prints become. The scene itself becomes sketchier, and the explanatory text lengthier.

The ship portrait originated almost simultaneously in Italy and Flanders in the second half of the fifteenth century. The Flemish Monogrammist WA (active ca. 1465-85 in Bruges and at the court of Charles the Bold, Duke of Burgundy) produced a group of nine extremely fine and instructive engravings of ships, including a carrack and a *baardze* (ill. 3). These prints are extremely rare, and only a few museums have specimens (the printroom of the Rijksmuseum, unfortunately, has none). The same applies to the ship prints made around 1460-80 in Florence and Venice (ill. 4).

Pieter Bruegel, the designer of the first series of ship portraits in this book (nrs. 1-5), very probably knew and assimilated the early Flemish and Italian ship prints. Comparison with earlier and contemporary paintings, miniatures, etc. shows that the prints after Bruegel are, on the whole, very accurate renderings, with many interesting details concerning the sails and the shape of the ships. However, in many cases we do not know what type of ship is being portrayed, just as we often do not know the appearance of ship types which are mentioned in the

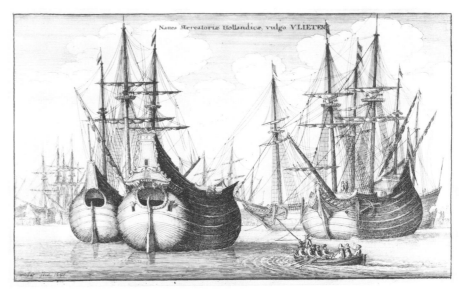

ILL. 4

ILL. 5

9

chronicles. The lack of inscriptions or captions on this series has therefore led to considerable confusion in identifying the ships (see nr. 4, for example). The anonymous engravings which have been associated with the Huys-Bruegel series also lack captions. There can be no doubt, though, that those anonymous prints were also intended as portraits of ship types, notwithstanding the fact that they are less accurately rendered.

The seventeenth-century series included in the book do have a text, and in many cases are our main source of information on seventeenth-century vessels.

The prints after Porcellis (nrs. 24-29), in addition to identifying the type, also give an indication of the vessels' cargo-carrying capacity, while the prints after Lons (nrs. 52-56) have an appropriate two-line verse. These series, published in 1627 and 1629 (?) respectively, concentrate on inland waterway vessels. The entire range of shipping, from foreign trade to ferry services, from East Indiamen to small horse-drawn barges, was depicted around the middle of the century by Reinier 'Zeeman' Nooms in several series. They constitute a high point of the genre, both artistically and historically. In a book published in 1970 on Zeeman's series entitled 'Verscheijde Schepen en Gesichten van Amstelredam' (Diverse ships and views of Amsterdam), it is pointed out that Nicolaas Witsen, the author of the first work on Dutch shipbuilding, took Zeeman's prints as the models for a number of his descriptions. In Witsen's Aeloude en hedendaegsche scheeps-bouw en bestier (Ancient and modern shipbuilding and ship management), published in 1671, two types which appear in the same print by Zeeman are often described one immediately after the other.

There was evidently a considerable demand for these series. Lons's prints, for example, were also published in a copied version. There were at least four editions of the series by Porcellis and Zeeman, the last in the eighteenth century, and the same is true of a series of etchings of Dutch ships made by a foreigner, Wenzel Hollar (1607-77, ill. 4).

After the series by David Kleyne (ill. 5) and Adolf van der Laan (nrs. 157-163) from the beginning of the eighteenth century, the genre was treated at its greatest length around 1800 in Gerrit Groenewegen's Verzameling van vier en tachtig stuks Hollandsche schepen (Collection of eighty-four Dutch ships; see nrs. 191-202). Groenewegen had trained as a ship's carpenter, so he was a particularly well-qualified interpreter. Many people have taken Groenewegen's etchings as their models because of their documentary fidelity, and even today they are constantly consulted by maritime historians.

The last prints in this category are those by le Comte and Greive. Pieter le Comte, a naval officer and amateur graphic artist, made lithographs of fifty ship types of his day, adding extensive commentaries on the types and their manoeuvres. In contrast, the more deliberately artistic Johan Conrad Greive depicted his ship types (mainly fishing boats and inland vessels) with a high degree of accuracy, but merely gave a bald identification of the type in his inscriptions.

Occasionally the portrait was of a specific vessel rather than a type, such as the ship built for the French in 1626 (ill. 6), or the Aemilia, the

flagship of Admiral Tromp at the Battle of the Downs in 1639. At a later period this type of portrait would be framed and hung in a ship-owner's office (ill. 7). These portraits were often very large, and this made it difficult to find a striking example suitable for reproduction in this book.

A brief word is in order about the prints depicting the building and use of sailing ships. A number of the prints show stages during the construction of a vessel, such as a launching, or maintenance and repair work. In some prints the artist set out to record the environment, with the ship playing a subordinate role (nr. 48). Others are decidedly instructive in their detailed depiction of a shipyard (nrs. 91, 120). Sieuwert van der Meulen is the only artist to have recorded, around 1700, the entire life of a ship, from the laying of the keel to the final journey to the breaker's yard (nrs. 138-153).

The operation of a particular type of ship is most strikingly illustrated in the numerous prints of herring fishing. An early illustration of this industry, which was so important to the Dutch, is found in an anonymous engraving published by Claes Jansz. Visscher (nr. 36). Adolf van der Laan devoted an entire series to the subject (nrs. 161-163), while de Sallieth made one large print (nr. 179). The two latter artists, incidentally, also depicted the more spectacular subject of whaling.

HISTORY PRINTS   As might be expected, the prints in this category deal with historical events. As far as sailing ships were concerned, this involved trading voyages and voyages of discovery, piracy, sea battles, shipwrecks and floods.

As early as the seventeenth century, but above all in the eighteenth, there were collectors who compiled what were known as historical and topographical atlases. The basic theme of these collections was generally topographical, but portraits and depictions of historical events were also included. The bulk of the history prints reproduced in this book come from the collection made in the nineteenth century by the bookseller and bibliographer, Frederik Muller (1817-81). He assembled a vast collection of prints, books and drawings devoted entirely to Dutch history, which is now in the printroom of the Rijksmuseum. When we came to select the prints for this book our preference was for the contemporary depiction of an historical event. There are, however, very few records made by eyewitnesses, as la Fargue maintained he was (nr. 168). In general, an artist depicting a history scene would give free rein to his imagination or adapt some earlier composition.

The first Dutch prints with a contemporary maritime subject date from the sixteenth century: Frans Huys's engraving of the Battle in the Strait of Messina after Pieter Bruegel, Frans Hogenberg's prints of the first period of the revolt of the Netherlands against Spanish rule, and the Defeat of the Spanish Armada in 1588 by an unknown artist (ill. 9).

The first history print in this book also dates from the Eighty Years' War, this being Cornelis Liefrinck's depiction of the voyage of the Leiden militia to the town of Grave in 1622 (nr. 18). The interpretation of some prints of an even earlier date is so debatable that it is doubtful whether they can be regarded as history prints at all. The works in

ILL. 6

ILL. 7

ILL. 8

question are a print of 1603 by Robert de Baudous, possibly depicting the departure of a fleet of ships on a voyage of discovery (nr. 11), and a print by Pieter Serwouter which may or may not be a record of the reception of the first Dutchmen to arrive at Bantam (nr. 21). Remarkably enough, this category contains no masterpieces from the middle of the seventeenth century, when Dutch art was in full flower. For example, no good prints were made of the important sea battles fought during the three Anglo-Dutch wars by such celebrated naval commanders as Maarten Harpertsz. Tromp, Michiel de Ruyter, and many others.

In the last quarter of the seventeenth century the activities of William III were the subject of numerous history prints. The majority of them are from the hand of Romeyn de Hooghe, who used his art to make propaganda for the House of Orange. One of his etchings is a crowded, ornate work depicting William's departure from England in 1688 to ascend the English throne (ill. 10). However grandiose in conception, van den Aveele's print of Mary, William's consort, setting sail in 1689 to join her husband appears simple and sober in comparison (ill. 11).

Our last seventeenth-century history print is, symbolically enough, of a mock battle on the River IJ held in honor of the visit of the Muscovite Legation and Tsar Peter the Great in 1697 (nr. 135). By this time the role of the Dutch as a sea power was virtually over. Only the Fourth Anglo-Dutch War of 1780-84 presented an opportunity for a few engagements at sea, and even then the only positive result was the modest success of the Battle of Dogger Bank (nrs. 169, 173).

As a result, the eighteenth-century history prints in this book are chiefly concerned with shipwrecks, floods, inexplicable explosions and even sheer incompetence (nrs. 170-173, among others). These prints often appeared as illustrations in pamphlets dealing with a recent event. The print was the ideal medium for scenes of this nature, since the techniques involved enabled the printmaker to keep pace with events. Moreover, the print had the not inconsiderable advantages of being easy to reproduce, relatively cheap and widely distributed, thus providing a means of communicating with and influencing the thinking of a large public. One particularly interesting example of a pamphlet illustration is the print by Jan Caspar Philips (nr. 164), which was used to depict a number of quite separate floods.

In the nineteenth century the Dutch developed a marked interest in their country's past, particularly the very distant past. We will end this survey of the contemporaneous history print with two lithographs by Pieter le Comte (nrs. 228, 229). They portray the heroic action of Lieutenant van Speyk, who blew up his ship (and himself with it) rather than let it fall into the hands of the enemy. This was one of the spectacular events which provided a source of inspiration for the romantic artists of the early nineteenth century.

TOPOGRAPHICAL PRINTS Topographical prints are, literally, prints depicting a geographical location. They could take the form of a map, a ground plan, a profile of a town, a view of a larger region, or of a particular spot in a town or village. This genre of print is well represented in the following pages, since views of harbors, roadsteads, landing

Classis Hispanica celeberrima quae anno celeberrimo MIDLXXXVIII inter Galliam Britanniamque venit & periit.

ILL. 9

Zeetocht van sijne Konincklijcke Hoogheyt WILLEM HENRICK de III: by de Gratie Gods Prince van Oranjen,
Erff-Stadthouder, Capiteyn en Admirael Generael des Vereenighden Staets, voor de Vryheyt en ware Godsdienst in Groot Brittangien:

ILL. 10

stages and the like are an important part of Dutch topography.

The first reliable topographical depictions in the Netherlands date from the early sixteenth century. It was in this period that people became aware of a distant, unknown and exciting world beyond the confines of their home town, and there was a great demand for maps, plans and other views to slake people's thirst for knowledge. Moreover, the expanding towns wanted plans which they could use when deciding on the provision of water supplies and the construction of roads, harbors, defense works, etc. One such view is the woodcut of 1544 by Cornelis Anthonisz., *The famous merchant city of Amsterdam, portrayed from life with all its waters* (ill. 2). However, since maps and plans tended to include ships only as an afterthought, none have been included in this book.

Shipping was depicted extensively and from a very early date in town profiles. The earliest Netherlandish town profile is the unique woodcut of 1515 with a view of Antwerp (Municipal Printroom, city of Antwerp), in which the massed shipping symbolizes the city's thriving commercial life, as was later the case in views of Amsterdam made around 1600. The atlases and travel books which appeared at the end of the sixteenth century were an important stimulus for the growth of topographical engraving. Albums with large numbers of attractive ground plans, such as Braun and Hogenberg's *Civitates orbis terrarum* (1572-1618, ill. 12), and Guicciardini's *Descrittione di tutti i Paesi Bassi*, published in Antwerp in 1581, made an important contribution to people's appreciation of the beauties of their own towns and country. Around 1600 Amsterdam moved to the forefront as the fastest growing and most prosperous of Dutch cities, and it was at this time that Pieter Bast made the first profiles of towns in the northern provinces, including two of Amsterdam (see nr. 19). Subsequent profiles which appeared in imitation of Bast were often very large indeed, with widths exceeding two meters on occasion. Many had an inscription in woodcut and a descriptive text in several languages, since they were also intended for export. The town profile is also found as just one element in a grander design, as was the case with Visscher's reworking of Bast's original (nr. 20). This type of composite work consisted of another map or ground plan (ill. 13), a description, and occasionally a number of smaller views associated with and amplifying the main motif (see, for example, the prints by Claes Jansz. Visscher, nrs. 30-35). There are some striking examples of this type of composite work later in the seventeenth century, such as the map of the River Maas and the Postal Map (nrs. 99-101) by Joost van Geel. Very few complete specimens of these composites have come down to us, for their large size and their use as wall maps made them particularly susceptible to wear and tear.

In addition to these documentary profiles and composite maps, there were a large number of topographical prints giving a more localized view of a town or region. A distinction must be drawn here between views within a town or village and prospects of them from outside. In both cases sailing ships were often included in the scene.

It was rare for a realistic view within a town to be published as an individual print in the seventeenth century. There were, however, series depicting 'real' buildings and views 'from life.' An early example of this is *The Overtoom near Amsterdam* by Simon Frisius (nr. 17). Various illustrated town descriptions were published in subsequent years, such as those by J. Orlers, *Beschrijvinge der stad Leyden* (Description of the town of Leiden; 1614), and S. Ampzing, *Beschrijvinge ende lof der stad Haerlem* (Description and glorification of the town of Haarlem; 1628). Around 1660 there was a flood of richly illustrated publications containing topographical views, chiefly of Amsterdam, and it was in this period that Zeeman made his topographical etchings of the city. They are eminently suitable for inclusion in the present work, for, with the exception of the series of city gates, they are mainly of canals and wharves. What is so remarkable about these fluently etched prints is that not only do they give a faithful depiction of the city, but they also reflect something of its bustle and liveliness.

Prints with a view of a place or building began to appear in large numbers from around 1600. Up until the middle of the century the artists generally placed the emphasis on nature, with the building serving merely as an element in the landscape. Well-known examples include the series by Esaias van de Velde. The topographical element is occasionally masked by an allegorical significance, as in the prints of castles and seasons by Hessel Gerrits (ill. 14). The views of villages along the River Lek (nrs. 121-132), which van Almeloveen etched after drawings by Saftleven some decades later, fall within this landscape category, for without the inscriptions there would be no way of identifying the locations.

There was another peak in the popularity of topographical prints around the middle of the eighteenth century. Public demand was met by a profusion of etchings, engravings and topographical volumes. They were the work of a relatively small group of specialist artists, such as Abraham Rademaker and Hendrik Spilman. These professional topographers concentrated almost exclusively on town and village views, and some of them soon lapsed into producing copies of their own work and that of others. Only a handful of the mass of prints produced in the second half of the eighteenth century have been selected for this book. They include Simon Fokke's '*View near the Old Yacht Basin*' (nr. 166) and H. P. Schouten's '*View of the Zeeregt building*' (nr. 177), both of which were executed for Pierre Fouquet's *Atlas*, the finest series of prints of Amsterdam ever published. Two prints by Matthias de Sallieth, views of Texel harbor and the River Maas at Rotterdam (nrs. 181-182), are from another important publication, the *Atlas van alle de zeehavens der Bataafsche Republiek* (Atlas of all the seaports of the Batavian Republic).

The close of the eighteenth century also saw the end of the publication of large albums of prints and illustrated descriptions of towns. The last major topographical works in this book date from around 1800, when Gerrit Groenewegen was producing his extremely accurate drawings and prints of Rotterdam and neighboring villages. Although recognizable locations do appear in the nineteenth-century scenes set in Spakenburg by Greive (nrs. 238-239), and in Jongkind's views of Honfleur (nrs. 248-250), these works demonstrate how nineteenth-century artists increasingly subordinated documentary significance to artistic expression.

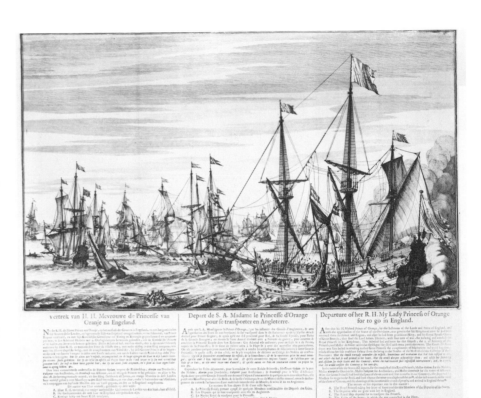

ILL. 11

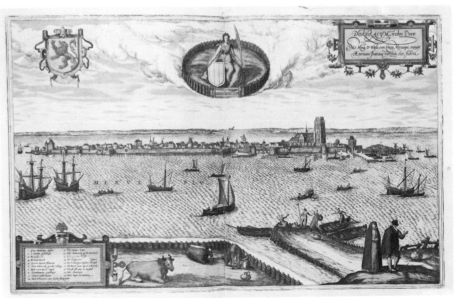

ILL. 12

Ill. 11 Johan van den Aveele, 'Departure of her R.H. My Lady Princess of Orange for to go in England,' 1689. Etching, engraving and letterpress, ca. 51 x 56 cm.

Ill. 12 Frans Hogenberg, Dordrecht. From Georg Braun and Frans Hogenberg, 'Civitates orbis terrarum,' 1572-1618. Etching, colored, 31 x 49.5 cm.

Ill. 9 Anonymous, Defeat of the Spanish Armada, 1588. Engraving, 38.3 x 51 cm.

Ill. 10 Romeyn de Hooghe, Departure of William III for England, 1688. Etching, 49 x 58 cm.

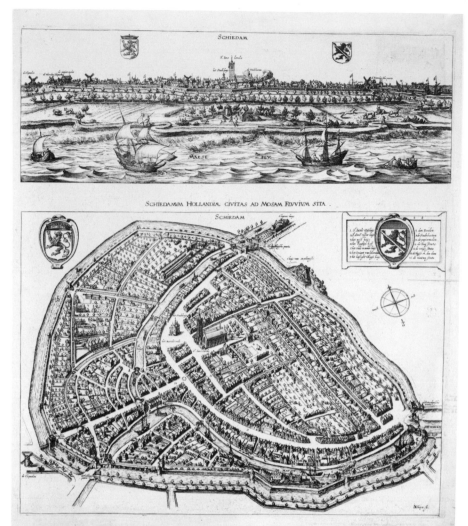

SCHIEDAMUM HOLLANDIÆ CIVITAS AD MOSAM FLVVIVM SITA.

Fervida ruricolas Aestas dum percoquit, arbor
Nobilibus gratas praebet opaca comas.

ÆSTAS

Venatu invigilant alii, citharam quatit alter:
Sunt quibus in lembo frondea facta casa est.

B.Bare inuent.
H.G. fe. et excu.
R.L.

PRINTS WITH AN ALLEGORICAL SIGNIFICANCE   By the middle ages the allegory had become a popular way of illustrating a wide range of concepts and thoughts in the guise of personifications. Well-known examples are the allegorical depictions of life and death, the stages of life, the elements, the seasons, peace, prosperity, freedom, fame, and so on. One would not tend to associate an allegorical significance with prints of sailing ships, and yet there are several examples which are worth considering. The majority date from the seventeenth century, when many of what we now regard as straightforward, realistic depictions of everyday events also contained a hidden, moral message for the people of the day.

Broadly speaking, there are two forms of allegorical scene related to a sailing ship. In the first it is the ship itself that bears the moral, and in the other it is the scene in which a sailing ship appears which illustrates an abstract concept or idea. In order not to make matters more complicated than they already are, this section will only consider prints whose meaning is explained in inscriptions or texts, not those with a hidden or equivocal significance.

One print depicting a specific concept is the early *Ship of St. Stony-broke* (ill. 1), by an anonymous artist. The verses on and beneath this woodcut of ca. 1520 call on topers and wastrels of every rank and station to board the ship 'named evil conduct' and sail to their patron, St. Stony-broke.

Even more unequivocal are scenes with the 'Ship of the Church,' the example included in this book being the print by Pieter van der Borcht (nr. 6). The church was being equated with a ship since the beginning of Christianity, the reasoning being that the church, like a ship, must be able to hold a steady course, and requires a resolute leader and a loyal crew. The comparison was extended to include the Cross as the ship's mast, with Christ or the pope as the helmsman, and deacons as the crew.

Similar comparisons were made in scenes of the Ship of State, which was another very popular allegorical image in the seventeenth century. It was used to depict the unity of the Dutch Republic after the Synod of Dordrecht in 1619, with the personification of the Seven Provinces, Prince Maurice, ecclesiastical figures and other allegorical and real personages sailing the seas together in the Ship of State (ill. 15).

There is far greater latitude for allegorical expression in the second group of prints, where it is not the ship that stands for a particular concept, but the scene in which a ship happens to be present. An early example of this is the series of four seasons which Robert de Baudous engraved after Claes van Wieringen (nrs. 13-16). In fact, this series is rather exceptional in that ships are also an important motif in both the summer and winter scenes. Ships were commonly included in prints of spring and autumn, since they gave the artist the opportunity of depicting the pleasures of boating and the hazards of violent storms.

The '*Aurora*' of Jan van de Velde (nr. 46), and the months of February and June by Dirk de Bray (nrs. 69, 70) belong to the same genre as the seasons. Zeeman, too, made a similar series of the four elements, in which fire, water and air are represented by marine views (ill. 16).

Towards the end of the eighteenth century Hendrik Kobell set out to depict less familiar concepts (nrs. 185-187). His small etchings have cryptic Latin texts, possibly written by the artist himself, explaining the underlying meaning of the scene. The admonitory tenor of those texts is in line with seventeenth-century moralizing scenes, in which the text is often more significant than the scene itself.

These allegorical prints drew their models from the emblemata published in the Netherlands, chiefly in the seventeenth century. These symbols, 'images of sayings' as Roemer Visscher called them, usually consist of a motto, an illustration and a commentary. The emblem can only be understood if these three elements are seen and read in conjunction. A fair number of emblemata derive their imagery from shipping. Love, for example, is compared to the sea, and the lover to the ship (ill. 17). In another print, entitled *Nothing ventured, nothing gained* (nr. 23), an association is made between the skipper of a fishing boat who, although he has returned with a disappointing catch, still has to re-equip his boat for the next voyage, and the person who must constantly seek his fortune without doubting that God will reward his steadfast faith.

Some scenes contain only the visual element of an emblem, with the result that the modern viewer, in particular, often misses the point.

PRINTS WITH MARINE AND RIVER VIEWS The prints in this last group, which make up one-quarter of the book, show ships in various situations, from riding peacefully at anchor in a roadstead to being tossed about in a storm. They are general works, and are not intended to portray a particular ship, roadstead or storm.

Marine and river views first appear as an independent theme in Dutch prints in the sixteenth century. It is noteworthy that they almost always contain a vessel, no matter how small or simple. The artists evidently used ships much as they did coastlines, or vegetation on river banks, namely as elements for ordering the space and creating a sense of depth. In doing so they were generally unconcerned about accuracy or detail. One of the few practitioners of this genre who was interested in ships was Cornelis Claesz. van Wieringen, who specialized in marine and river views around 1600. Van Wieringen took the trouble of ordering the various elements in his work into compositions which give every appearance of being realistic. However, one must beware of falling into the trap of regarding these views, which lack any text or clear topographical or historical background, merely as decorative illustrations, although that they certainly are. It has already been pointed out in the discussion on allegorical prints that sixteenth- and seventeenth-century prints, in particular, often embody a meaning, exhortation or warning. For example, it was a common device to liken the voyage of a ship to a person's journey through life. In both cases there are encounters with a variety of hazards and difficulties. According to Hendrik Poot, who lived in the eighteenth century but who drew mainly on earlier sources for his *Groot natuur, en zedekundigh werelttoneel of woordenboek* (Great nature, and ethical world stage and dictionary), one had to arm oneself against those hazards 'with virtue and a stout heart, …there being so many parallels with the encounters of a ship, which have to be detected

ILL. 15

ILL. 16

Ill. 13 Jacob de Gheyn, Schiedam, 1598. Engraving, 48 x 41.4 cm.

Ill. 14 Hessel Gerrits after David Vinckboons, 'Aestas' or Summer, with Loenersloot Castle, ca. 1610. Etching, 18.9 x 24.3 cm.

Ill. 15 Frans Schillemans after Jacob Oorloge and Adriaan van de Venne, The ship of state, 1620. Engraving, ca. 46.5 x 61 cm.

Ill. 16 Reinier Nooms, 'Le feu' or fire, ca. 1655. Etching, 8.5 x 21.6 cm.

Al zijt gy vert „ noyt uyt het hert.

DE ongebaende Zee vol spoekooze baren,
Doet tusschen hoop, en vrees mijn lievend herte varen;
De Liefd is als de Zee, den Minnaer als het Schip;
De weêr-liefd als een baek, de afkeer als een klip;
In dien het Schip vervalt, door afkeer komt te strande,
Zoo is de hoop te niet van veylig te belande;
Toon my in Liefdens Zee, uw weêr-liefd tot een Baek,
Op dat ik zoo, mijn Lief! in liefdens Have raek.

ILL. 17

by the cautious helmsman; so must one exercise all diligence in this life if one wishes to avoid shipwreck and the loss not only of one's temporal possessions but also of one's precious soul.' In the Dutch translation of Cesare Ripa's *Iconologia*, a guide to meanings in art, which was published by D.P. Pers in 1644, we find the following sentence accompanying 'Ill Fortune:' 'The ship is our mortal life, which every man endeavours to bring to a safe haven.'

There are also scenes with a more abstruse message, as in the case of the ship, the barrel and the whale depicted by the Monogrammist AB (nr. 58). This print, which at first sight appears to have no clear meaning, contains an emblem in the visual element. The scene only becomes comprehensible when one knows of other works containing the same element accompanied by an explanation. One then discovers that there is a dual meaning. In the first place one must not allow oneself to be distracted from one's goal by transitory pleasures, and secondly that a person will sometimes have to abandon everything in order to save his life.

As the seventeenth century progressed so these admonitory secondary meanings began to disappear, and by the time we reach the work of Zeeman, the maritime specialist, they are no longer to be found. In later periods the main representatives of this group were artists like Schotel and Jongkind. Their 'sole' aim was to depict what they regarded as a striking marine or river view according to the dictates of their personality or the artistic norms of their day.

Ill. 17 Jacob Savery [?], 'Although you may be far away, you are in my heart always.' From J.M. Krul, 'Pampiere werelt,' 1644. Engraving, 11.5 x 13.8 cm.

Een Vriefche Kaegh,   Een Gelderfe Kaegh,

ILL. 18

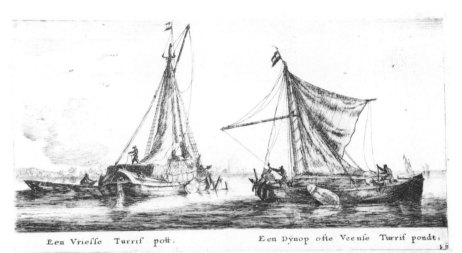

Een Vrieffe Turrif pott,   Een Dynop ofte Veenfe Turrif pondt,

ILL. 19

en Boortman de Zeelande die geetelick prov de Harlingen. || Een Zeuws Boortman uit Geetfteck by Harlingen || a Birthman of Zeland uid the geetetek naar Harlingen

ILL. 20

Ill. 18   Reinier Nooms, 'A Frisian kaag...'
Etching, 13 x 24.5 cm. Netherlands National
Maritime Museum.

Ill. 19   Reinier Nooms, 'A Frisian peat pot...'
Etching, 13.6 x 25.2 cm. Netherlands National
Maritime Museum.

Ill. 20   Adolf van der Laan after Willem van
Oordt, 'A Zeeland passage boat...' Engraving,
21.2 x 34 cm. Netherlands National Maritime
Museum.

The ships *by Robert Vorstman*

'Particularity of use dictates diversity of design,' wrote Nicolaas Witsen in 1617 in his *Aeloude en hedendaegsche scheeps-bouw en bestier* (Ancient and modern shipbuilding and ship management). In other words, the design of a particular type of vessel is governed by its function, the cargo it is to carry, and the waters it is to sail.

When we were compiling this book we endeavoured to select prints of ship types which would give a representative picture of that 'particularity of use.' Inevitably, though, our canvas has been limited, for when the earliest prints of sailing ships were made the ships themselves, both inland and seagoing vessels, were already the product of an evolution going back hundreds of years. In addition, the choice of theme has necessarily excluded other categories of ship, such as those driven by mechanical power or propelled by oars.

The scene of Dutch windmills in a print by Jongkind (nr. 246) calls to mind a remark made by G. C. E. Crone in 1926. 'Ships on the water have suffered the same fate as the windmills in our landscape. They have been supplanted, inexorably, by more and more factories, steam pumping stations and electrical operation. The old ships and the windmills are vanishing. Many of them have gone already; they have had their day.'

E. W. Petrejus expressed a similar thought in 1971: 'Nevertheless, he [the writer] is painfully aware that the Dutch waterways have lost much of their tranquility and beauty, for the disappearance of sail has meant the loss of the gentle splendor of the inland vessel.'

In order to make the prints more comprehensible to the non-specialist reader, the remainder of this introduction is devoted to a general description, illustrated with examples, of the main elements of the hull and rigging of inland waterway vessels and seagoing ships. This is followed by a brief explanation of certain manoeuvres.

Our first illustration (ill. 18; see also nr. 83) shows a Frisian and a Gelderland *kaag*, a flat-bottomed type of inland vessel in which the side strakes (planking) and bottom strakes meet at a definite angle. The other hull category is the round-bottomed type, in which the side strakes gradually curve round to form the bottom planking.

The *kaag* has a stem and a sternpost, heavy wooden beams in the bow and stern of the vessel to which the strakes are fastened. The two vessels in ill. 18 are carvel-built, i.e. the side planks are flush, as opposed to clinker construction, where the planks overlap.

Both vessels have a wale. This is a thicker plank protruding from the hull which has the twofold purpose of providing longitudinal reinforcement and of protecting the hull from damage. The *kaag* on the right has hung-out fenders to protect the wale.

The *kaag* has leeboards, in common with most inland vessels. The shallow depth of the Dutch waters precluded the use of ships with deep, fixed keels, and so in the second half of the sixteenth century the lee-

een Smakje of Tjalk met een Ferry tuig.

C · II

ILL. 21

een Jacht met een bezaanzeyl.

F · II

ILL. 22

een Smak Schip.

A · 7

ILL. 23

Ill. 22 Gerrit Groenewegen, 'A yacht with a Dutch gaff sail.' Etching, 13.8 x 15.4 cm. Netherlands National Maritime Museum.

Ill. 21 Gerrit Groenewegen, 'A small smack or tjalk with a ferry rig.' Etching, 12.1 x 15 cm. Netherlands National Maritime Museum.

Ill. 23 Gerrit Groenewegen, 'A smack.' Etching, 13 x 14.7 cm. Netherlands National Maritime Museum.

FEN HOLLANDS OORLOG SCHIP NA DE MANIER DER ENGELSE GEBOUWT VOERENDE 44 STUKKEN KANON

Ill. 24 Adolf van der Laan, 'A 44-gun Dutch warship built in the English manner.' Engraving, 61.3 x 94.3 cm. Netherlands National Maritime Museum.

▶ *Ill. 25 Gerrit Groenewegen, 'Three-masted hooker running before the wind.' Etching, 12.7 x 15.3 cm. Netherlands National Maritime Museum.*

Ill. 26 Gerrit Groenewegen, 'A Greenlander running free.' Etching, 15 x 12.6 cm. Netherlands National Maritime Museum.

▶ *Ill. 27 Gerrit Groenewegen, 'Barquentine close-hauled.' Etching, 15 x 12.7 cm. Netherlands National Maritime Museum.*

Ill. 28 Gerrit Groenewegen, 'A cat or timber-carrier weighing anchor.' Etching, 15 x 12.9 cm. Netherlands National Maritime Museum.

Driemart Hoeker Zeylende voor de wind

ILL. 25

Greenlandsvaarder zeylende van de wind

ILL. 26

board was introduced to prevent the vessel making leeway and to improve its headway through the water. The *kaag* has a broad rudder, which is operated by a tiller. Both *kaags* have a deck-house. Aft of the deck-house on the anchored vessel there is a horizontal reel, the windlass, which was used for working ropes. The plume of smoke from the chimney forward of the mast shows that there is a galley below deck.

Both *kaags* are spritsail-rigged. The spritsail takes its name from the sprit, the spar running diagonally from the bottom of the mast to the peak (top outer corner) of the sail. The foot, or heel, of the sprit is held at the base of the mast in an iron collar, known as a snotter. The purpose of the two ropes, or vangs, running from the top of the sprit (sprit arm) to the port and starboard sides of the vessel is to prevent the sprit from swinging too far outboard. The mast is braced fore-and-aft by a forestay and backstays, and laterally by shrouds. On the anchored vessel the spritsail and the fore staysail have been lowered and covered by a tarpaulin. The *kaag* on the left is under sail in a light breeze coming from astern. The set of the spritsail is controlled by a length of rope known as a sheet. At the bottom of the spritsail is a bonnet, an additional strip of canvas laced to the foot of a sail which could be removed if the wind started freshening. Brails run from the leech (after edge) of the sail to the luff (leading edge) and the head (top edge). A foresail has been set on the stay forward of the mast. At the top of the mast there is a small square topsail, the sheets of which run aft from the yardarms down to the deck. Jutting out over the bows is a jib boom, on which another headsail, the jib, can be carried. Before the spritsail could be lowered the setting of the sprit itself had to be altered. This was done by slacking off on the rope attached to the heel of the sprit so that it slid up the mast, bringing the sprit arm down on deck. The sail could then be detached from the arm and furled. This operation is clearly illustrated in ill. 19 (see also nr. 84), where the deckhand in the bows of a *dijnop* is slacking off on the heel rope while the skipper is busily reeling it off the windlass.

In the peat boat on the left of the illustration the sprit has been fully topped, and the sail is hanging slack against the mast. Another way of reducing sail was by brailing up. The sail, instead of being lowered, was gathered in to the mast like a curtain using the brails. When fully brailed up the sail ran from the sprit arm to the hounds, wooden plates attached to the upper part of the mast, and then down to the deck. (Ill. 20 shows a Zeeland passage boat with its spritsail brailed up in this way.)

The peat boat anchored just to the right of the passage boat in ill. 20 is wearing a ferry rig, which was a variant of the spritsail rig. In the ferry rig the sprit is shorter, and the topping lift is fixed not to the middle of the sprit, but to the sprit arm. The sail in the illustration has been run out to the sprit arm by an outhaul, and has been hoisted half way.

The smack in ill. 21 also has this ferry rig, and is carrying a mizzen on a smaller mast in the stern. In this rig the mizzen is laced to a short gaff at the top of the sail, and to a longer boom at the bottom. The mizzen is hoisted into position by a halyard. Although the mizzen on this smack is more of an auxiliary sail, many small vessels carried a sim-

ilar, *bezaan* sail, as a mainsail. This *bezaan*, or Dutch gaff rig, can be seen on the *spiegeljacht* (transom yacht) in ill. 22, which is running free with the wind on its starboard quarter. The sail is worked by a mainsheet attached to the boom.

Ill. 23 shows a smack with its mizzen lowered and the mainsail brailed up. The mainsail is attached to a long gaff at the top, but is loose-footed, i.e. it is not laced to a boom. This is known as a standing gaff sail, for unlike the spritsail or Dutch gaff sail it was not lowered but remained attached to the mast. If it was necessary to reduce sail, the brails were used to gather the sail partly or fully in to the mast. The hands forward are lowering the jib. The smack also carries a square foresail forward of the mast, with a square topsail above it. Square sails are set athwartships, while sails like the spritsail, gaff sail and Dutch gaff sail are set fore-and-aft. The horizontal yards to which the square sails are attached are worked by braces, ropes running aft from the yardarms (outer ends of the yard) down to the deck.

Although several types of inland vessels had square sails, it was generally seagoing ships that were square-rigged. Ill. 24 shows a square-rigged, forty-four gun Dutch frigate anchored in the Amsterdam roads off the Tollhouse. The underwater section of the hull is shown by a dotted line. The frigate has two gun decks, the lower deck and the main deck. Forward and above the main deck is the forecastle deck. Aft of this, broken by the waist, is the quarterdeck, which extends from the mainmast to the stern. The ship's head, right up in the bows, is decorated with a lion. In addition to the bowsprit, the length of which can be extended with a jib boom, the frigate has three masts: from fore to aft the foremast, mainmast and mizzenmast. The foremast and mainmast consist of three spars: a lower mast, a topmast and a topgallant mast. The mizzenmast has only one upper spar, the mizzen topmast. These spars are held together by caps, wooden blocks at the top of each spar with a hole through which the next spar could be drawn or lowered. The masts and upper masts are supported fore-and-aft and athwartships by thick ropes known as the standing rigging. Ropes used to work the yards and sails are known as running rigging. The shrouds providing lateral support for the lower masts are fastened to the channels, thick wooden planks projecting horizontally from the hull. The foot of the topmast shrouds are attached to the outside edges of the tops, platforms at the bottom of the topmasts, and the topgallant shrouds to the topgallant crosstrees, a construction of wooden beams around the top of the topmast and the foot of the topgallant mast which, together with the cap, holds the two spars together. In ascending order from the deck, the square sails on the foremast are the foresail, the fore topsail and the fore topgallant sail; on the mainmast: the mainsail, main topsail and main topgallant sail; and on the mizzenmast: the mizzen topsail.

The sail furled on a yard slung below the bowsprit is the spritsail. In addition to these square sails, the frigate can also set triangular or trapezium-shaped fore-and-aft sails on its stays. These include the jibs, which are hauled out on the jib boom at the end of the bowsprit, the

21

Pink dryvende

sails set on the stays between the masts, and the mizzen, which is carried on a yard on the mizzenmast.

The combination of sails set depended on the force of the wind, the course the ship was steering, or the manoeuvre it was engaged in. The force of the wind was denoted by the name of the square sail which could still be carried in that wind.

Ill. 25 shows a three-masted hooker carrying a main topgallant sail, so the ship is sailing in a topgallant breeze. Other terms are a topsail breeze, a reefed topsail breeze and a lower course breeze.

The inscription on this print states that the hooker is running before the wind, i.e. it is steering a course such that the wind comes from directly astern. With the wind over one of the stern quarters the ship is said to be running free. This is the case with the *bootschip, De Goede Hoop* (ill. 26), where the wind is coming over the starboard quarter, as indicated by the position of the flag in the stern. If the ship were to alter course so that the wind came at an angle of 90° to the fore-and-aft line, then it would be reaching with the wind abeam. With the wind ahead of the beam the ship is said to be sailing close-hauled, as is the case with the barquentine in ill. 27. On this course the sails are still drawing fully. If the angle between the fore-and-aft line and the direction of the wind is reduced even further, the sails will start to shiver and the ship will be lying into the wind. With that angle reduced to zero the ship is lying head to wind and can make no more progress through the water.

Generally speaking, a ship in this position will be engaged in weighing anchor, like the cat in ill. 28. In this print the wind is already coming in over the port bow. The crew are using the capstan to haul in the anchor cable, and the main topsail has been backed. This has the effect of pushing the ship backwards through the water, making it easier to break the anchor out of the bottom. As soon as the anchor is clear of the bottom the ship will begin to make sternway. In the meantime the fore topsail, which had been braced to port in order to make the ship's head fall off to starboard, is now braced round to starboard. The jib has also been hoisted to provide additional pressure on the ship's head. Once the ship has fallen off sufficiently the other sails can then be braced to the wind.

The pink in ill. 29 is already under sail. The main topsail has been removed from the yard, and the mizzen and jib have been hoisted. Here, though, the ship is making use of the current rather than the wind in order to clear the river. This is known as backing and filling. The ship is kept broadside on to the current, with its bows and stern pointing towards either bank. Depending on the bends in the river and various other factors, the jib can be hauled taut in order to make the ship's head pay off, or the mizzen can be hauled taut in order to make the ship luff up into the wind. The ship's headway can be arrested by backing the main topsail. This manoeuvre is used when the wind is coming from an awkward angle and the narrowness of the river makes it impossible for the ship to tack out to sea.

Ill. 29   Gerrit Groenewegen, 'Pink backing and filling.' Etching, 15 x 12.7 cm. Netherlands National Maritime Museum.

Ill. 30 illustrates a manoeuvre known as going about, or tacking. This is done in order to take the ship's head through the wind to put it on the opposite tack. The ship in this print was originally sailing close-hauled on the port tack. First the rudder is put over to port to bring the head up into the wind. The jib sheet is released to reduce the pressure on the bows, and the mizzen sheet is hauled in to increase the pressure on the stern. As the ship begins to luff up the sails start shivering and will eventually lie against the masts. As soon as the ship brings her head to wind the main yards are braced about ready to catch the wind on the new tack, and the jib is backed. As a result of the pressure on the forward part of the ship the bows fall off to port, the sails on the mainmast begin to fill, and those on the foremast can be hauled round. This is the moment depicted in ill. 30. The snow's head is already through the wind, the foremast yards still have to be braced about, and the staysails and jibs can then be trimmed to the wind.

The final manoeuvre is the anchoring of a three-master. Ill. 31 shows a frigate carrying out this operation after it has sailed close-hauled up to the point chosen for anchoring. The lower courses and the topgallant sails have been furled, the jib has been lowered, and the mizzen brailed up. The anchor has been veered out beneath the cathead in the bows, and is ready to be dropped. A few ship lengths from the anchorage the topsail yards are braced athwartships in order to take the way off the ship. As soon as the ship begins to make sternway the command is given to let go the anchor. Once the anchor has caught hold the ship will swing round head to wind, safely anchored, and the sails can be furled.

Ill. 30   Gerrit Groenewegen, 'Snow going about.' Etching, 12.4 x 15 cm. Netherlands National Maritime Museum.

Ill. 31   Adolf van der Laan, 'A 4th rate Dutch man of war, English built, coming to an anchor.' Engraving, 13.8 x 21.6 cm. Netherlands National Maritime Museum.

Five prints from a series depicting ship types

Around 1561-62 Pieter Bruegel made drawings of a number of ship types. These drawings were probably commissioned by publisher Hieronymus Cock, who wanted them as models for engraver Frans Huys. Bruegel presumably based these drawings, none of which has survived, on detailed studies made during his stay in Italy (1551-55). The ships in the print of the *Battle of the Strait of Messina,* which was engraved by Huys after Bruegel and published by Cock in 1561, are closely observed and may be elaborations on the same studies. Either Bruegel or Cock (who was himself an artist and had also visited Italy) may have modelled the design of this series on fifteenth-century ship prints by the Flemish Monogrammist WA and by several anonymous Venetian and Florentine artists.

Until recently it was assumed that Huys's series was executed in 1565, the year given on the prints. However, I. de Ramaix's discovery that Huys died before April 1562 shows this dating to be incorrect. The date may indicate the year in which Cock first published the series.

The series probably consisted of ten prints originally. In 1568 the famous Antwerp printer, Christopher Plantin, noted in his accounts that he had received 'all the ten ships f°' from Cock. There is also a note of 'the twelve ships of Bruegel, twelve plates' in the inventory drawn up in 1636 of the property of the deceased artist-publisher Theodore Galle and his widow. Both references almost certainly pertain to this series, to which two prints had evidently been added before 1636. Van Bastelaer, who compiled the best-known catalogue of prints after Bruegel, believed that there were eleven prints in all, but nowadays one of those prints, a composition with sixteen ships, is no longer regarded as being after a Bruegel original. In recent years, though, attempts have been made to augment the series with a number of vaguely related prints (see nrs. 37-40).

It is clear from the sixteenth and seventeenth-century sources cited above, and from the inscriptions on the prints, that there were at least two printings of the entire series, one by Hieronymus Cock and the other by Theodore Galle.

A hulk and a boeier on the Zuider Zee off Enkhuizen

Engraving. Muller 418 As(8). Van Bastelaer 98. De Ramaix, Lebeer 41. First state of two.

Dated *1565* in the waves in the foreground, and with the words *Dit scip. 1564* on the ship's stern. The date has been superimposed over the continuous lines of the waves, and was removed in the second state. Before the surviving impressions were printed, a large, radiant sun was burnished out of the sky, although traces of it can still be seen.

The lack of any inscriptions on this and the following four prints makes it impossible to say with any certainty what the ship types are. Attempts to do so over the years have led to a plethora of varying identifications. The large ship in the foreground was called a 'nef de bande ou de haut-bord' by van Bastelaer (1908), a 'hulk' by Benthem (1913), a 'Dutch hulk' by Buyssens (1954), a 'three-masted Dutch merchantman' by Smekens (1961), and an 'Amsterdamer Kauffahrsteischiff' by Müller-Hofstede (1961). Although van Beylen wrote in 1970: 'it is not at all certain what type of ship this is, but it is certainly not a fly-boat,' only six years later he was calling it a 'hulk, possibly of the "large hulk" type used by the Dutch in the siege of Zierikzee in 1576.'

The following features of the ship are worth noting. The bottom wale only runs as far as the point where the stern begins to curve upwards, whereas the wale above it follows the curvature up to the transom. There are two counters above the transom. There are three openings in the lower counter: one on the port side with the muzzle of a cannon protruding through it, a helm port in the middle for the tiller, which is attached to a long, narrow rudder, and a port on the starboard side, through which a bucket is suspended on a line reeved through a block. The design on this counter may be of a unicorn. On the beam separating the two counters is the inscription *Dit scip. 1564*.

The upper counter bears two coats of arms: a shield with the arms of Amsterdam on the port side, and the arms of Enkhuizen on the starboard side. In the bottom left corner of this counter there is another aperture. The topmost section of the stern is the taffrail, and the spar protruding through the circular opening is a bumpkin, which was used for sheeting the mizzen. Above this opening is the coat of arms of Hoorn. A dark patch on the hull amidships, between the third and fourth wale, could be a side port. Below it is the bottom, or orlop deck, and above it the main deck, whose level is indicated by the six cannon protruding through circular gunports in the ship's side. The upper deck consists of a quarterdeck, running aft from the mainmast, with the poop above it. The deck in the bows is the topgallant forecastle. The arched opening beneath it provides access to the forecastle itself. Light swivel guns are mounted on the topgallant forecastle and the poop. Those on the topgallant forecastle cover the waist of the ship and the stern castle should the ship be boarded.

The ship has a bowsprit and three masts. The tackle hanging from the bowsprit is for a small square sail known as the spritsail. The foremast and mainmast have topmasts and tops. A crewman in the maintop is hauling in the main topsail. The mizzenmast and the upper masts are supported on either side by shrouds without any ratlines. Bonnets are attached to both mainsail and mizzen. Martnets are attached to the leeches, or outer edges of the square sails. The red, white and red flag of Hoorn flies from the head of the mainmast. On the foremast is a flag with the Burgundian or St. Andrew's cross. The flag flying from the mizzen yardarm is a signal pennant.

A boeier to the right of the hulk is running before the wind under spritsail, fore staysail and a square topsail. A mizzen can also be set on the mizzenmast on the raised afterdeck.

A corpse is floating in the water in the right foreground.

The illustration is slightly reduced; the actual size of the print is 22 x 29 cm.

2

FRANS HUYS after PIETER BRUEGEL

Armed three-master, with Daedalus and Icarus in the sky

Engraving. Muller 418 As(4). Van Bastelaer 101. De Ramaix, Lebeer 44. First state of two.

Signed *.F.H.bruegel* at bottom left, and marked *.Cum.priuileg* in the margin at bottom right. In the second state the margin also has the address of the publisher, Theodore Galle. Daedalus is flying in the sky. Above him his son Icarus has flown too close to the sun. The wax on his wings has melted, and he is shown tumbling down towards the sea. Three other prints in this series have a similar combination of a ship with a scene from classical antiquity (cf. nr. 4).

Once again, the lack of an inscription has led to a variety of identifications. Van Bastelaer (1908) called the ship a 'nef de bande,' Buyssens (1954) referred to is as a 'nao,' Müller-Hofstede (1961) as a 'carrack,' Smekens as an 'armed three-master,' and van Beylen (1970) as a 'meersschip,' or ship with tops. This was the old term for square-rigged vessels, which was the strict definition of the word 'ship,' analogous to the French *navire* and the Portuguese *nao*. The ship in this print has a square, or transom stern, with the strakes ending at the counter.

The throwing spears and round shields in the tops indicate that it is a warship, as do the lighter guns in the fore and stern castles and the heavier pieces protruding through the gunports in the side. Spread above the waist, the space between the fore and stern castles, are the nettings, which were designed to prevent boarders gaining access to the waist and at the same time enabling the crew to attack them from below. There are topgallant masts on the mainmast and foremast. The flags flying from the mastheads are divided into diagonal fields and bear the imperial device of the double-headed eagle. On the end of the bowsprit there is a pomegranate, a symbol of imperial power. The combination of diagonal fields with a shield bearing a double-headed eagle very strongly suggests the Austro-Burgundian royal house of Spain. The diagonal fields are an allusion to the dynastic realm of 'old Burgundy.' The pomegranate may be a reference to Granada.

The illustration is slightly reduced; the actual size of the print is 22 x 29 cm.

FRANS HUYS after PIETER BRUEGEL

Armed four-master putting to sea

Engraving. Muller 418 As(2). Van Bastelaer 102. De Ramaix, Lebeer 45.

Signed .*F.H.bruegel* at bottom left, and marked .*Cum.priuileg* in the margin at bottom right.

Here too, attempts to identify the type of ship have produced mixed results. Van Bastelaer (1908) called it a 'nef de bande,' Buyssens (1954) a 'four-masted Portuguese nao,' Smekens (1961) an 'armed four-master,' and Müller-Hofstede a 'Viermastiger Küstenfahrer.'

The masts are pole masts, i.e. they have no separate topmasts. The vessel is square-rigged on the foremast and mainmast, with lateen sails on the mizzenmast and bonaventure mizzen. The trucks in the main shrouds, four at the top and four at the bottom, were used as guides for the running rigging. The figures below the bowsprit are handling the spritsail on its yard. The inboard end of the bowsprit has been padded with baggywrinkle to prevent chafing of the foot, or bottom, of the foresail.

A flag with the Burgundian or St. Andrew's cross flies from the head of the foremast, there is a Portuguese flag with an armillary sphere at the head of the mainmast, and the flag of Porto at the head of the mizzenmast. A flame-banner extends from the poop. The warlike nature of the vessel is amply borne out by the fifty or so guns of various caliber, the bundles of spears in the tops, and the grappling iron slung under the bowsprit. The two barrels hanging down the side of the stern castle served as privies for the crew. The ship's head is decorated with an outstretched hand. Beneath it there is a bumpkin for hauling down the tacks of the foresail. Members of the crew are climbing the shrouds while the four-master, under foresail alone, leaves the roads of a town which could very well be Antwerp.

The illustration is slightly reduced; the actual size of the print is 22 x 29 cm.

.*Cum.priuileg*

Fig. 4a *Jan Luyken, 'Spanish carracks or galleons.' From Cornelis van Yk, 'De Neder-landsche scheeps-bouw-konst,' 1697. Etching, 29.9 x 37.7 cm.*

4a

Three caravels in a rising squall, with Arion on the dolphin in the foreground

Engraving. Muller 418 As(6). Van Bastelaer 105. De Ramaix, Lebeer 48. Second state of five.

Signed *.F.H.bruegel* at bottom left, and marked *.Cum.priuileg* in the margin at bottom right. This is the only state to have the address, *.H.Cock ex,* in the sky at top right. In the first state it had not yet been inserted, and it was removed again in the third. In the fourth state the print acquired the number *4,* but this too was removed in the fifth. The figure on the back of the middle dolphin is Arion, the Greek poet whose skill with the lyre was legendary. As Herodotus tells the story, Arion was returning by ship in 625 BC from a music contest in Sicily, where he had enjoyed a great triumph and had been showered with gifts. During the voyage, however, he was overmastered by the crew, who were intent on robbing him. He was allowed to sing a final song, and then he jumped overboard, where a school of music-loving dolphins had gathered, attracted by his playing and singing. One of them bore him away to safety on its back.

The print shows three four-masted vessels scudding before the wind. Sailors on the two leading ships are climbing the shrouds in order to shorten sail. The ships are probably caravels. They are certainly very similar to a type of ship depicted in a prospect of Antwerp (1515), which J. van Beylen described as a caravel in 1976. As B.E. van Bruggen rightly observed in 1975, the names which have been given to the ships in this illustration down the years have created a certain amount of confusion.

The first writer was van Yk (see nr. 120), who included a print in his book on shipbuilding (1697), in which he brought together various ships by Huys, which he identified in his inscription as 'Spanish carracks or galleons' (fig. 4a). R. van Bastelaer (1908) called this type a 'nef,' B. Morton Nance (1912) a 'hulk,' E. Keble Chatterton (1923) a 'galleon,' O. Buyssens (1954) a 'mahona' and a 'nao,' while B. Landström (1972), like B.E. van Bruggen, referred to it as a merchant caravel!

The illustration is slightly reduced; the actual size of the print is 22 x 29 cm.

H. Cock ex

FH bruegel

Cum priuileg

4

FRANS HUYS after PIETER BRUEGEL

A fleet of galleys escorted by a caravel

Engraving. Muller 418 As(5). Van Bastelaer
107. Lebeer 50. First state of two.

Signed *.F.H.* at bottom left, with the name
bruegel at bottom right, and marked *.Cum.
priuileg* in the margin. In the second state,
which bears the address of Theodore Galle,
the plate has been trimmed by about 1.5 cm.
on the left, removing Huy's monogram.

Even in the early impression reproduced
here (see, for example, the careful initial out-
lining of the *C* of *Cum*, which is clearly visible here but has worn away in later impressions) one can see the weak area in the top left
corner which was later to result in that entire
corner breaking off.

A copy from the hand of Lambert Cornelisz. (active ca. 1594-1621 in Amsterdam)
forms the title print of Jan van Linschoten's
*Itinerario, Voyage ofte schipvaert van Jan
Huygen van Linschoten naar Oost ofte Portu-
gaels Indien*, Amsterdam 1596 (fig. 5a). The
first English edition of this work appeared in
1598 under the title *Description of a voyage
made by certaine ships of Holland into the East
Indies*.

The square-rigged caravel is of the same
type as the ships in nr. 4, most closely re-
sembling the ship on the left, which, unlike
the other two, also has a high forecastle. Although it lacks a ram, the grappling iron
slung beneath the bowsprit indicates that it is
a warship. It carries a square spritsail and has
its lower courses set.

The flags flying from the heads of the foremast and mainmast have four fields. The
swallow-tail pennants flying below these flags
and from the tops might indicate that the
ship is Spanish. The banner beside the tent
over the afterdeck of the galley on the left has
a field with lilies, together with a cross in the
center formed by a reversed crosier and a
key.

The illustration is slightly reduced; the actual size of the print is 22 *x* 28.5 cm.

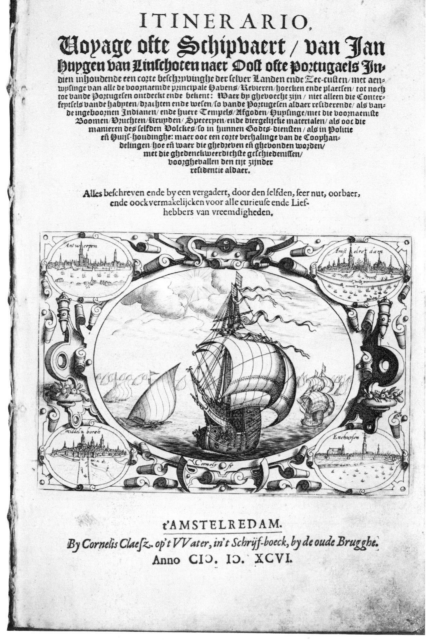

*Fig. 5a   Lambert Cornelisz., title print of
'Voyage ofte schipvaert van Jan Huygen van
Linschoten,' 1596. Engraving, 12.7 x 18.1 cm.*

5a

NAVIS ECCLESIÆ MILITATIS.

Vide Catholice Spectator, quam concinno ordine Petri Nauicula adhuc in terra fortiter militans, a Petri Vicario
gubernetur cunctisq; sacris ministerijs, licet inimicis ventis et vndis, fluctuans, Christi summi
naucleri gubernaculo sanctorumq; suorum triumphantium auxilio dirigatur.

Docto, pioq; Domino D. Joanni Andreæ Collegiatæ Ecclesiæ S. Gudilæ Canonico, Domino suo, Henricus Costerius Antuerpiæ Pastor D.D.

6

6

PIETER VAN DER BORCHT IV [?]

'Navis ecclesiae militātis' (The ship of the church militant)

Etching, with engraving in the shaded areas. Muller 448. At bottom center is the address *A.Huberti ex.*

In the first centuries after Christ the church came to be compared to a ship that had to weather storms, just as the church had to withstand a multitude of problems and threats to its existence.

This satirical print on the Reformation also employs a ship as the symbol of the church. The artist's intention is explained in the numerous captions by the figures. Christ and the apostles are seated in the uppermost platform on the mast, which is itself identified as the *Malus crucis*, or upright of the cross. The platform below them holds Mary and the holy virgins. A Jesuit is climbing the rigging to help hoist the mainsail, which is labelled *Zelus Catholicorum*, or Catholic zeal. The ship itself is manned by a mixed crew of churchmen. A cardinal is letting go the anchor of faith, while monks fire the cannons of prayer and mutual assistance.

The Pope holds the tiller, while some of the crew are engaged in repelling boats packed with proponents of false doctrines, heretics and devils approaching over the *Undae adversitatis*, or waves of opposition. In the sky the Flesh, the World, the Devil and *Falsa doctrina* (in the person of Luther) are belching forth opposing winds.

The inscription reads as follows: 'The Ship of the Church Militant | See, faithful onlooker, how harmoniously the ship of Peter, still bravely doing its duty here on earth, is steered by Peter's representative, and how, kept afloat with the aid of all holy servants, it holds its course no matter how hostile the wind or sea, guided as it is by Christ, skipper supreme, assisted by his victorious saints.'

7

HENDRICK GOLTZIUS [?] after CORNELIS CLAESZ. VAN WIERINGEN [?]

Two three-masters off a coastline

Woodcut, printed on blue paper. Weigel 363. Hirschmann, Hollstein 383. Strauss 413. First state of two. In the second state, which was invariably printed on white paper, the same line block was used in combination with two tone blocks, such as light and dark green. The artist has added highlights in the clouds and in the waves around the ships. These white touches, done with the brush, were designed to provide added contrast. However, the space left for these highlights when cutting the tone blocks was not done as precisely as one could wish.

Until recently, this and the following print were always attributed to Goltzius. Doubt has now been thrown on this attribution (van Thiel, Keyes), since they are coarser in execution than the chiaroscuro woodcuts with landscapes which bear Goltzius's monogram. It has been suggested that van Wieringen made the prints himself.

8

HENDRICK GOLTZIUS [?] after CORNELIS
CLAESZ. VAN WIERINGEN [?]

*Merchantmen, inland vessels and a rowboat off
a coastline*

Woodcut, printed on blue paper. Bartsch
246. Hirschmann, Hollstein 382. Strauss 414.
First state of three. Signed *CW* at bottom
right. In the second state the line block was
combined with two tone blocks, such as light
and dark brown. The third state bears the address of the printer, Willem Jansen. White
paper was invariably used for the later states.

   The monogram is of Cornelis Claesz. van
Wieringen. As in the preceding print, some
highlights have been added.

   The ship is the foreground also appears, reversed, in a print by Segers (nr. 45), while the
ship on the right is found in a print by Jan
van de Velde (nr. 50).

16.   ORBIS LONGITVDINES REPERTÆ È MAGNETIS À POLO DECLINATIONE.

Magnete paulum vtrinque sæpe deuia   *Dat inuenire portum vbique Plancius.*

9

HANS COLLAERT after **JOHANNES STRADANUS**

'Orbis longitvdines repertae è magnetis à polo declinatione'

Engraving. Hollstein 129-48. At bottom left is the name of the artist, *Ioan. Stradanus invent*. At right, below the bows of the ship, is the address *Phls Galle excud*. Numbered *16* below the border at bottom left.

This is one of a series of twenty prints after drawings by Jan van der Straat, known as Johannes Stradanus. Theodore Galle and Hans Collaert each engraved ten prints for the series, which bore the general title of *Nova reperta* (New discoveries; fig. 9a). The discoveries include Columbus's landing in the New World, the invention of gunpowder, a book printing shop, silk production, etc. Some of Stradanus's drawings for this series have survived, but not the drawing for this print.

The inscription reads as follows: 'Determining distances on earth by the declination of the compass. | The needle deviates a little to either side, | As Plancius told us would give our course to every port.'

In the days before it became possible to determine longitude at sea accurately, ships that sailed out of sight of land did so at grave risk. The Plancius mentioned in the inscription was a geographer and churchman who set himself to solving this problem around 1594. The method he developed was unfortunately based on a false premise, namely that there was a connection between the degree of compass deviation and the observer's longitude. It was not until John Harrison designed the ship's chronometer in 1759 that the problem was finally solved.

The cannon on the poop are mounted as field guns, rather than on the usual ship's gun carriage. It is here that the subject of the print is depicted. The figure seated at the table is taking a sun sight using a declination compass. His action is dramatized by the very peculiar ray of light linking his compass with the sun.

The purpose of the netting in the waist of the ship is explained in the commentary to nr. 2 above.

The illustration is slightly reduced; the actual size of the print is 20.5 x 27.5 cm.

Fig. 9a   Theodore Galle, title print of 'Nova reperta,' ca. 1600. Engraving, 20.6 x 26.7 cm.

THEODORE GALLE after **JOHANNES STRADANUS**

Ship surrounded by sea monsters

Engraving. Previously unpublished. The names of the artist and publisher appear at bottom right: *Ioan. Stradanus inuent*. and *Phls Galle excud*.

The scene is explained in the Latin inscription: 'The master who sails in Indian waters | Hangs great bells from bow and stern, | Whose tolling frightens the vast sea monsters | And keeps the whale away from the ship's hull.'

No other depiction of this intriguing theme is known.

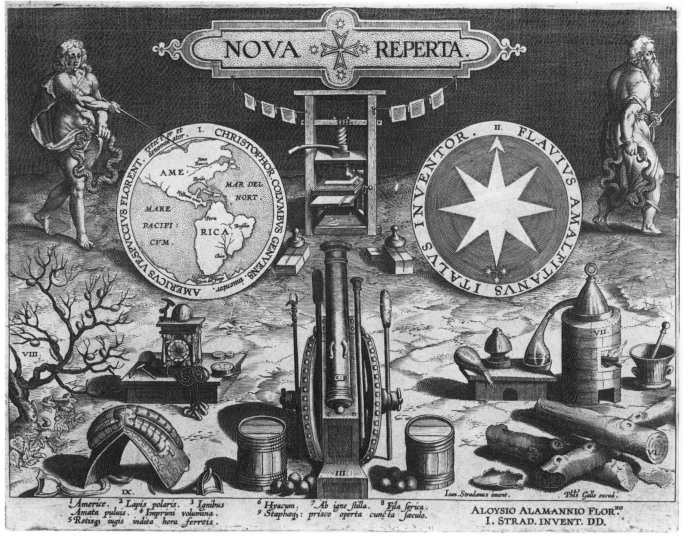

Nauita Erythræum pauidus qui nauigat æquor,   Tintinnabula : eo sonitu prægrandia Cete,
In proræ et puppis summo resonantia pendet   Balenas, et Monstra marina à nauibus arcet.

10

Henr. Hondius excud.
Cum priuilegio.

Plaus tra alii jactent et equos magno'sque Elepha
Quique onera huc illuc ferre referre solent:

Iactet Hamaxobius currus. se Nauita credit
Navi, quâ Batavis est via ad Antipodes.   .1603.

Ships in a roadstead

Engraving. Muller 1192. Below the border at
bottom left is the address and inscription
Henr. Hondius excud. Cum priuilegio. Dated
1603 at bottom right. Although the print is
unsigned it seems probable, on the basis of a
comparison with the following print, that it
was engraved by Robert de Baudous. Frederik Muller assumed, probably incorrectly,
that the scene shows the sailing, in 1603, of
the Amsterdam contingent of the first fleet of
the Dutch East India Company (founded
1602), under the command of Admiral Steven van der Hagen.

  The inscription reads as follows: 'You can
brag of horse-drawn carts, of elephants, |
You who carry heavy loads hither and thith-
er; | Carriers boast of wagons, but seamen
trust their ships, | The ships with which the
Batavians voyage to the Antipodes.'

ROBERT DE BAUDOUS after HENDRIK
VROOM

Ships in the Rammekens roads

Engraving. Hollstein 78. Third state of four.
The rectangle at bottom right contains the
dedication by Hendrik Vroom and the signature and address *R. de baud. sculp. et exc.*,
which were added in the second state. In the
third state, shown here, there is a new address in the waves at bottom center: *H.laur.
exc*. This was altered to the address of Jan
Jansz. in the fourth state.

The print is dedicated to Johan Huyssen
(1566-1634), Lord of Cattendyke. It is interesting to note that Huyssen is also praised
as a connoisseur of prints in the inscription
on a portrait engraved of him by Hendrik
Hondius in 1598. Zeeburg Castle, or Rammekens as it was later called, dates from
around 1550. Behind it is the island of Walcheren, with the towns of Veere and Middelburg. It was from this roadstead that
Charles V sailed for Spain in 1556, having
handed over his Netherlands dominions to
his son, Philip II of Spain. It was here, too,
that the ships of the East India Company
used to lie waiting for a fair wind.

The flag of Zeeland flies from the head of
the mainmast of the ship on the left, with the
flag of Flushing at the foremast head. The
two ships in the foreground are firing guns to
announce their departure from the roadstead.

Spectabili. Ornatiss.^{mo} vico ac Domino Joh. Huyssen
J.C.° Zeellandiæ Ordin. fœderat. Belgij rebus. Neptu-
nianis apud Middelburgenses Mattiacarum à Consilijs
Apellinæ scientiæ maximè studioso, Mecœnati mihi
faventissimo. Posui.   Henricus Vroom
        R. de baud. sculp. et exc.

ROBERT DE BAUDOUS after CORNELIS
CLAESZ. VAN WIERINGEN

The four seasons

Wurzbach 13. Hollstein 80-83. Numbered
1-3 at bottom right, the last sheet unnumbered.

The seasons were a popular subject in the
sixteenth and seventeenth centuries, but
there were few series in which all four seasons were depicted as maritime scenes. Generally speaking, established stereotypes were
used for each season. Some took the form of
personifications, summer being represented
by a woman or man with ears of grain and
winter by an old man warming his hands before a fire. Most depictions of the theme al-
luded to the cycle of nature, and to human
activities dictated by that cycle. In spring, for
example, people were shown shearing sheep,
pruning, or simply enjoying the fresh young
greenery in a pergola. Summer is the time for
haymaking and reaping, and in autumn there
is the wine harvest. In winter stores of food
were laid in, and people went skating.

Some of these motifs are to be found in the
following four prints, but they have been
linked to maritime activities. In summer, for
example, we see the hay being transported by
boat, and in winter, when the ships are frozen
in, the sailors enjoy their enforced leisure
playing games on the ice. In spring there is
the bustle of making ships ready for sea.

13

ROBERT DE BAUDOUS after CORNELIS
CLAESZ. VAN WIERINGEN

*'Ver,' or Spring: a merchantman being caulked
and provisioned*

Engraving. Hollstein 80. Second state of two.
In the first state the print was simply signed
Corn. Nicolai inv. Robb. de Baudous sculp.,
but this was amplified in the second state
with the address and date: *et excudebat Joan-
nes Janssonius A° 1618.* Numbered *1* at bottom right.

The Latin inscription is by the Amsterdam
physician, Nicolaes van Wassenaer, and
reads as follows: 'Spring | New spring; brave
mariners hoist high the sails, | And almost
before the waves have subsided does the
new-caulked keel kiss the open sea.'

The arms on the ship's taffrail are those of
Haarlem. The animal painted on the counter
appears to be a dog. To the right is a heavy-
duty crane.

The illustration is slightly reduced; the actual size of the print is 19 x 26.5 cm.

Corn. Nicolai inv. Robb. de Baudouz sculp. et excudebat Ioannes Ianssonius A° 1618.

Vere novo indomitus suspendit lintea malo **VER** *Navita, compostas volet uncta Carina per undas*
N. a Wassenaer

ROBERT DE BAUDOUS after CORNELIS
CLAESZ. VAN WIERINGEN

*'Aestas,' or Summer: an inland vessel sailing
with the wind large*

Engraving. Hollstein 81. Only state (?).
Numbered *2* at bottom right. Typical sum-
mertime activities, such as bringing in the
hay, are taking place while the sun emerges
from behind a cloud. The inscription reads as
follows: 'Summer | While the summer sun
still blazes down, safely choose the open sea, |
Gentle summer breezes blow, with mind at
ease, leave land's lee.'
   The illustration is slithtly reduced; the actual size of the print is 19 *x* 27 cm.

Tutius est æstu medio se credere Ponto,   ÆSTAS *Cum molles Zephyri suadent dare Carbasa vento.*

ROBERT DE BAUDOUS after CORNELIS
CLAESZ. VAN WIERINGEN

*'Autumnus,' or Autumn: three-masted
merchantmen and an inland vessel shortening
sail in a rising squall*

Engraving. Hollstein 82. First state of two.
Numbered *3* in the water, at right. In the
second state the second *r* in *horrisono* has
been inserted in its proper place. The initial
delineation of the letters in the inscription,
which is still clearly visible, shows just how
carefully the letters were traced onto the copper plate (this is generally true of the composition as well, but that can no longer be seen
in the finished print). Only then was the final,
deep incision made with the burin.

The small ship on the left is flying the banner of Amsterdam from its masthead: red,
black and red, with white crosses on the black
field.

The inscription reads as follows: 'Autumn |
Batavians, those water folk, exult to voyage
on the high seas, | A panorama of full-
stretched canvas driven on by the howling
wind.'

The illustration is slightly reduced; the actual size of the print is 19 *x* 27 cm.

Sic Neptunicolas Batavos juvat ire per altum,   AUTUMNUS.   Agminaq̃ horisono velorum expandere Cauro.

16

ROBERT DE BAUDOUS after CORNELIS
CLAESZ. VAN WIERINGEN

'Hyems,' or Winter: icebound ships in a harbor

Engraving. Hollstein 83. First state of two.
Classo, which is incorrect, was changed to
classe in the second state. The harbor is the
scene of various winter activities: skating,
riding on sledges and horse-drawn sleighs,
playing *kolf* (related to golf and, according to
some, the origin of the game) and another
game which closely resembles curling. A rink
was marked out on the ice and massive disks,
probably made of wood with a peg for a han-
dle, were sent skimming over the ice. In its
earliest form the object was to see who could
slide the disk the furthest.

It was later refined into a game of skill, the
object being to hit another player's disk or to
get as close as possible to a particular mark.
Brooms were used to keep the rink smooth.
The print also shows how the broom was
used to get the disks back to the base line by
rotating them on their pegs.

The inscription reads as follows: 'Winter |
Chill December clamps the ships in its grip;
the sailors, freed of care, | Bind runners to
their feet and carve thin furrows in the ice.'

The illustration is slightly reduced; the actual size of the print is 19 x 27 cm.

Navita sic gelido subductâ classo Decembrj   HYEMS   *Securus glaciem ferratâ compede sulcat.*

Fig. 17a   *Anonymous after Roelant Roghman,*
'The Overtoom,' ca. 1650. Etching, 13.2 x 25
cm.

SIMON FRISIUS

'The Overtoom near Amsterdam'

Etching. Burchard 4e. Hollstein 36. Numbered 5 in two places: above the word *Am-*
sterdam and in the margin at bottom right.

This is one a series of five views in and
around Amsterdam, the others being of St.
Anthony's and Reguliers Gates, the village of
Houtewael, and Kostverloren Mansion. The
addresses on the first sheet (St. Anthony's
Gate) identify the successive publishers of
the series as Robert de Baudous, H. Laurens
and N. Visscher. The series can be dated
around 1610, and must certainly have originated before the rebuilding of St. Anthony's
Gate and the destruction of Reguliers Gate
by fire in 1617-18.

Until the beginning of the fifteenth century, inland vessels sailing from Amsterdam
to Leiden and towns further south had to
travel via Haarlem, to the west. In order to
shorten the passage between Amsterdam and
Leiden, and incidentally to avoid paying toll
dues at Haarlem, Amsterdam dug a waterway
to Haarlem Lake (the waterway followed the
course of present-day Kostverlorenvaart and
Schinkel). Haarlem had no intention of los-
ing such a profitable source of income, and
retaliated by blocking the new channel with a
dam. Amsterdam reacted by building an
overtoom into the dam, consisting of a bed of
timbers over which ships were hauled with
windlasses. It was not until 1609 that the
squabble between the two towns was patched
up, when they agreed to tolerate both dam
and *overtoom*. The waterway and the surrounding neighborhood eventually took their
name from this *overtoom*.

In the left foreground is the Leiden Ferryhouse. In the center a ship is being winched
over the Great Overtoom, at a point where a
dam separates the Schinkel and the Overtoomse Vaart. On the right is the Lesser
Overtoom, which provided access to the
Slotervaart. There are numerous depictions
of this point at the end of the Overtoomse
Vaart, which was filled in 1902 and is known
today as Overtoom (see also fig. 17a and the
print by Nooms, nr. 88).

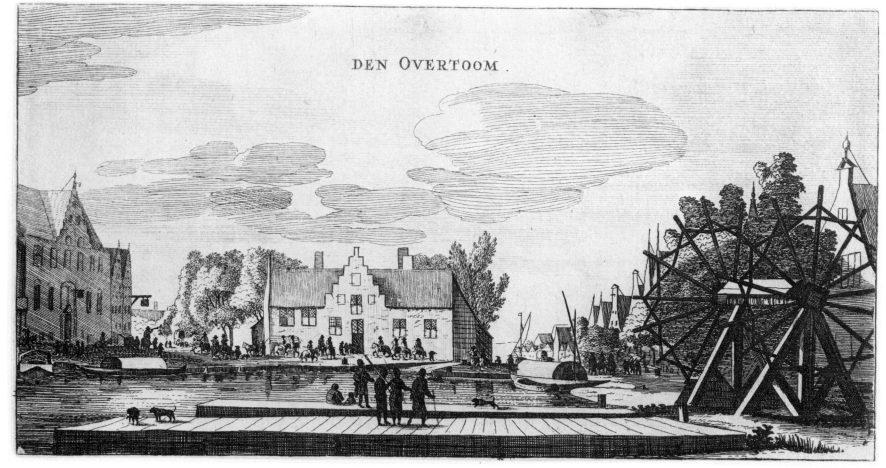

DEN OVERTOOM.

Den OVÉRTOOM bij Amsterdam.

5

17

Oppijnen

WAEL

De acht Karviel scheepen gelijckse
op stroom alle avonts Laghen.

Visscher excudit

Thiel

F L U.

Liefrinck fecit

The Leiden militia en route from Leiden to Grave

Etching. Muller 1472, Ib. Burchard, p. 46, note 2. Hollstein 2. Second state of three. Signed *CLiefrinck fecit* at bottom right. Left of center is the address *CJVisscher excudit*. There is no address on the first state, while in the third state Visscher's address was changed to that of P. Goos.

This is one of a series of three prints depicting the journey of the Leiden militia to Grave, below Nijmegen, in 1622. The other two prints show the march across Mooker Heath, and the town of Grave. The event took place during the Eighty Years' War with Spain. Prince Maurice called upon the citizens of Leiden to garrison Grave while he led the Grave garrison to relieve the town of Bergen op Zoom, which was being besieged by General Ambrosio Spinola. The militiamen and their supplies were carried by ship up the River Waal until the wind and current brought them to a halt at a point between Tiel and Oppijnen, where they disembarked and marched overland to Grave.

There are impressions of these three prints on yellow silk. No publisher is mentioned on those impressions, but there is an inscription above the scene: *Tocht ofte Reyse, van de Schutters van Leyden naer de stadt Grave, gedaen in de Maent van September, 1622* (Journey or voyage of the Leiden militia to the town of Grave, undertaken in the month of September, 1622). There is an explanatory text at the bottom of the print. Muller considers these silk impressions to be unique, and thinks that they were probably made for the commander. In the same period Amsterdam militiamen travelled to Zwolle, and the Haarlem militia went to the aid of Hasselt, in the province of Overijssel.

The inscription on the print reproduced here reads: *The eight carvel boats as they lay each evening.* Carvel was the earlier name for *smal* and *wijd* ships (literally: narrow and broad ships; see Glossary). The term was introduced when the Dutch adopted carvel construction, where the planking of the hull is flush, as opposed to clinker construction, where the strakes overlap, in imitation of a Spanish or Portuguese ship type known as a carvel, and later as a caravel.

PETR BAST au'a sculp et excudebat
1599

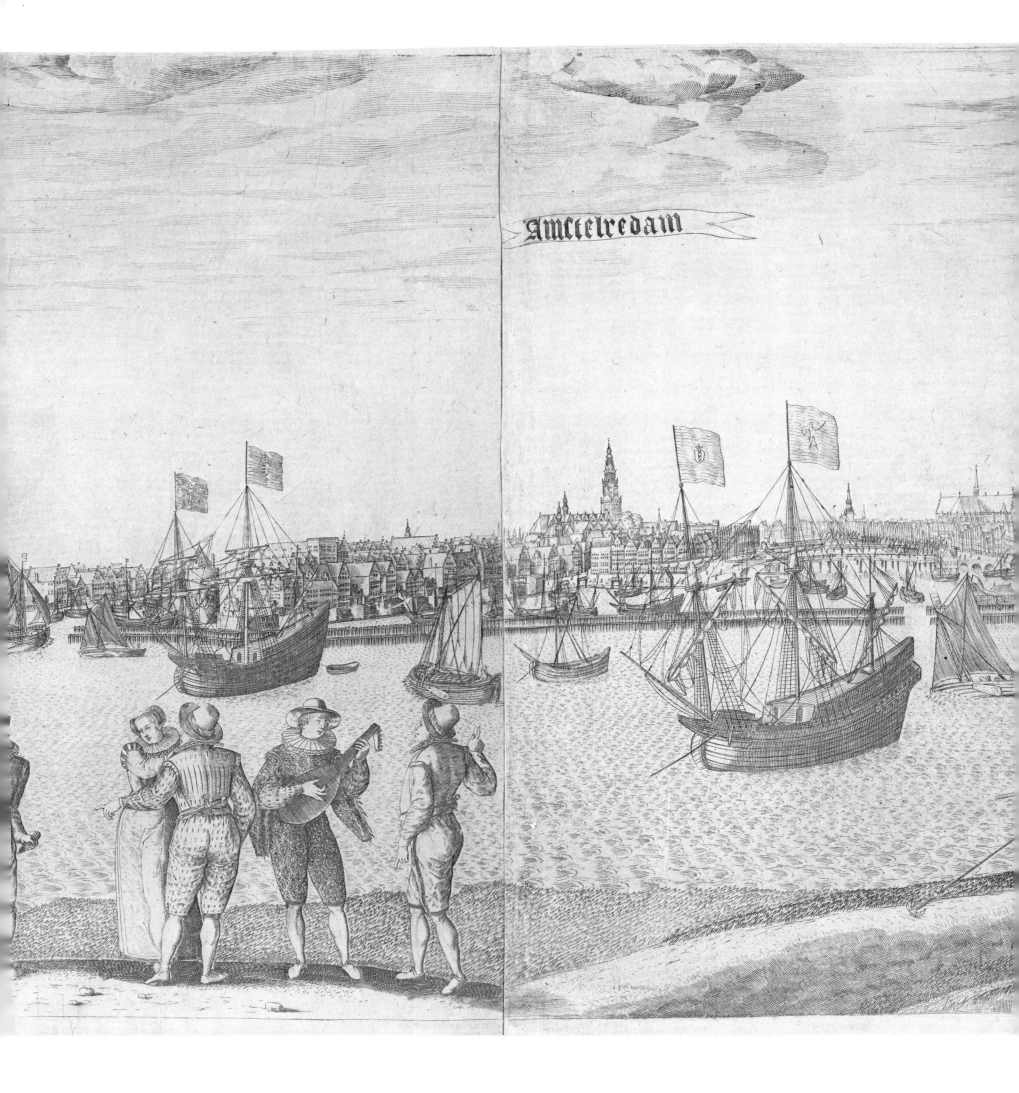

Amsterdam seen from the north bank of the River IJ

Engraving. D'Ailly 6. Hollstein 8. At bottom center of the left-hand sheet are the signature, address and date, *Petr Bast au et sculp et excudebat 1599*. On the right-hand sheet is the address *Et excudit*. To the right of this there are traces of another address, *Et exc* (?), which was probably removed in order to prevent it appearing in mirror image on the print. The composition was so large that it had to be printed from two copper plates, the two sheets then being glued together to form the complete print.

At top left are the arms of Holland, and at top right those of Amsterdam. Around both shields there are traces of earlier trials for other coats of arms, or for cartouches to contain a dedication. Since these outlines would have extended over the present edges of the print it can be deduced that the plates were originally wider.

Various figures, conversing or making music, form a repoussoir in the foreground. A contrast is provided at the right, on the spit of land known as De Volewijk, where condemned criminals are seen hanging from the town gallows. The Amsterdam landmarks visible in the background are, from left to right, Pepper Wharf, Weepers' Tower, Oude Zijds Chapel, Old Church, the Town Hall, New Church, and the former Haarlem Gate on Singel. This townscape was reworked by Claes Jansz. Visscher in 1611 (see nr. 20).

Various types of ship are depicted in the print. The rowboats carrying passengers were ferries taking people out to the ships in the roads or to the far bank of the River IJ. The boats being poled along are small lighters carrying cargo to and from the large merchantmen lying at anchor. The small spritsail-rigged vessels are passenger ferries. The slightly larger ships with the same rig and curved hatches over the hold are cargo vessels. Finally, there are the small and large three-masted merchantmen, some at anchor and others under sail. A number of them have a stern gallery. Opposite Oude Waal a ship is firing a gun as it enters the roads. From the mainmast head flies the flag of Amsterdam, consisting of a shield with the town's arms in the white field. The flag of Orange flies from the foretop. Another ship of the same type, but without a stern gallery, is under sail opposite Martelaarsgracht. A *waterschip* is anchored to its right.

Amsterdam seen from the River IJ

Etching and engraving. D'Ailly 17. Simon 160. Signed and dated on two bales in the left foreground: *n° HA 1611*. and *i CJV n* (reversed). The *p* and the *s* in the Latin text in the cartouche on the left are corrections made with the pen.

This profile view consists of four sheets glued together after they had been printed from four separate copper plates. The angels in the sky bear the arms of Holland, Amsterdam and Prince Maurice. The print is dedicated to Amsterdam in the cartouche on the left by the publishers, Claes Jansz. Visscher and Herman Allarts. On the right is an inscription explaining how religion, trade, the arts and good government have spread the name of Amsterdam all over the world.

Visscher used Pieter Bast's prospect of Amsterdam (nr. 19) for the two center sheets. He added a number of ships, and joined the sheets up with the new sections he made on either side. In the foreground he designed an allegory on the theme of Amsterdam as a mercantile center. The personification of Amsterdam is seated in the middle. On her left hand the nation's products are brought forward, while merchants from all over the world approach her on the other side bearing their more exotic trading goods. They include a Lapp with a reindeer, negroes, a camel and a penguin.

The numbers and figures on the print refer to the accompanying guide, which also provided a brief account of the physical expansion of Amsterdam down the centuries. This broadsheet was illustrated with a number of views by Visscher, chiefly of places associated with trade, such as Dam Square, the Exchange, etc.

It is possible that Visscher and Allarts published a more complex form of this prospect view in 1611. It had the same profile, text and illustrations, but added to them were two prints by Bast, one being an updated ground plan of Amsterdam, and the other a view of the town from the landward (southern) side.

The main landmarks in this prospect include, from left to right, Rijzenhoofd (B), Pepper Wharf (C), numerous ships in the Waal near Montelbaan Tower (D), the tower of the South Church (K), Weepers' Tower (H), the towers of Old Church (O), the Town Hall (aa) and New Church (bb), and Herring Packers' Tower (kk).

The illustration is slightly reduced; the actual size of the print is 25.5 x 112 cm.

21

PIETER SERWOUTER after PIETER
SIBRANTSZ.

Dutch ships off Bantam

Engraving. Wurzbach 14. Second state of
two (?). The name of the artist, *P. Sibrantsz:
Inv:*, is given at bottom center, together with
the address *Excusum Amstelodami apud. DP:
voskuijl*. Signed *PS: scal:* at bottom right.
There are faint traces of an inscription after
the address which has been deleted in this
state.

Dutch seamen are being received by an
Eastern ruler on the spur of land in the
foreground. The ships behind them are
flying a variety of flags, including those of
Amsterdam and Hoorn. It is not clear who
the seamen are, but a similar meeting must
have taken place when the first Dutch ships
sent out by the First Company of Far Lands
under the command of Cornelis de Houtman
anchored at Bantam in 1596. Bantam was
ideally situated for trade, lying at the north-
western tip of Java on Sunda Strait. After
1619, however, Bantam declined as Batavia
(present-day Jakarta) rose in significance.

The personification of Asia is seated in the
clouds above the fortified town, which is
identified as Bantam. On her left stand figures from eastern lands, where the Dutch
traded in spices and other products: India,
China, Sumatra, Arabia and Java. On Asia's
right are figures from more westerly regions:
Moses holding out the tables of the law, a
Tartar, a Persian, a Muscovite (Russian), and
the Portuguese explorer, Vasco da Gama,
who opened up the east when he landed in
India after voyaging round Africa in 1497-
99.

The Latin inscription goes some way
towards explaining how the Dutch arrived in
these parts, following in the footsteps of
explorers in classical times: 'When
Alexander the Great arrived in India | His
inquiring mind led him to explore Asia's
cities. || Soon afterwards the same longing
gripped Romulus's people, | And Sri Lanka
became a familiar land to them. || Finally,
after an interval of many centuries, | Lord
Vasco da Gama travelled the same route. ||
After clearing the cape of Africa and Japhetia
| He taught mankind to direct their sails
here.'

The illustration is slightly reduced; the
actual size of the print is 30 x 33 cm.

'*Sit oneri, erit usui:*' *A present burden is a future blessing*

Etching. De Vries 53. Plate 14 from the 'Eerste schock' (First sixty) of Roemer Visscher's emblem book, *Sinnepoppen*, published in 1614 by Willem Iansz. op 't Water inde Sonnewyser.

Each of the 183 emblematic prints in the book is accompanied by an aphorism in Dutch, Latin or French, together with an explanatory text. The text in this print reads as follows: 'When a ship puts to sea its boat is stowed in the ship itself, where it takes up much room and obstructs the crew. And yet they must suffer its presence, despite the inconvenience, for they will need it to go ashore when next they reach port. Thus it is rightly said: "He who saves, has."'

'*Nothing ventured, nothing gained*'

Etching. De Vries 53. Plate 49 from the 'Tweede schock' (Second sixty) of *Sinnepoppen*. See also nr. 22.

The accompanying text reads as follows. 'A buss shoots its nets, and has barrels of salt, victuals and other equipment, all of which have to be paid for before the skipper can even look for either profit or catch, which is often so meager that it barely covers the costs. So, in hope of better things, he fits out again for the next harvest. All men must give if they are to seek fortune once again, never doubting that God will show mercy and bestow prosperity on all who trust steadfastly in him.'

CLAES JANSZ. VISSCHER after JAN
PORCELLIS

*Title print of 'Icones variarum navium
hollandicarum' (Illustrations of various Dutch
vessels)*

Etching and engraving. Muller 1985 (Visscher?). Simon 112. Hollstein 21 (after Porcellis). Second state of four. Numbered *1* at
bottom right. A sheet of paper nailed to the
wooden piles around the islet bears the address *Amsterodami Impressae, apud I. Bormeester. Excudit.*

In the first state this title print had Visscher's address and the date *1627*. The printing reproduced here was published by
Jochem Bormeester towards the end of the
seventeenth century. Later editions bear the
addresses of G. Valck and B. Cleynhens
respectively, and the following text has been
added: *Diverse Navires dont on se sert dans les
Provinces Unies.* Nr. 39 in the 1779 inventory
of Cleynhens's estate records: '12 plates,
ships, by Johannes Percelles with 23 specimens,' so there was evidently considerable interest in these obsolete ship types until well
into the eighteenth century.

Visscher made this title print for a series of
eleven ship prints after Jan Porcellis which
he wished to publish. The following five
prints come from that series. Porcellis chose
to depict humble fishing boats, ferries and
various inland craft, rather than large, awe-
inspiring warships. This series can be regarded as the first of its kind since the series engraved by Huys after Bruegel.

CLAES JANSZ. VISSCHER[?] after JAN
PORCELLIS

'Damlopers of some 16 lasts'

Engraving. Muller 1985 (Visscher?). Hollstein 23 (after Porcellis). First state of two.
At bottom left are the artist's initials, *I.P. in,*
and at bottom right the address *CJV.ex.*
Numbered *3* below the border at bottom
right. See also nr. 24.

Although the address of Claes Jansz. Visscher was retained on later editions of the
prints, other publishers were mentioned on
the various title prints. When Valck published the prints he added a French translation of each of the Dutch inscriptions.

The drawing by Porcellis which served as
the model for this print is now in the Fondation Custodia (Frits Lugt collection) in Paris.
The only other surviving drawing by Porcellis for this series is that for nr. 8 (not included
in the present work), *'A Zeeland cog'* (Vienna,
Albertina).

The *damloper* was originally a small type of
inland vessel, and got its name from its use in
waterways where there were dams and dikes,
since it could be hauled across dams via an
overtoom. The *damloper* increased in size in
the course of the seventeenth century as
waterways became easier to navigate.

Damloopers groot omtrent 16 Last

3

CLAES JANSZ. VISSCHER [?] after JAN
PORCELLIS

'Overijssel pots of some 36 lasts'

Engraving. Muller 1985 (Visscher?). Hollstein 25 (after Porcellis). First state of two. At
bottom left are the artist's initials, *I.P. in.*,
and at bottom right the address *CJV.ex.*
Numbered *5* below the border at bottom
right. See also nr. 24.

Although these prints after Porcellis do not
capture all the qualities of the original drawings, they do retain much of the subtle inter-
play between light and shade. Above all,
though, they display the tranquility and
breadth with which Porcellis enriched Dutch
art of the period.

The *pot* was an inland vessel of the Overijssel region. Only two seventeenth century
depictions of it are known: the print reproduced here, and a print in the series *Verscheijde Schepen en Gesichten van Amstelredam*
(Diverse ships and views of Amsterdam), by
Reinier Nooms (nr. 84). Both versions are
clinker-built, have a *staatsie*, or peaked taffrail, and are spritsail rigged. The *pot* carried
peat from the eastern provinces to the west of
the country. However, as this engraving after
Porcellis shows, they were also used as ferries.
E. W. Petrejus, in his *Oude zeilschepen en hun
modellen* (Old sailing ships and their models),
had the following to say about this particular
depiction of the *pot*. 'I feel that Porcellis has
been rather unsuccessful in his illustration of
the *pot*. Admittedly it does have the straight
Overijssel stem, but the stern is very inaccu-
rate.'

I.P. in.

Overÿsselsche Potten groot omtrent 36 Last

27

CLAES JANSZ. VISSCHER[?] after JAN PORCELLIS

'A dogger of some 8 lasts'

Engraving. Muller 1985 (Visscher?). Hollstein 30 (after Porcellis). First state of two. At bottom left are the artist's initials, *I.P.in*, and at bottom right the address *CJV.ex*. Numbered 9 below the border at bottom right. See also nr. 24.

Doggers were fishing boats specially designed for cod fishing on the Dogger Bank in the North Sea. The rig was almost identical to that of the pink, i.e. square-rigged on the two masts, with the foremast stepped just abaft the stem. Other features include the high stem and the low upper planking above the gunwale, which is interrupted at the stern, leaving an open space at the point where the tiller comes inboard.

This print provides a good illustration of the care Porcellis took in choosing the right setting for his ships. In the prints of inland craft there are always towns or villages in the background. In this print of the *dogger*, which mainly worked the North Sea, there is the more suitable backdrop of a hilly and rocky coastline which could not possibly be mistaken for that of Holland.

Een Dogh-boot groot omtrent 8 Last

9

CLAES JANSZ. VISSCHER[?] after JAN
PORCELLIS

*'A ferry kaag of some 6 lasts sailing from
Amsterdam to Leiden'*

Engraving. Muller 1985 (Visscher?). Hollstein 31 (after Porcellis). First state of two. At
bottom left are the artist's initials, *I.P.in*, and
at bottom right the address *CJV.ex*. Numbered *10* below the border at bottom right.
See also nr. 24.

The ferry is shown crossing Haarlem Lake,
with Haarlem and the coastal dunes in the
background. In the course of time Haarlem
Lake gradually swallowed up more and more
land. An engineer, Jan Adriaansz. Leeghwater, submitted the first plan for draining the
lake to Prince Frederick Henry as early as
1635. However, there were to be many more
floods before the decision was finally taken
to drain the lake in 1839.

Kaag boats had been used for ferrying
people and goods between Amsterdam and
Leiden since time immemorial. Another
print in the series shows '*A cargo kaag of
some 6 lasts.*' Both vessels have the distinctive
straight stem raked at an angle of about 45°.
Various writers, such as Crone, Petrejus and
van Beylen, have pointed out the similarity
to the schokker, which also had a straight,
raked stem. The vessel in the print reproduced here is the smaller type of *kaag*. Larger
versions can be seen in prints by Reinier
Nooms (nrs. 74, 83, and in the introduction,
p. 17, ill. 18).

I.P in   ℈.ex

Een Veer-kaghe varende van Amsterdam op Leyden groot omtrent 6 Last   10

CLAES JANSZ. VISSCHER [?] after JAN
PORCELLIS

'A hoy of some 20 lasts'

Engraving. Muller 1985. Hollstein 32 (after
Porcellis). First state of two. At bottom left
are the artist's initials, *I.P.in.*, and at bottom
right the address *CJV.ex*. Numbered *11*
below the border at bottom right. See also
nr. 24.

The hoy was an inland craft which was
mainly found on the waterways of Zeeland
and South Holland, where it was used for
carrying goods and passengers. J. van Beylen,
in his *Schepen van de Nederlanden* (Ships of
the Netherlands) concludes that the hoy depicted by Porcellis 'would not be recognized
as such were it not for the inscription, or if
one relied on other depictions of hoys.' This
is the smaller version of the type, and is evidently doing service as a passenger ferry.

Een Heude ofte Heu groot omtrent 20 Last

11

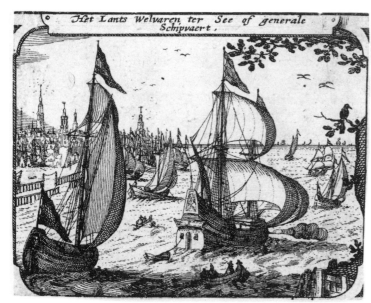

30

*'The nation's prosperity at sea, or general
shipping'*

Etching. Muller 1108. Wieder 1915, p. 36
and 1918, nr. 35. Simon 177.

The scene is set in the Amsterdam roads.
This and the following two prints are from a
series of ten illustrating Dutch customs, historical events, national costumes and town
views. Together they formed the upper and
lower borders of a map signed by Abraham
Goos and entitled *'Comitatus Hollandia.
't Graefschap Holland... Van nieus uitgegeven
ende vermeerdert door Pieter Vanden Keere,
Plaetsnyer tot Amstelredam... Anno 1610'*
(Comitatus Hollandiae. The county of Holland... Newly published and enlarged by
Pieter Vanden Keere, engraver at Amsterdam... Anno 1610). The upper border com-
prised the three prints reproduced here, together with a fourth in the top right corner
showing a horse-drawn plow, which was entitled *'The manner of cultivating land in the
County of Holland.'* The lower border consisted of six smaller scenes showing a water
mill and the Dutch way of fishing, the Honds-
bos sea defences, *'A Countess of Holland giving
birth to 360 children during a single confine-
ment,'* a mermaid captured in Lake Purmer,
Brittenburg, a submerged town near Katwijk,
the remains of which were exposed by the
tide on several occasions during the sixteenth
century, and peat cutting and cow milking in
Holland. The two sets of six town views on
either side of the map were also by Visscher,
and showed Dordrecht, Delft, Amsterdam,
Rotterdam, Alkmaar and Enkhuizen on the
left, and Haarlem, Leiden, Dergou (Gouda),
Den Briel (Brill), Hoorn and Hof van Holland
(The Hague) on the right.

There was also an inner border, containing
the coats of arms of thirty-two towns. The
only complete specimen of this map known
today is in the Palacio Real in Madrid (fig.
30a). It measures 43.5 x 55 cm.

*Fig. 30a Abraham Goos (?), Comitatus Hol-
landia, 1610. Engraving, 43.5 x 55 cm. Madrid,
Palacio Real.*

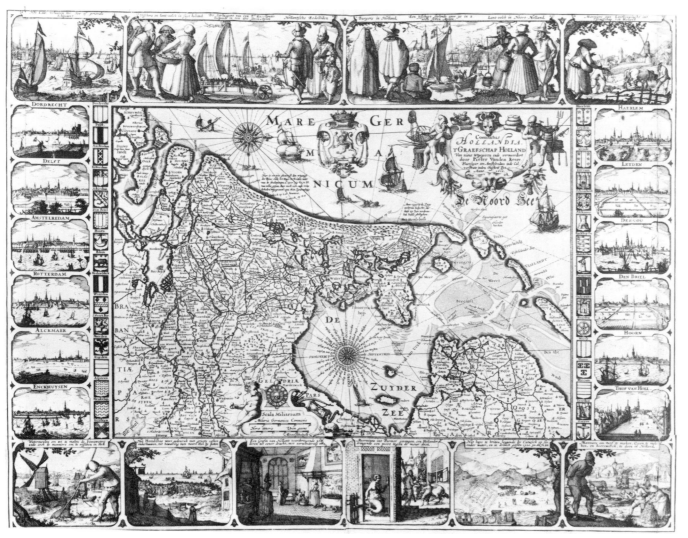

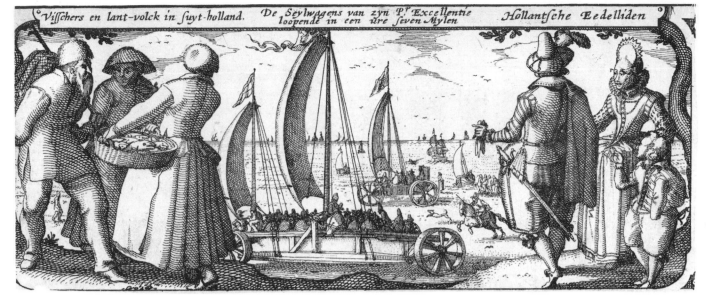

'The land yachts of His Excellency the Prince covering seven miles in an hour'

Etching. Muller 1108. Wieder 1915, p. 36 and 1918, nr. 35. Simon 177. See also nr. 30.

To the left and right stand two groups of three figures dressed in clothes which identify their social standing: '*Fishermen and country folk of South Holland,*' and '*Dutch nobility.*' In the center the land yachts of Prince Maurice are seen bowling along a beach.

Visscher's drawing for this print, which is reversed left for right, is in the Ingram collection, Chesham, Buckinghamshire (England). The drawing is similar in content to a print by Willem Isaacsz. Swanenburgh showing a land yacht making a trip between Scheveningen and Petten around 1600 (fig. 31a). Visscher had previously used a very similar scene as a border illustration above a map of the County of Holland published by Willem Jansz. Blaeu in 1608.

The seven miles mentioned in the inscription are Dutch land miles of 5,555.6 meters, so the total distance would be almost thirty-nine kilometers. The distance from Scheveningen to Petten is approximately eighty kilometers, which could certainly be covered in little more than two hours, and this fits in with the text beneath Swanenburgh's print, which speaks of a distance of fourteen miles. That journey was made in two 'wind carriages' with the wind from the southeast. Passengers on the 'ship' included Prince Maurice, who took the helm, Prince Frederick Henry, the French ambassador de Busenval, ambassadors from the emperor, and Admiral Don Francisco de Mendosa, who had been captured at the Battle of Nieuwpoort in 1600. Dutch, French, English and Danish nobles also went along for the ride. In all there were twenty-eight people on board the yachts.

The land yacht was not invented by Simon Stevin, as is so commonly maintained. Jan Huygen van Linschoten had earlier reported seeing similar vehicles in China.

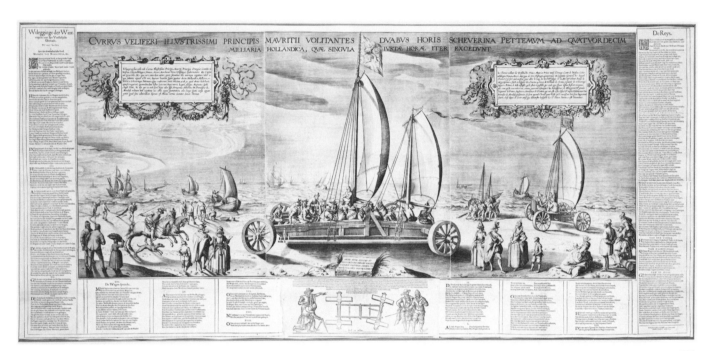

Fig. 31a Willem Swanenburgh and Cornelis van Sichem after Jacques de Gheyn, Land yacht, about 1600. Engraving, woodcut and letterpress, about 70 x 150 cm.

31

31a

32

'An ice-boat sailing over the ice, covering seven miles in two hours'

Etching. Muller 1108. Wieder 1915, p. 36 and 1918, nr. 35. Simon 177. See also nrs. 30–31.

To the left and right stand two groups of three people dressed in clothes identifying them as *'Burghers of Holland'* and *'Country folk of North Holland.'*

Visscher's (reversed) drawing for this print is in the Ingram collection, Chesham, Buckinghamshire (England).

This etching by Claes Jansz. Visscher is one of the few depictions of an ice sailing boat. Before the streamlined version of this boat was developed in the present century, the hull and rigging followed the traditional pattern. Adam van Breem depicted an ice boat with a lateen sail, but Reinier Nooms and Adriaen Loosjes showed it with a Dutch gaff and foresail. The boat in the etching reproduced here has a spritsail and a foresail. The flag at the masthead has the arms of Amsterdam. The vessel was fitted with three skates: a steering skate attached to the bottom of the rudder, and two others at either end of a runner mounted athwartships beneath the bottom of the boat.

33

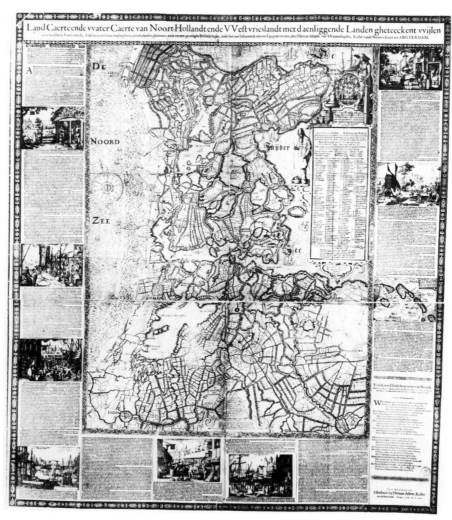

33a

CLAES JANSZ. VISSCHER

Fishing port with fish market

Etching. Muller 1109. Wieder 1918, nr. 28. Simon 119 and 176. Numbered *2* at bottom center.

This and the following two prints are from a series of eight depicting occupations typical of Holland, such as the dairy industry, fishing, flax working, washing and bleaching cloth, peat cutting, etc. These prints formed the border illustration in the text either side of and beneath the 1608 edition of the '*Land-Caerte ende water-Caerte van Noort-Holland ende West vrieslandt*' (Map of the land and waters of North Holland and West Friesland; fig. 33a). This map was first published in 1575 by Joost Jansz., a surveyor, and it is generally believed nowadays that it was commissioned by the Spanish. Various facts support this theory. The patent was granted by Requesens, commander of the Spanish forces after the departure of the Duke of Alva. Moreover, various earthworks and forts around Leiden are given Spanish names, and the waterways are particularly accurately drawn. This was vitally important to the Spanish, who were at a disadvantage in not knowing these waterways, and so were unaware of when they were running into danger. However, the only impressions to have survived are those from 1608, 'newly published, with many improvements and a detailed commentary, and decorated with suitable new figures, by Harman Allartsz. van Warmenhuysen, Sexton of the New Church at Amsterdam.'

In addition to the eight prints already referred to, the border also contained a print of the northern tip of North Holland and a few of the Wadden Zee islands, which had previously been omitted.

The text beneath the etching reproduced here tells of the good catches to be had from Lake Purmer, the Zuider Zee and the North Sea. It goes on to explain how the fish could be kept perfectly fresh in floating baskets, which can be seen in the print. The map, complete with borders, measures 116 x 105 cm. The drawing for this print is in the E. J. Otto collection, Celle (West Germany).

Fig. 33a Joost Jansz.(?) and Claes Jansz. Visscher, 'Map of the land and waters of North Holland and West Friesland' (1575), 1608 edition. Engraving, etching and letterpress, 116 x 105 cm. University Library, Amsterdam.

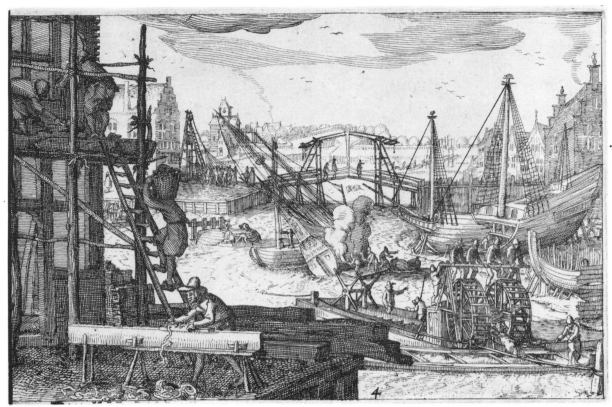

House-building and shipbuilding

Etching. Muller 1109. Wieder 1918, nr. 28.
Simon 121. Numbered *4* at bottom center.
See also nr. 33.

There are traces of letters in the lower margin which originally formed a text which was
evidently printed onto the paper after the impression had been made. Both the map and
the borders consist of several pieces of paper
which were glued together after printing. The
text beneath the print relates how, in Enkhuizen alone, three hundred ships were built
in a very short space of time during the
'seizures by the King of Spain of the ships of
Holland and Zeeland.'

◀ 35

CLAES JANSZ. VISSCHER

Trade in the port

Etching. Muller 1109. Wieder 1918, nr. 28.
Simon 123. Signed and dated *16 CJV 08* on
one of the bales in the left foreground. Numbered *6* at bottom center. See also nr. 33.

The associated text at the bottom of the
map proudly relates how the ports of Holland, and notably Amsterdam, were international trading centers, where large consign-
ments of textiles, wine, spices, etc. were disembarked and shipped on to other destina-
tions.

r excu.

36
ANONYMOUS, CA. 1600

Busses on the fishing grounds, escorted by two armed three-masters

Engraving. Previously unpublished. Second state of two? At bottom center, in the waves, is the address *CJ Visscher excu.* Visscher very probably added his address to an earlier plate which had come into his possession and from which he published prints.

For the technique of herring fishing, see nr. 179.

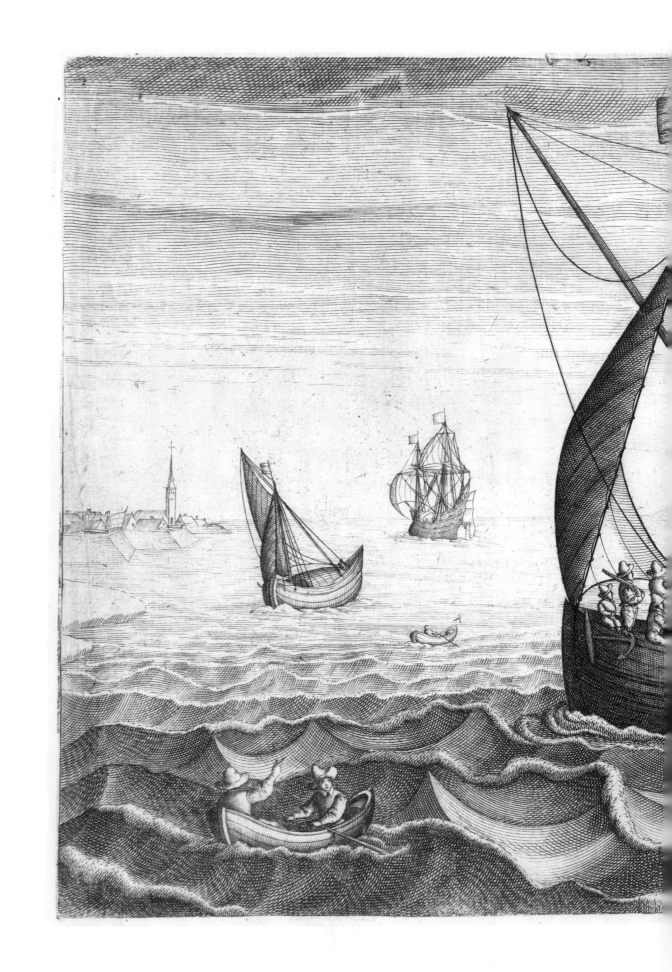

Ferry with soldiers

Engraving. Craddock & Barnard, cat. 111, 1966, nr. 51, pl. IV (as anonymous after Bruegel).

This and the following three prints are from a series of six, or possibly seven, ship prints. Four of them were published separately, and for the first time, in the present century, and it was not until 1966 that Craddock & Barnard added another two and identified them as a group. The print which might possibly be regarded as the seventh in the series is in the Waldburg collection, Wolfegg (West Germany).

It was originally assumed that these prints belonged to the series engraved by Frans Huys after Pieter Bruegel (nrs. 1–5). However, the far less imaginative composition and the rather stiff style of engraving and hatching argue against an attribution to either Bruegel or Huys. What is true is that some of the ships are very similar to those in the Huys series, and may even have been copied from them.

The soldiers include pikemen, a drummer, and a man armed with a firelock. The ship is sailing with its weather leeboard let down into the water, and is running before the wind under foresail alone.

Two seagoing ships and two inland craft, at anchor and under sail

Engraving. Campbell Dodgson 1931 (as Huys after Bruegel). Lavalleye, nr. 136 (as after Bruegel). Craddock & Barnard, cat. 111, 1966, nr. 51, pl. 11 (as anonymous after Bruegel). See also nr. 37.

The specimen reproduced here has a vertical printing fold running down the middle. This was caused by the paper being folded up on itself during printing, leaving a white line.

From left to right the vessels are an anchored fishing boat drying its nets, a spritsail-rigged inland vessel with its weather leeboard lowered, a rowboat with a fish basket, an armed three-master at anchor with a rowboat on a painter astern of it, a rowboat with a passenger, and a three-master running before the wind.

39

ANONYMOUS, CA. 1600

Three-master under spritsail, foresail and mainsail

Engraving. Sotheby auction, March 17, 1966, nr. 52 (as anonymous after Bruegel). Craddock & Barnard, cat. 111, nr. 51 (as anonymous after Bruegel). See also nr. 37.

ANONYMOUS, CA. 1600

English four-master in Indian waters

Engraving. Colnaghi, cat. 1963, nr. 19, pl. VI
(as Flemish, ca. 1565). Craddock & Barnard,
cat. 111, nr. 51 (as anonymous after Bruegel).
See also nr. 37.

A similar flag is depicted in Carel Allard,
Niewe Hollandse scheepsbouw (New Dutch
shipbuilding; 1705).

ANONYMOUS after CORNELIS CLAESZ. VAN
WIERINGEN

Ships in Spaarndam [?] harbor

Etching. Wurzbach 2(?). First state of two.
The artist and publisher are mentioned at
bottom left: *C Wieringen Inuen* and *H le Roy
excu*. Numbered *3* at bottom right. In the
second state le Roy's address was replaced
with that of a certain Roguié.

This and the following three prints are
from a series which probably consisted of
twelve landscapes and river scenes. Wurzbach mentions six etchings which could
belong to this series, but he regards them as
being from van Wieringen's own hand. The
series was also copied, but in less detail.

Van Wieringen still adhered to a mannerist
way of drawing, with markedly undulating
and unbroken lines. The prints can probably
be dated shortly afer 1615, which is when
Esaias and Jan van de Velde began to pop-
ularize this oblong format.

42

43

44

42

ANONYMOUS after CORNELIS CLAESZ. VAN WIERINGEN

Inland vessel on a river

Etching. Wurzbach 3(?). First state of two. The artist and publisher are mentioned at bottom right: *C Wieringen Inuen* and *H le Roy excū.*, together with the number *6*. See also nr. 41.

The rents in the vessel's sail would seem to indicate that the skipper had fallen on hard times.

43

ANONYMOUS after CORNELIS CLAESZ. VAN WIERINGEN

Ships moored near a small town with a tower

Etching. Wurzbach 3(?). First state of two. Numbered *8* at bottom left, together with the names of the artist and publisher: *C Wieringen inu H le Roy ex*. See also nr. 41.

44

ANONYMOUS after CORNELIS CLAESZ. VAN WIERINGEN

Ships outside the boomed entrance to a harbor

Etching. Wurzbach 3(?). First state of two. Numbered *9* at bottom left, together with the names of the artist and publisher: *C Wieringen Inuen H. le Roy ex*. See also nr. 41.

Booms topped with iron spikes were laid across harbor entrances at night and removed again the following morning.

The small ships

Etching. Springer 56. Haverkamp Begemann
50.
   Printed in dark gray on paper prepared
with gray-green. The ships and their shad-
ows were later colored gray with the brush.
Trimmed on the left.
   The specimen in the printroom of the
Rijksmuseum is one of the two fragmentary
impressions to have survived. The other, in
Dresden, adds to the scene on the left, with a
small overlap in the center, bringing the
overall width to 32 cm.
   Two of the ships (one being the large ship
in the left foreground) are copies in reverse of
the ships in a woodcut after van Wieringen
(nr. 8).

45

46

JAN VAN DE VELDE

'Aurora,' or Dawn: timber yard with ships

Etching. Franken–van der Kellen 187. Third state of three. Signed *J.V.Velde fecit* in the margin at bottom right, with the address *CJVisscher exc.*, and numbered *1*. In the first state there was no inscription at all, while in the second only the signature and the address were missing.

This print is one of a series of four. The others are *'Meridies'* (Noon), *'Vesper'* (Evening) and *'Nox'* (Night). All, with the exception of *'Meridies,'* show the influence of Hendrick Goudt's prints after Adam Elsheimer in the use of deep black areas.

A fire is being fed in the left foreground against the chill of the early morning. Beyond the fire men are already at work in the timber yard, which is sited by the waterside for ease of transport.

The inscription reads as follows: 'Dawn, who scorns Tithonus' lukewarm bed, | Drives off chill night before the morning star. | Clad in glorious, emblazoning attire, she routs | Dull slumber; welcome light spreads wide across the land.'

Peat boats by a river bank

Etching. Franken–van der Kellen 361. First
state of two. Numbered *3* with the pen at
bottom right. In the second state the number
has been etched into the plate. The diagonal
line between the trees on the left is due to a
slip of the etching needle. In the second state
it is nearly invisible.

This is one of a series of four landscapes.
The first sheet bears the signature and
address of Jan van de Velde, but the series
was also published at a later date by Claes
Jansz. Visscher.

Moored by the bank of a river is a *beitelaak*,
or 'chisel barge,' so-called because of its
chisel-shaped bow. *Aak* was the general
name for barges whose bottom planking was
extended right up to the nose of the vessel,
which consequently had no stem. They were
mainly used for carrying bulk cargo. In this
case the chisel barge is laden with peat.

Shipyard

Etching. Franken–van der Kellen 414.
Signed *I.V.Velde fecit* at bottom right, with
the address *CJVisscher excudit*. Visscher
evidently saw no reason to destroy the plate,
despite the scratches and irregularities in the
sky.

I.V. Velde fecit Vischer excudit.

JAN VAN DE VELDE after CORNELIS
CLAESZ. VAN WIERINGEN

Fishermen hauling in their nets

Etching. Franken-van der Kellen 421. First
state of two. Numbered *2* at bottom right in
the second state. This and the following two
prints probably belonged to a series of at least
six river scenes.

Van Wieringen's preparatory drawing, in
the printroom of the Rijksmuseum (fig. 49a),
bears the marks of the needle used to trace
the contours onto the plate.

The fishermen are hauling in a seine net,
the method being to encircle the fish and
then draw them in to land. The seine was
used for netting salmon and various other
types of fish.

Fig. 49a   Cornelis Claesz. van Wieringen,
Fishermen hauling in their nets, ca. 1625. Pen
and brush, 12 x 25.3 cm.

49a

50
JAN VAN DE VELDE after CORNELIS CLAESZ. VAN WIERINGEN

Ferryboat putting out from the shore

Etching. Previously unpublished. See also nr. 49.

Van Wieringen's drawing, which was formerly attributed to Hendrik Vroom, is in the Staatliche Graphische Sammlung, Munich. There is a drawing of a very similar scene in the Fitzwilliam Museum, Cambridge (England), which is sometimes attributed to either Jan or Bonaventura Peeters, as well as to van Wieringen. Although that drawing is far larger and was certainly not the direct model for the print reproduced here, it does have the same small pine tree on the end of the ferry's bowsprit.

51
JAN VAN DE VELDE after CORNELIS CLAESZ. VAN WIERINGEN [?]

An inland vessel passing a windmill

Etching and, in the sky, engraving. Previously unpublished. See also nr. 49.

This print, too, is probably after a van Wieringen drawing, hitherto unidentified.

50

51

'*A boeier*'

Engraving. Muller 1985A (as Nooms? after Lons). Hollstein 3 (as Lons). First state of two. Below the border enclosing the scene are the address and date, *P. Goos Excudit. Anno 1642*. Numbered *1* at bottom right. In the second state the address on this first sheet has been changed to that of C. Allard.

This and the following four prints are from a series of ten, the majority of them depicting ferries. They are copies by an anonymous artist after a rare series which may have been the work of Dirck Eversen Lons. Two of the only known specimens from the original series bear the handwritten date *1629* (J. van Beylen collection, Antwerp; fig. 52a), which might be the date of publication by Claes Jansz. Visscher.

The copies are mirror images of the originals. The hatched corners around the ovals were introduced by the copyist. Seven of the ten copies were made after the eight prints known to us, so there must have been more than ten prints in the original series.

The inscription reads as follows: 'With main and fore winged either side, | Making good time in a stiff breeze.'

The boeier was a cargo vessel generally used in the coastal trade. It originally carried a spritsail, but at the beginning of the seventeenth century this rig was superseded, in the boeier and other coastal vessels, by the standing gaff rig. The boeier in this print is running before the wind with its mainsail to port and its foresail to starboard. It also carries a square spritsail on the bowsprit and a square topsail.

Fig. 52a   Dirck Eversen Lons, 'A pleasure yacht,' 1629(?). Etching, ca. 22 x 16.5 cm. J. van Beylen collection, Antwerp.

Een Boeyer

Het Seyl en Fock elck op een zij
Met stijve koelt maeckt goede tij

P Goos Excudit.   Anno 1642.

ANONYMOUS, CA. 1640

'*A ferry serving Hoorn, Enkhuizen, Friesland and inland sea ports*'

Engraving. Muller 1985A (as Nooms? after Lons). Hollstein 4 (as Lons). Numbered *2* at bottom right. See also nr. 52.

The inscription reads as follows: 'With sheet and vang veered out wide, | The ship comes smartly into stride.'

The ferry is running before the wind with the mainsheet and vang veered right out. The foresail has been goose-winged to starboard, and is held out with a hook. Although the shape of the hull bears some similarity to that of the boeier on the previous page, the tall rudder, the higher superstructure and the rigging indicate that this a *smalschip* or *wijdschip*. These two names denote a single type of vessel which was built 'with an eye to conditions at Gouda,' the one being narrow and the other beamy. Ships with a beam less than 4.68 meters (*smalschips*) were able to pass through the Donkere Lock in the center of Gouda, but broader-beamed vessels (*wijdschips*) had to bypass the center and use the Mallegat Lock in the west of the town.

Een Veerschip op Hoorn, Enckhuysen Vrieslant of overzee
Als Schoot en gaerdt wert uyt geviert
Het Schip dan Sustich henen Swierdt

Een Speel-jacht
't geen dickwils t'varen heeft vermeert
Wert dus al varende verteert

Vißcher   Excudebat

52 a

ANONYMOUS, CA. 1640

'*A Delft, Rotterdam, Gouda or Hague ferry*'

Engraving. Muller 1985A (as Nooms? after Lons). Hollstein 9 (as Lons). Numbered *7* at bottom right. See also nr. 52.

The inscription reads as follows: 'Sailing is better than rowing, | And so one saves one's oars.'

Schuit was a general name for craft which could differ greatly as regards their construction. *Schuits* designed to carry large numbers of passengers generally had a long hull with little sheer, the bows meeting at a sharp angle above a straight, raked stem. In the first half of the seventeenth century they were open, undecked vessels which could be either sailed or towed, depending on the circumstances. Lons's ferry *schuit* is of this type. It is sailing before the wind under spritsail and square foresail.

Een Delſse, Rotterdamſe, Goutſe of Haeghſe veerſchuyt

Dit ſeylen is van beter aert
Als t'roeyen dus u riemen ſpaert

'*A Buiksloot ferry, or steigerschuit*'

Engraving. Muller 1985A (as Nooms? after
Lons). Hollstein 11 (as Lons). Numbered *9*
at bottom right. See also nr. 52.

The inscription reads as follows: 'A stiff
schuit and a following breeze, | what could be
more designed to please?'

The *steigerschuit* serving Buiksloot, across
the River IJ from Amsterdam, was a small,
single-masted vessel with a small spritsail
and a fore staysail (see nr. 158 and Glossary).

Een Buyckslooter Veer ofte Steygerschuyt

Een stijve Schuyt en vlack voor windt
Daer toe een Jder is gesindt

Een Speel-jacht

T'geen dickwils t'varen heeft vermeert
Wert dus al varende verteert

56
ANONYMOUS, CA. 1640

'*A pleasure yacht*'

Engraving. Muller 1985A (as Nooms? after Lons). Hollstein 12 (as Lons). Numbered *10* at bottom right. See also nr. 52.

The inscription reads as follows: 'Earnings which are often increased by sailing in trade | Are consumed again in sailing for pleasure.'

The word 'yacht' was applied at the beginning of the seventeenth century to vessels whose main feature was their speed. It was only later that the word took on its present specific meaning of a pleasure craft. The earliest depictions of a pleasure yacht show a vessel with a transom stern, a low bow section, with the strakes rising towards the stern. It carried a traditional Dutch type of gaff sail, with a very short gaff, on its two masts.

57
CRISPIJN DE PASSE II

'*Portrait of the celebrated hero, Pieter Pieters. Hein, General, etc.*'

Engraving. Franken 648. Muller 1596A. Hollstein 60. Second state of three. The first state lacked the motto above the figure of Hein, '*Goudt voor Silver | Eer voor all*' (Gold above silver, honor above all). In the third state the age given beneath the 'true likeness' of this naval hero was changed to *47*.

Piet Hein (1577–1629) was appointed Admiral of the Dutch fleet in 1626. He was an extraordinarily able and fair leader of men, and from 1629 to his death held the country's highest rank, that of Lieutenant-Admiral.

The cartouche at the bottom shows the battle in the Bay of Todos los Sanctos (Brazil) in 1624, which resulted in the fall of the virtually impregnable fort of San Salvador, largely due to the efforts of Piet Hein. His fame, which lasts to the present day in the Netherlands, rests on his capture of the Spanish silver fleet on September 8, 1628, in Matanzas Bay (east of Havana, Cuba; depicted in the upper cartouche). Hein had drawn up a plan for the regular interception of the Spanish silver flotillas as early as 1626.

58

MONOGRAMMIST AB

A galliot at sea, with a whale spouting

Etching. Nagler, *Monogrammisten* I, nr. 160,
1. Signed *AB* in the water at bottom left.

The vertical white line down the center was
caused by a crease during printing.

The underlying motif of this scene is the
belief that whales deliberately rammed ships
and knocked them on their beam ends. The
approved remedy was to throw a barrel overboard to distract the whale while its real target, the ship, made its escape. Bruegel used
this motif in his *Storm at sea* of 1569 (Vienna,
Kunsthistorisches Museum) as a symbol for
being distracted by vain and transitory pleasures and failing to keep one's real interests in
view. The motif is also enshrined in the emblem literature, but with a different meaning,
notably in Johannes Camerarius's *Symbolo-
rum et emblematum ex aquatilibus et reptilibus*,
which appeared in 1604. The accompanying
text tells us that it is sometimes necessary to
sacrifice all one's treasures in order to save
one's life.

Although the ship's hull is certainly reminiscent of a galliot, the rig is not. As far as we
know, galliots had two masts, with a gaff sail
on the mainmast. The ship in this print, however, has three masts, and is square-rigged on
the mainmast.

59

MONOGRAMMIST AB

*Christ appearing to the disciples on the shore of
the Sea of Galilee*

Etching. Nagler, *Monogrammisten* I, nr. 159
and nr. 160, 2. Hollstein 1. Second state of
two. Signed *ABf* at bottom left. According to
Nagler the print also appeared without the
monogram.

The mast and the half-lowered sprit form a
cross, possibly with the aim of presenting the
ship as a symbol of the church (cf. nr. 6).
There is, however, another interpretation. A
ship was often used as a symbol of man, driv-
en sometimes by the gentle breezes of life and
sometimes by raging storms. Since the ship's
anchor rope in the print appears to be
attached to Christ, the scene could symbolize
man's bond with and dependence on the
Christian faith.

MATTHIJS VAN PLATTENBERG

Storm at sea

Etching. Robert-Dumesnil, Hollstein 4. First state of three. Signed *Montaigne fecit* at bottom left, outside the circular border, and with the address *Morin Ex. Cum Priuil. Re.* at bottom right. Morin's address was removed in the second state, and horizontal lines were added to fill the space between the scene and the edges of the plate. A number and a letter were added in the third state.

This print is from a series of six circular seascapes and river scenes.

Montaigne fecit   Morin Ex. Cum Priuil. Re.

60

MATTHIJS VAN PLATTENBERG

Shipwreck

Etching. Robert-Dumesnil, Hollstein 23.
Second state of three. Signed *M. Montaigne
in et fe* in the margin at bottom left, and
marked *cum priu Reg* at bottom right. Numbered *A.5* at top left. In the first state the
statement of printing rights was preceded by
the address of Jean Morin, traces of which
can still be seen in the state reproduced here.
In the third state the plate had been reworked, and the white patch in the top left
corner filled in with cross-hatching.

WILLEM BASSE

The Battle of Gibraltar

Etching. Hollstein 64. This is one of the
seventeen illustrations which Basse made for
Elias Herckmans's *Der Zee-vaert lof* (In
praise of sailing), published in Amsterdam in
1634. The eighteenth print in that work is by
Rembrandt (see nr. 63).

The text on p. 191 of *Der Zee-vaert lof*
identifies the scene as the sea battle which
took place in 1607 off Gibraltar between the
Dutch and Spanish fleets. Although both
commanders, Jacob van Heemskerk and Don
Juan Alvarez d'Avila, lost their lives, the
Spanish fleet suffered a crushing defeat, opening up the way for the Dutch to achieve their
immediate objectives. These included bringing pressure to bear on the Spanish to conclude a provisional peace, protecting Dutch
trade, and preventing the enemy from under-
taking punitive expeditions to the Netherlands or the Dutch East Indies.

One of the flags flying from the ship on the
right contains the 'hooked cross in d'Avila's
banner.' On the left cannon are firing from
one of the forts covering d'Avila's fleet as it
lay in Gibraltar roads.

M. Montaigne in et fe   cum priu Reg

The ship of fortune

Etching. Bartsch, Hollstein 111. Second state
of two. The signature (partly burnished out)
and the date on the boat read: *Rembrandt. f.
1633*. The signature is clearly visible in the
first state, the only specimen of which is in
the Bibliothèque Nationale in Paris. That
state is also 2 cm. wider on the left.

This and the preceding print served as
illustrations in Herckmans's *Der Zee-vaert lof*
(see nr. 62). The text accompanying this
print on p. 97 of that work describes the
closure of the Temple of Janus (top left) after
the defeat of Mark Antony (left foreground)
in 31 BC at the Battle of Actium. Octavian,
the victor, ordered the closure of the temple,
which was always left open in time of war for
people to come and offer sacrifices for peace.

Herckmans's six-book poetic work is an
account of the maritime history of the world.
He repeatedly urges his contemporaries and
countrymen to take the lessons of history to
heart, and to treasure unity above all. It is felt
that Rembrandt, too, was more intent on presenting an allegorical comment on contemporary politics than on producing a straightforward depiction of an event from classical
antiquity. Between December 1632 and
December 1633 peace negotiations took place
between the Dutch and the Spanish, with the
Dutch failing to present a united front. The
negotiations had been made possible by the
Dutch victory at the battle on the Slaak between the Dutch and Spanish fleets in 1631.
The encounter resembled the Battle of Actium in that the side which initially had the
upper hand was eventually defeated, due to
the weather and other factors. Fortune thus
turned her back on the exhausted Spain,
shown here as a horse, and it appeared that
the temple doors could soon be closed. The
bearded Neptune, leaning on his trident and
seated in Fortuna's ship, alludes to the prosperity which shipping could enjoy after peace
was signed.

62

63

64

BONAVENTURA PEETERS

The round bastion

Etching. Van der Kellen, Hollstein 1. First state of two. Signed *B.P.* in the water at bottom left, and with the address *Ioan. Meysens exc.* in the margin at bottom left. The address was removed in the second state.

65

BONAVENTURA PEETERS

The tower

Etching. Van der Kellen, Hollstein 5. First state of three. In the second state more shading has been added to the thickest post in the water. In the third state birds were added in the sky left of the tower, and the wall around the tower was made darker.

66

BONAVENTURA PEETERS

The castle on the shore

Etching and engraving. Van der Kellen, Hollstein 6. Second state of two. Signed *B.P.in.* on the land in the foreground. This piece of land had already been worked up with the burin in the first state. More vegetation has been added in the second state, as have the birds in the sky.

67

BONAVENTURA PEETERS

The storm

Etching. Van der Kellen, Hollstein 7. As van der Kellen has noted, a thicker needle was used for this print than was the case with Peeters's other etchings.

68

BONAVENTURA PEETERS

'*The redoubt at Willemstad*'

Etching. Van der Kellen 8. Hollstein 9. Second state of three. Signed *B. Peeters.fecit.* after the title. In the first state the line beneath the scene was still incomplete. In the third state the address of Johannes Meysens was added in the margin to the left of the title.

Willemstad, in the province of North Brabant, was built in 1583 and was fortified by William the Silent in order to protect communications between the provinces of Holland and Zeeland in time of war, and in order to prevent an enemy crossing from Brabant.

A redoubt was originally a small field fortification. Here it is the jetty-head, controlling the entrance to Willemstad from the Hollands Diep channel.

The ship on the left is flying a flag whose central field has a shield with three St. Andrew's crosses. This is probably the flag of Willemstad. The flag on the ship at the right could be that of Rotterdam, with green and white fields.

69

DIRCK DE BRAY [?]

'*Febrvarivs, Sprockel:*' the storm on the Sea of Galilee

Woodcut. Previously unpublished.

In the top right corner is the zodiacal sign of Pisces, which begins in February. After the Latin name of the month is the Dutch expression '*Sprockel,*' or *sprokkel* month. This came about by an association between the *sporkel* month, when the *spurcalia* took place, and *sprokkelen*: gathering brushwood. The *spurcalia* was an exuberant heathen festival, while gathering firewood was necessary at this time of year in order to replenish the store depleted during the winter. The stormy weather being braved by the little ship and those on board is typical of February.

This woodcut is from a series of twelve months which appeared in a small almanac. Most of the scenes are from the Bible. September is represented by the Raising of Lazarus, and December by the Nativity.

70

DIRCK DE BRAY [?]

Boating on a river

Woodcut. Previously unpublished.

The sign of Cancer and boating are customary symbols for the month of June. This woodcut is from a series of the twelve months, showing country activities like haymaking and gathering in the harvest in July and August, and ice and showers in January and March.

64

65

66

67

69

70

Redout van Willemstadt. B. Peeters fecit.

68

Skirmish at sea

Etching. Bartsch, Weigel, Dutuit 2. Muller 2051. First (?) state of two. Signed *Zeeman* in the water at bottom right. The original margin probably had the address of Dancker Danckerts at bottom right. In this impression, however, the margin has been cut off and replaced with another strip of paper.

Bartsch states merely that the portrait is that of a skipper, Kees de Jonge. The incident depicted in the print, however, is described in detail in a pamphlet containing another print of the same subject (Muller 2050; fig. 71a): '*A skirmish at sea between an English and a Dutch fishing boat on August 9,*

1652.' The skipper of the Dutch vessel, Jonge Kees of the island of Vlieland, sailed to fish for cod in his small hooker fishing boat. Arriving at the fishing grounds, he spoke an English boat which was fishing and asked if he could buy some bait, since he was planning to fish with a long-line rather than a net. The English skipper suspected a trick (the two countries were at war) and flew into a rage. A bloody fight ensued, with the two crews hurling firewood and stones at each other. The Dutch finally boarded the English vessel, 'and all sliced and carved at each other right lustily.' The Dutch managed to drive the English fishermen down into the hold. They then nailed down the hatches and brought the vessel in to Amsterdam. The Noble Lords of the Amsterdam Admiralty

rewarded Jonge Kees with the gold medal which he is seen wearing in the portrait.

The illustration is slightly reduced; the actual size of the print is 19 x 28.5 cm.

Fig. 71a   Hugo Allardt(?), Skirmish at sea, 1652. Engraving, 13.9 x 19.6 cm.

71a

Ferries in open water

Etching. Bartsch, Weigel, Dutuit 33. First
state of two. Numbered *3* below the border at
bottom right. This print is from a series of
eight bearing the general title: '*Tweede deel.
Verscheyde Binne-waters…*' (Second part.
Various inland waters). The successive title
prints bear the addresses of publishers Dancker Danckerts, Clement de Jonghe, Johannes
de Ram, and W. de Broen. In the final edition
there is a double border around the scene.
Zeeman rarely dated his prints, but the *1656*
on the title sheet of the '*Eerste deel*' (First
part) gives an approximate idea of the origin
of the series.

Het veer van de uyterse schietschuyten

73

Het Leytsche Veer

74

'Mooring stage of the schietschuit ferry service to Utrecht'

Etching. Bartsch, Weigel, Dutuit 51. First state of two. Signed *Zeeman* on the quay wall at right. The title of the print and the number *5* are pencilled in beneath the scene in an eighteenth-century hand. In the second state the title and number have been engraved on the plate.

This and the following print are from a series of eight entitled *Verscheide gesichten binnen Amsterdam* (Various views in Amsterdam). In the second state the print bears the address of Clement de Jonghe, but this was later changed to that of publisher F. de Wit.

According to Wagenaer the ferry lay on the east side of Singel, between Gasthuismolensteeg and the former Kruissteeg.

The first part of the word *schietschuit* has two meanings: to move swiftly (to shoot), and to move in a straight line. The shape of the hull, with a length to breadth ratio of 7:1, certainly made these vessels swift sailers. They plied the route from Amsterdam to Utrecht, carrying cargo. Passengers were carried in tow barges which left from a landing stage on Achtergracht. The *schietschuit* followed the pattern of the *kaag* in having a vertical stem and sternpost. There was no wale around the hull, but instead there were two harpings, or bow wales, which can be seen on the *schietschuit* on the right. These boats carried two masts, square-rigged on the mainmast and with a Dutch gaff sail on the foremast. A windlass mounted just aft of the hold (visible on the vessel on the left) was used to hoist the main yard. Curved hatches covered the hold.

'The Leiden ferry'

Etching. Bartsch, Weigel, Dutuit 53. First state of two. Signed *Zeeman* on the leeboard of the ship in the foreground. In the second state the title and the number *7*, which are pencilled in on this impression, have been engraved on the plate. See also nr. 73.

In addition to the ferry landing stages in Amsterdam, the series contained views of the Naarden ferry and of the St. Anthony's, Northern and Apple markets.

The Leiden ferry sailed from Singel, between Heiligeweg and Kalverstraat. The tower of the Mint can be seen above the sails of the moored *kaags*, and in the right background is the mansion of Burgomaster Huidekoper. *Kaags* had traditionally provided the ferry service between Amsterdam and Leiden. 1647 marked the beginning of a period of decline with the introduction of an outside ferry service, which sailed from Damrak via Spaarndam to Leiden. This was followed in 1657 by the inauguration of a tow-boat ferry service, which also left from Singel. In an attempt to reverse this decline it was decided to move the departure point of the *kaag* ferry to beyond the Overtoom (see nr. 88). The tow-boat ferry, however, remained on Singel.

Title print of the 'First part' of 'Diverse ships and views of Amsterdam'

Etching. Barth, Weigel, Dutuit 63. First state of four. Numbered *1* in the margin at bottom left, with the address *C: Danckerts. Exc:* at bottom right. The print was numbered *1a* in the second state. Later states have the addresses of Dancker Danckerts and Clement de Jonghe.

This and the following five prints are from a series of twelve, the majority of them depicting warships, merchantmen, fishing boats and inland vessels.

The 'Watch house,' or 'Chamber of the Noble Lords of the Water Company' on the left, places the scene on present-day Prins Hendrikkade, near Damrak (see also nr. 177).

The white line down the center is due to a printing crease.

'*Two new frigates, equipped for war against the Parliament of England*'

Etching. Bartsch, Weigel, Dutuit 65. Second state of two. Numbered *a 3* in the margin at bottom right. In the first state the prints comprising the 'First part' of *Diverse ships and views of Amsterdam* lacked the *a* before the numbers 1-12. See also nr. 75.

Many warships were decommissioned after the elimination of the Spanish menace at sea with the fall of Dunkirk (1646) and the end of the Eighty Years' War in 1648. This put the Dutch at a dangerous disadvantage to the English, who had larger and heavier ships. On the outbreak of the First Anglo-Dutch War (1652-54) the various admiralties of the United Provinces were forced to augment their fleets with large merchantmen, despite the fact that their construction and speed made them unsuitable for their new task. After a great deal of bickering it was decided, while the war was still going on, to lay down larger warships. The ships depicted in this print appear to be these new frigates, which were probably built at Amsterdam.

'*Herring busses*'

Etching. Bartsch, Weigel, Dutuit 69. Second state of two. Numbered *a 7* below the border at bottom right. See also nr. 75.

The print shows a fleet of herring busses lying to their nets in the open sea. Fishing was done at night, to reduce the risk of the fish seeing the nets. Here it is evidently early morning, with the sun only halfway above the horizon. Some of the crew of the buss in the left foreground are hauling in the net via the roller fairlead set in the ship's side. The float line (see nr. 179) is being hauled aboard in the bows. In the seventeenth century busses were broad-beamed vessels with a taffrail over the helm port. An older type of buss, with a transom stern, can be seen just right of center.

'*Tochtschuits, or Spaarndam fishing boats*'

Etching. Bartsch, Weigel, Dutuit 70. Second state of two. Numbered *a 8* below the border at bottom right. See also nr. 75.

Tochtschuits were small trawlers from the area around Zaandam, northwest of Amsterdam, the River IJ and the Zuider Zee. The trawl was attached to two spars extending either side of the ship. This fishing method shows the relationship between these vessels, which Nicolaas Witsen called '*tochtschuits or drijvers,*' and which Soeteboom called '*drijvers* or *quacks,*' and the nineteenth-century Volendam *kwak*, which used the same kind of net.

Twee Nieuwe Fregatten. geruft ten Oorloogh. tegen t' Parlement van Engelandt,

Harinck-Buÿſen,

Tocht Schuÿten of Sparendammer Viſſers,

'*Bicker's Island*'

Etching. Bartsch, Weigel, Dutuit 71. First state of two. Numbered *9* below the border at bottom right. See also nr. 75.

Bicker's Island, one of three small islands in the west of Amsterdam, was brought within the city boundaries as a result of the 1612 expansion program. It was later named after the merchant, Dr. Jan Bicker (1591-1653), who bought the island from the city in 1631 and established a shipyard there. He also built a number of warehouses and houses on the island, as well as a stately mansion for himself.

On the left is Bicker's shipyard, and behind it are the sails of the windmill on Blauwhoofd bastion. On the right is the small watchhouse beside the opening in the palisade of mooring posts near Nieuwe Waal.

'*A damsout*' and '*A smalschip*'

Etching. Bartsch, Weigel, Dutuit 73. Second state of two. Numbered *a 11* below the border at bottom right. See also nr. 75.

In this etching Reinier Nooms brought together two ship types which, according to Nicolaas Witsen, had a great deal in common: '*Damsouts* are not dissimilar to *smalschips*, only smaller.' The *damsout* depicted by Nooms is a small, broad-beamed vessel reaching with the wind large under a spritsail and fore staysail. It is not clear from the print whether it also had the peaked taffrail, or *staatsie*, which can be seen on the *smalschip*. According to Witsen, the *smalschip* was used as a lighter for loading and discharging larger ships, and for carrying cargo out to ships in the roads. See also nr. 53.

'*The Vrijheijt, a man-of-war*' and '*The Hasewint, a Spaniarder*'

Etching. Bartsch, Weigel, Dutuit 77. Second state of two. Numbered *b 3* below the border at bottom right.

This and the following three prints come from the 'Second part' of *Verscheijde Schepen en Gesichten van Amstelredam* (Diverse ships and views of Amsterdam). In the second state the twelve prints comprising the 'Second part' have the letter *b* before the number.

As explained in the commentary on nr. 76, the Dutch admiralties were forced to charter large merchantmen on the outbreak of the First Anglo-Dutch War in order to bring the fleet up to strength. The *Hasewint* (Greyhound), a flute, was probably one of those vessels. The term 'Spaniarder' means that it traded on the Spanish run. The red, or 'bloody' flag flying from the poop, and the States flag at the head of the mainmast, indicate that the ship was equipped for war. This is borne out by the trophy decoration of drum and flags on the ship's side.

The *Vrijheijt* (Liberty) was a frigate built in 1651 for the Amsterdam Admiralty. In later years it served as a model for other capital ships. It saw action in the First and Second Anglo-Dutch Wars in fleets commanded by Maarten Harpertsz. Tromp and Michiel Adriaensz. de Ruyter. In 1675 it was destroyed by fire in a battle with the French off Palermo.

Bickers Eylandt,

Een Damſout,   Een Smalſchip,   a jj

De Vryheyt een Oorloogs Schip,   De Haſewint een Spaens Vaerder,

b 3

Een Staten Iacht,   Een uytlegger of Watte Convoyer, ♭4

Een Vriefche Kaegh,   Een Gelderse Kaegh, ♭10

'A States yacht' and 'A guard-ship or Wadden convoy ship'

Etching. Bartsch, Weigel, Dutuit 78. Second state of two. Numbered *b 4* below the border at bottom right. See also nr. 81.

States yachts were official vessels used by members of the States-General and the provincial States (parliaments). They had a transom stern, with a stateroom aft, another room amidships, and a pantry and a galley in the forecastle. The yacht, which is sailing close-hauled, has a spritsail. This had become a rather outmoded rig by this date, and had generally been replaced in this type of vessel by the more modern standing gaff rig. The Wadden convoy ship, on the other hand, does have this gaff rig. Nicolaas Witsen described the Wadden convoy vessels as 'ships fitted out for war which were used in shoal waters. They have a flat, transom stern and carry leeboards. There is a mainmast with a gaff sail, and a mizzen.' The convoy ship in this print lacks the leeboards mentioned by Witsen.

'A Frisian kaag' and 'A Gelderland kaag'

Etching. Bartsch, Weigel, Dutuit 84. Second state of two. Numbered *b 10* below the border at bottom right. See also nr. 81.

The *kaag*, along with the *smalschip* and the *wijdschip*, was one of the commonest inland craft of the Netherlands, being found in North and South Holland, Friesland, Groningen and Gelderland. The Frisian and Gelderland *kaags* in this print are in open water. W. A. Winschooten described the *kaag* as 'a type of inland vessel suitable for carrying cargo and for use in heavy seas.' It is perfectly true that *kaags* were used as lighters for transferring cargo from seagoing ships lying in the roads off the islands of Texel and Vlieland. However, they could not carry as much as the *smalschip*, and so in the course of the seventeenth century they were built with straighter stems and broader bottoms to give them a greater cargo capacity. In the process the *kaag* increasingly came to resemble the *smalschip*.

'A Frisian peat pot' and 'A dijnop or fenland peat pont'

Etching. Bartsch, Weigel, Dutuit 85. Second state of two. Numbered *b 11* below the border at bottom right. See also nr. 81.

In this etching Nooms has brought together two craft with a very similar function: a Friesland *pot*, which carried peat across the Zuider Zee, and a *dijnop* or *pont*, which carried peat from South Holland to Amsterdam. However, there is a considerable difference in the construction of the two vessels. The *pot* has a peaked taffrail, while the other vessel does not. Nicolaas Witsen described *ponts* as 'peat boats, square of build, their sails being hoisted with the aid of a windlass in the stern.'

Een Vrieſſe Turrif pott;   Een Dÿnop ofte Veenſe Turrif pondt;

'*Launching a ship*'

Etching. Bartsch, Weigel, Dutuit 86. Second state of two. Numbered *b 12* below the border at bottom right. See also nr. 81.

The etching shows a ship being launched bows first at the East India Company shipyard, when it was still located on Rapenburg Island in the Amsterdam port quarter. In other countries ships were launched stern first.

'*Rokin, with the Exchange*'

Etching. Bartsch, Weigel, Dutuit 88. First state of two. Numbered *2* in the margin at bottom right. It is numbered *3* in the second state. Johannes de Ram renumbered the prints for his edition, after the series had been published by C. Danckerts and Clement de Jonghe.

This and the following three prints are from the 'Third part' of *Verscheijde Schepen en Gesichten van Amstelredam* (Diverse ships and views of Amsterdam). This series of twelve prints is devoted to smaller barges and tenders. The Exchange building in the background was built between 1608 and 1611 by Hendrik de Keyser, and was the first building in the city specifically designed as a meeting place for merchants. Part of the building consisted of five arches over the River Amstel, the central arch being high enough to allow shipping to pass through.

From the sixteenth century, ferries sailing to towns in South Holland like Gouda, Delft, The Hague and Rotterdam berthed on the west side of Rokin, opposite Nieuwe Zijds Chapel, the entrance to which can be seen on the left. The ferry service was provided by horse-drawn barges which could also move under sail. Nooms also depicted these boats as night ferries (see nr. 87).

'*Hague, Delft and Rotterdam night ferries*'

Etching. Bartsch, Weigel, Dutuit 91. Only state (?). Numbered *5* in the margin at bottom right. See also nr. 86.

The night ferries sailed from the landing stage on Rokin when the evening bell rang in the Exchange. They were designed to carry a large number of passengers, who were accommodated either in the wooden cuddy on deck (first class), which could take eight people, or down in the hold, which seated twenty-six. The cuddy and the hold together formed the pavilion, the stanchions of which were fastened to the sides of the vessel. The spaces between the stanchions could be closed off with tarpaulins.

Het Afloopen Van een Schip,

b 12

Het Rockin, mette Beurs,
2.

Haegse, Delfse, en Rotterdamfe, Nacht~Schuyten,
5.

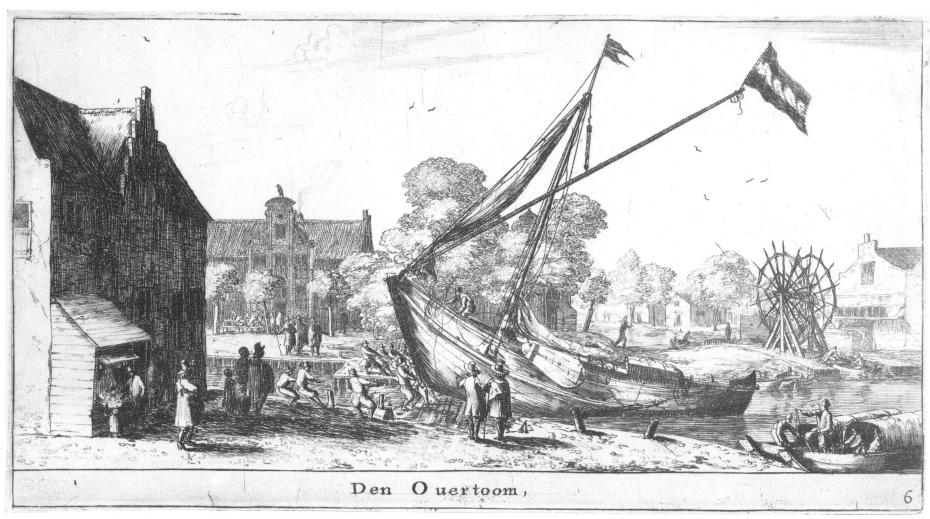

Den Ouertoom,

6

Schol-Schuÿties of Pinckies,

9

'*The Overtoom*'

Etching. Bartsch, Weigel, Dutuit 92. First state of two. Numbered *6* in the margin at bottom right. Renumbered *7* in the second state. See also nr. 86.

This scene is very similar to the one depicted by Simon Frisius some fifty years previously (see nr. 17, where the function of an *overtoom* is explained). If one compares the prints one sees just how representative the two artists were of the ideas of their day. Nooms focuses on a single event: a vessel being hauled over the *overtoom*, while Frisius

felt it necessary to include a wealth of detail and separate elements.

Inland craft increased in size in the course of the seventeenth century. The small *overtoom*, the size of which had been specified in an official agreement between Amsterdam and Haarlem, proved such an obstacle that shipping avoided the city center altogether. The ferry houses and inns, where people waited while the ship was hauled over the dam, now became departure and arrival terminals. New buildings have sprung up around the *overtoom* in the period between the two prints, among them the De Valck inn on the far side of the dam on the left (on present-day Sloterkade).

'*Plaice boats or pinks*'

Etching. Bartsch, Weigel, Dutuit 95. Only state (?). Numbered *9* in the margin at bottom right. See also nr. 86.

The pink was a beach-launched boat used for coastal fishing. It generally had two masts, but single and three-masted versions are also known. Since the coastal fishing villages had no harbors, the craft was specifically designed to operate from the beach. The pinks in this print are homeward-bound with their catch, and are about to beach at high tide.

A sea battle during the First Anglo-Dutch War

Etching. Bartsch, Weigel, Dutuit 101. First state of two. Signed *Zeeman* on the flag flown by the ship in the foreground. The second state is numbered *3* in the waves at bottom right.

This is one of a series of eight prints entitled *Nieuwe Scheeps Batalien* (New sea battles). The title print bore the addresses of the successive publishers: Clement de Jonghe, F. de Wit, G. Valck and B. Cleynhens.

The illustration is slightly reduced; the actual size of the print is 18 x 26.5 cm.

A shipyard

Etching. Bartsch, Weigel, Dutuit 107 and
140. It is not clear from Dutuit's description
whether he saw more than one state.

This is the first sheet of a series of thirteen
prints, to which the following two numbers
also belong. In 1675 the series was published
in London by Arthur Tooker, who probably
acquired the plates from Zeeman himself. In
that edition this sheet was replaced by a copy,
with a dedication to Samuel Pepys, Secretary
to the Admiralty, on the flag, and the statement that the following twelve sheets were by
Zeeman. The next time the series was published the numbering had been changed, and
the address replaced by that of the Amsterdam publisher, Carolus Allard. Hendrik de
Leth was the last to publish the series.

The print shows a number of activities associated with shipbuilding. On the left a
plank is being bent over a fire. A workman is
wetting the upper surface of the plank with
what looks like a swab. One end of the plank
is resting on a fire iron and is wedged under
something. The other end, which is not visible, is weighted down.

Two frigates

Etching. Bartsch, Weigel, Dutuit 112 and 145. First state of five (?). According to Dutuit an inscription was added in the margin in the second state, while in the third state the entire margin was trimmed off. The fourth state has Zeeman's signature, the number 6, and Tooker's address. The fifth state has Allard's address. By that stage the plate had become so worn that it had to be reworked in various places. See also nr. 91.

93
REINIER NOOMS

Two frigates and a transom yacht

Etching. Bartsch, Weigel, Dutuit 115 and
148. First state of five (?). The number 9 was
added later. See also nr. 91.

Rigging and caulking a frigate

Etching. Weigel, Dutuit 170. Second state of
two. The address, *Dancker Danckerts Exc.*, in
the margin at bottom right, is missing in the
first state.

The illustration is slightly reduced; the actual size of the print is 17.5 x 26.5 cm.

95a

MICHIEL MOUSIJN after JAN LIEVENS and
HERMAN VAN ALDEWERELT and REINIER
NOOMS

'Marten Harpertsz Tromp'

Engraving (portrait and frame) and etching
(seascape). Muller portr. 5446. First state of
three. Below the portrait is the name of the
artist after whom Mousijn made his engraving: *J. Lievens Pinxit.* The name of the
draftsman, *H v. Alde [werelt] ᵭ Invent*, is in
the left of the frame, and the name of the engraver, *M. Mouzyn sculpsit*, in the right of the
frame. The seascape at the bottom is signed
Z.M. At the very bottom of the print is the address: *'t Amsterdam, bij Lodewyck Lodewycksz
Boeckbinder en Printvercoper, inde Heerestraat
in 't Cunstboek* (At Amsterdam, at the premises of Lodewyck Lodewycksz, book-binder
and print-seller, in the Art Book on Heren-
straat).

   This print is the work of several artists.
Matters became even more complicated in
the second state, when the oval containing
the portrait was sawn out of the plate. The
portrait of *Michiel de Ruyter, Aᵒ 1654* was
then engraved on a new piece of copper and
inserted in the empty frame (fig. 95a). In the
third state the seascape etched by Zeeman
had become so worn that much of it had to be
reworked. The publisher of the third state
was Frederick de Widt. The frame was then
used for a whole series of oval portraits of
naval heroes, including de Ruyter again, Jan
Evertsen, Cornelis Tromp and Witte de
With.

   Maarten Harpertsz. Tromp (1597/98–
1653) had served under Piet Hein (see nr.
57), and in 1637 he was made Lieutenant-
Admiral of Holland and West Friesland, and
in 1652 commander-in-chief of the Dutch
navy. He became famous for his defeat of the
Spanish fleet in the Downs, and he is rightly
regarded as one of the greatest of Dutch
admirals.

   The illustration is slightly reduced; the actual size of the print is 31.5 x 21.5 cm.

*Fig. 95a   Michiel Mousijn after Herman van
Aldewerelt and Reinier Nooms, Michiel de
Ruyter, 1654. Engraving and etching,
31.5 x 21.5 cm.*

MARTEN HARPERTSZ TROMP.
RIDDER, L. Admiraal van Hollandt
en West-Vrieslandt, etc.

J. Lievens Pinxit.

Alde ᵭ Invent.   M. Mouzyn sculpsit.

Ick heb mijn vlijt gedaan, u cierlijck af te maalen___   Tot lof der Helden trou en 't Rijck der Admiraalen.
't Amsterdam, by Lodewyck Lodewycksz Boeckbinder en Printvercoper, inde Heerestraat in 't Cunstboeck.

*Two frigates, one at anchor and the other under
sail*

Etching. Weigel, Kunst Cat. 21382 (as Backhuizen). Nagler, *Monogrammisten* I, nr. 225,
4 and 2534. Hollstein 4. Signed *ABk* in the
water at right. This and the following print
are from a series of ship prints which probably totalled six in all. Nagler states that the
only print without the monogram has the address *Carel Allardt op den Dam inde Caardt
Winkel* (Carel Allard on the Dam, in the Map
Shop). This would indicate a dating to the
last quarter of the seventeenth century.

The frigate Zeelandia of the Amsterdam Admiralty

Etching. Nagler, *Monogrammisten* I, nr. 225, 5. Hollstein 5. Signed *ABk fe* on the barrel floating in the water at the right. See also nr. 96.

The *Zeelandia* (in the foreground) was built in 1643, and had thirty guns and a complement of one hunderd and twenty men. The ship participated in various actions, including Dungeness (1652), Lowestoft (1665), Schooneveld and Kijkduin (1673). The flag of Amsterdam flies from the mainmast.

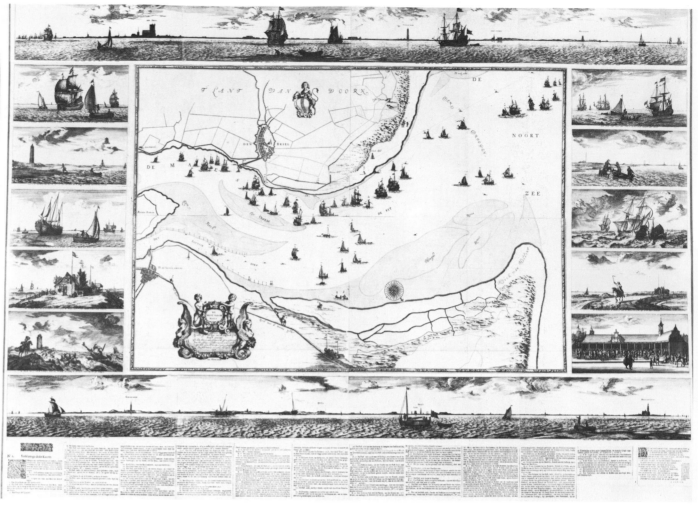

Fig. 98a Joost van Geel, The Postal Map, 1665. Etching, 119 x 166 cm. Municipal Archives, Rotterdam.

98a

het Postjagt ontmoet de inkoomende Scheepen en neemt de Naam op van Schip en Schipper en ontfangt de Memorie

'The mail packet meets the incoming ships and notes the name of the ship and her captain, and receives the register'

Etching. Dutuit 6 (as R. Roghman). Hollstein 1. Second state of two. In the first state there was no inscription, and the print was numbered *1*.

This and the following three prints are from the 'Postal Map,' which was published in 1665 (fig. 98a). The patent (valid for fifteen years) to publish this map and the chart of the River Maas was granted by the States of Holland to one Jacob Quack. Quack was a leading Rotterdam merchant who did valuable work in organizing the postal service to France and England. In 1663 he set up a shipping news service for Rotterdam, the object of which was to get reports and information on ships lying in or near the mouth of the Maas to Rotterdam as fast as possible by mail packets and mounted couriers. During the Second Anglo-Dutch War Quack's postal service carried mail, sailors and provisions to and from the fleet. The Postal Map measures 119 *x* 166 cm. It consists of the following elements, the drawings and plates for which were commissioned from Joost van Geel: a chart of the mouth of the Maas, with above and below it profiles of the western and northern banks, and flanked by ten scenes illustrating the work of the news and postal service. The columns of text at the bottom of the map amplify certain details shown in the map and prints. Nrs. 18 and 19 explain the scene illustrated here. '18. A flute approaches from the sea. The mail packet comes alongside the flute and asks for the captain's name, the name of the flute, and whence it has come. It also inquires whether there are any other vessels standing in towards land, and asks the captain for his bill of lading. The packet heaves across a leather pouch for the register, as seen in detail in panel nr. 1.'

The buildings on the horizon, from left to right, are identified on the map as Stone Beacon and the church of East Voorn.

The illustration is slightly reduced; the actual size of the print is 14.6 *x* 28.8 cm.

'A herring buss aground on the Crabbe, while its anchor is laid out by the mail packet'

Etching. Dutuit 5 (as R. Roghman). Hollstein 3. Second state of two. Numbered *3* in the first state. See also nr. 98.

The Crabbe was a shoal area off the town of Brill, which can be seen on the horizon. In order to prevent the buss being driven higher up the sandbank, and at the same time to enable it to kedge itself off as the tide rises, the mail packet is taking the buss's anchor out to deeper water.

The operation is also depicted on the chart of the mouth of the Maas. The relevant text reads: '8. A herring buss aground on the Crabbe. It shows a piece of linen attached to an oar or boathook aft of the poop, signalling for the mail packet to come to its assistance, or to hand over a letter for its owners, as shown in detail in panel nr. 3. . . . 9. The mail packet, arrived alongside the herring buss, takes its anchor out, as illustrated in panel nr. 3.'

The illustration is slightly reduced; the actual size of the print is 14.5 *x* 28.9 cm.

Een Haring buis sit op de Krabbe en 't Post Jagt zeylt zyn Anker uyt.

*'The mail packet indicates the best holding
ground for the anchor'*

Etching. Dutuit 7 (as R. Roghman). Hollstein 6. Second state of two. Numbered 6 in
the first state. See also nr. 98.

This operation is also illustrated on the
large chart of the mouth of the Maas. The
text reads: '12. A flute is aground on the
Crabbe, and signals as described above. 13.
The flute's boat prepares to lay out the anchor. The mail packet, in answer to the signal, comes up to the flute, and one of the crew
points out the best place to drop the anchor,
as shown in detail in panel nr. 6.'

The illustration is slightly reduced; the actual size of the print is 14.6 *x* 29 cm.

Het Post Jagt wyst aan waar 't Anker best uytgebragt dient

JOOST VAN GEEL

'The pilot boat transferring a pilot to a flute'

Etching. Dutuit 8 (as R. Roghman). Hollstein 8. Second state of two. Numbered *8* in
the first state. See also nr. 98.

The same hazardous operation is depicted
on the chart of the mouth of the Maas. The
text reads: '28. A flute enters the Maas in
rough weather under its lower courses, and
hoists a doubled flag aft, signalling for a pilot.
A 28. The pilot boat, in answer to the signal,
comes up to the flute, and with great difficulty
transfers a man, who grasps hold of a rope, as
shown in detail in panel nr. 8.'

The illustration is slightly reduced; the actual size of the print is 14.6 *x* 28.9 cm.

de loots Boot geeft een Loosman over aan een Fluitschip

Fishing boat in a harbor

Etching. Hollstein 5.
   This and the following four prints come from a series of thirteen views of the environs and port of Messina, entitled '*Vrbis Messanae. Eivsqve maris. Varivs. prospectus.*' Casembrot, who described himself as a Belgian, is listed on the first sheet as designer, etcher and publisher of the series.

A papal ship in a harbor

Etching. Hollstein 7. Signed *A. Casembrot. in. et. f.* below the archway on the right. See also nr. 102.

Galley in front of a house surrounded by a wall

Etching. Hollstein 9. Signed *Ab.C.f.* in the water at left. See also nr. 102.

103

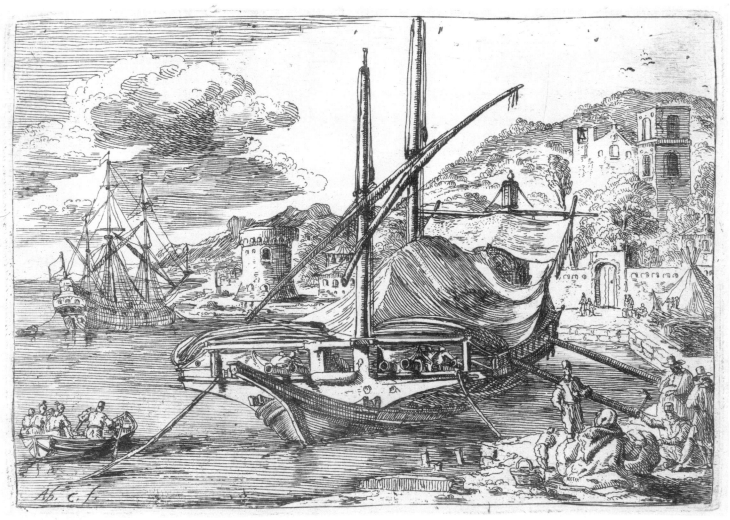

104

105

105
ABRAHAM CASEMBROT

Galley before the fort of Messina

Etching. Hollstein 11. Signed *Ab.C.f.* at bottom left. See also nr. 102.

106
ABRAHAM CASEMBROT

The storm

Etching. Signed *Abramo C.in. et fe.* in the water at bottom right. See also nr. 102.
   The fury and drama of the storm are heightened not only by the shipwrecked sailors in the foreground, but above all by the effect of masts, spars and oars jutting out at all angles, with the ship towering over the entire scene.

107
CORNELIS BOL IV

View of 'Vere'

Etching. Hollstein 6-11.
   This print is from a series (extent unknown) which Hollstein combined with several Italian town views and landscapes. The more logical approach would be to separate this and the following two prints, as well as a small view of Flushing (not reproduced here), from the others.
   Above the walls of Veere, a small port town in Zeeland, are the towers (on a rather exaggerated scale) of the Church of Our Lady and the Town Hall.

108
CORNELIS BOL IV

A spritsail-rigged inland vessel off a rocky coast

Etching. Hollstein 6-11. See also nr. 107.

109
CORNELIS BOL IV

View of 'Brill'

Etching. Hollstein 6-11. Signed *C bol fecit* at bottom right. See also nr. 107.
   The main feature identifying this as Brill (Den Briel) is the unfinished, massive tower of the Great Church.

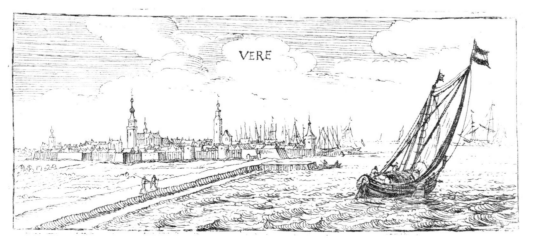

107

106

108

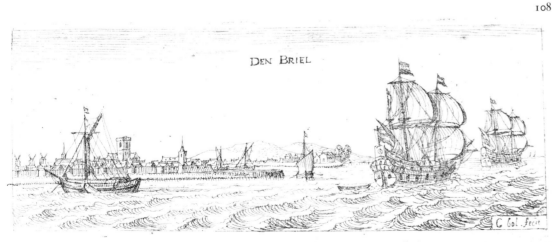

DEN BRIEL

C Col. fecit

109

The personification of Amsterdam riding on a triumphal car in the River IJ

Etching. Bartsch, Dutuit, Hollstein 1. Second state of two. Signed *L Bak* (reversed) on the barrel floating in the water at bottom right, and *LB* on the stern of the large ship on the right. The signature appears yet again in the margin at bottom left, together with the address and statement: *L. Bakhuizen fecit et exc: cum Privil: ord: Hollandiae et West-Frisiae.* This is absent in the first state. The verse below the scene was printed from a separate copper plate. This and the following five prints are from a series of ten etchings of river views with shipping. They were the only prints ever made by the celebrated marine painter, Ludolf Backhuizen, and were done when he was seventy years old. The series was augmented with a sheet with the etched title '*D' Y Stroom en Zeegezichten geteekent en geëtst door Ludolf Bakhuizen, Anno 1701…*' (The River IJ and seascapes drawn and etched by Ludolf Backhuizen, Anno 1701…), and a portrait of the artist by Jacob Gole.

Backhuizen has used a variety of devices in this print to highlight Amsterdam's role as a maritime center. In the foreground the personification of Amsterdam, with the city's coat of arms resting on her knee, is seated in a car drawn by sea-horses and nereids. Neptune, who is clearly favorably disposed towards her, rides on the back of the car with his trident grasped in his hand.

Drawings for this etching are in the Dutuit collection, Petit Palais, Paris, and in the British Museum, London.

The verse below the scene reads as follows: 'Thus they build here, on the ship-rich IJ, | The queen-post of the state and cities, | For the benefit of the community and the members | Of the East India Company; | So pearls are brought from one land to another, | Where Christ's doctrine was taught, established and took root.'

On the right is the *Amsterdam* man-of-war of the Amsterdam Admiralty, across the river from the shipyard and depot (reversed left for right) of the East India Company. The identification of the ship is based not only on the coat of arms on the taffrail, but also on the name '*Amsterdam*' written, in mirror image, in the white field of the Prince's flag and in the cartouches over the gunports. This ship of the line was built in 1688, under the supervision of shipbuilder Hendrik Cardinaal. It mounted sixty-four guns and had a crew of three hundred and twenty-five. The *Amsterdam* fought at the Battle of Barfleur as part of the combined Anglo-Dutch fleet against the French.

L. Bakhuizen fecit et exc: cum Privil: ord: Hollandiæ et West-Frisiæ.

Zoo bouwt men hier aan 't Scheepryk Y
De Moerbalk van den Staat en Steeden,
Ten besten van 't gemeen, en Leeden
Van de Indiaansche Maatschappy:
Zoo brengt men peerlen, wyd van 't een in 't ander Landt;
Daar Kristus Leer, geleert, gesticht werd, en geplant.

Ludolf Bakhuizen.

A transom yacht of the States-General and a boeier shortening sail

Etching. Bartsch, Dutuit, Hollstein 3. Third state of three. Signed *LB* on the flag flying from the mainmast of the yacht in the foreground. The signature appears again in the margin at bottom left, together with the address: *L. Bakhuizen Fec: et exc:*. Marked *cum Privil: ord: Holland: et West Frisiae*. There are three states for each of the Bartsch nrs. 2 to 8. In the first state the text below the scene is lacking. In the second state the text and the numbers 1 to 7 have been added, and there is some reworking in the scenes. The title sheet and the last sheets, however, remained unnumbered. In the third state the numbers were removed again. See also nr. 110.

Shipping on the IJ at Amsterdam

Etching. Bartsch, Dutuit, Hollstein 4. Third
state of three. Below the border at bottom
left are the signature, address and statement:
L. Bakhuizen fec: et exc: cum Privil: ordin:
Holland: et West Frisiae. See also nr. 110.

 A preliminary study for this etching is in
the British Museum, London. The ships,
from left to right, are a flute, a *kaag*, an unknown type of vessel, a rowboat, a ship of the
line, and a *wijd-* or *smalschip*.

L. Bakhuizen fec: et exc: cum Privil: ordin: Holland: et West Frisiæ.

Shipping on the Maas at Rotterdam

Etching. Bartsch, Dutuit, Hollstein 5. Third
state of three. Dated *1701* (reversed) on a
piece of timber in the water at bottom left,
and signed *LB* on the leeboard of the ship on
the right. The signature is repeated below the
border at bottom left, together with the address and statement: *L. Bakhuizen fec: et exc:
cum Privil: ord: Holland: et West-Frisiae.* See
also nr. 110.

The ships, from left to right, are a spritsail-
rigged inland vessel, an English yacht, an
English frigate, and a boeier.

L. Bakhuizen fec: et exc: cum Privil: ord: Holland: et West-Frisiæ.

Shipping in an unidentified roadstead

Etching. Bartsch, Dutuit, Hollstein 6. Third
state of three. Signed *LB* on the flag flying
from the stern of the ship in the center. The
signature is repeated below the border at bottom left, together with the address and statement: *L. Bakhuizen fec: et exc: cum Privil:
ord: Holland: et West Frisiae*. See also
nr. 110.

   A preliminary study for this etching is in
the British Museum, London. In the foreground, from the left to right, are a boeier,
which is reducing sail, and a transom yacht of
the States-General sailing close-hauled.

L. Bakhuizen fec: et exc: cum Privil: ord: Holland: et West Frisiæ.

Pinks in the surf

Etching. Bartsch, Dutuit, Hollstein 8. Third
state of three. Signed and dated *L Bakh 1701*
(reversed) on a piece of timber in the sand at
bottom right. The signature is repeated below
the border at bottom left, together with the
address and statement: *L. Bakhuizen fec: et
exc: cum Privil: ord: Holland: et West-Frisiae.*
See also nr. 110.

L. Bakhuizen fec: et exc: cum Privil: ord: Holland: et West-Frisiæ.

116
RICHARD ADAM

Ships moored at the foot of a tower

Etching. Meyer 1 (as Philipp Adam). First
state of two. Signed *RAdam:inu: et fe* below
the border at bottom left. The number *1* was
added in the second state, as was the address
of Johannes de Ram.
   This and the following two prints are from
a series of six river views in a southern or
possibly eastern country.

117
RICHARD ADAM

Carrying freight by water

Etching. Meyer 2 (as Philipp Adam). First
state of two. Signed *RAdam inu et fe* below
the border at bottom left. Numbered *2* in the
second state. See also nr. 116.

Ships on a river and by the river bank

Etching. Meyer 3 (as Philipp Adam). First
state of two. Signed *R Adam inu et fe* below
the border at bottom left. Numbered *3* in the
second state. See also nr. 116.

On the left of the print a small, spritsail-
rigged cargo vessel is sailing away from the
bank at a bend in the river. It is clear from
the position of the flags and sails that the two
ships on the right have the wind dead ahead,
which is why the ship on the extreme right is
being towed. The towing is being done by
three men, instead of the usual horses. The
absence of a roller guide post, which served
as a lead for the towrope at river bends, suggests that the towpath does not continue behind the tower, and that the ship's destination is the wharf at the foot of the tower.

Rdam inu et fe

118

Title print of the 'Life and exploits of Cornelis Tromp'

Etching. Van Eeghen 1284. Signed *I.Luiken*
at bottom right, with the address and date:
't Amsterdam Gedrukt voor den Auteur 1692.
(Printed at Amsterdam for the author, 1692)
at bottom center.

There are three more prints by Jan Luyken
in the book: one of the tomb of Cornelis's
father, Maarten Harpertsz. Tromp, another
of Cornelis being made a Knight of the Danish Order of the Elephant, and the third showing his funeral procession.

Cornelis Tromp (1629-92) was the son of
Maarten Harpertsz. Tromp (see nr. 95), and
rose from the rank of Lieutenant to become
Lieutenant Admiral-General of the Dutch
navy. He saw action in numerous battles in
the Mediterranean and the North Sea, including Elba, Leghorn, Lowestoft, the Four
Days' and St. James's Day Battles, and the
battle off Schooneveld and Kijkduin. He
served in the Danish navy as General-
Admiral from 1676 to 1678, and commanded
a combined Danish and Dutch fleet which
defeated the Swedes off Öland. He also assis-
ted Frederick William, Great Elector of Bran-
denburg, in a number of seaborne landings.

In addition to his Danish order, Cornelis
was also awarded the Order of the Garter by
the King of England.

Title print of 'Dutch shipbuilding unveiled'

Etching, with engraving in the shaded areas.
Van Eeghen 1653. First state of two. Signed
J. Luyken. below the border at bottom right.
In the second state the title of the book was
inserted at the top of the curtain, while the
address and date: *'T Amsterdam By Ian ten
Hoorn Boekverkoper 1697* (At Amsterdam, at
the premises of Jan ten Hoorn, bookseller,
1697), were added beneath the scene.

This well-known book by ship's carpenter
Cornelis van Yk contained a further fourteen
prints – twelve by Jan Luyken, chiefly of Siamese vessels, and two by Caspar Luyken.

In this title print the personification of
Shipping, on the left, points proudly at the
activity taking place in a shipyard.

In his dedication Cornelis van Yk states
that he was apprenticed at a shipyard at the
age of twelve, at the urging of his grand-
father, his father and his uncles, all of whom
were shipwrights. After training as a ship's
carpenter for several years he moved to the
yard of the East India Company at Delfshaven, near Rotterdam, which was managed
by Leenders Symonsz. Heerman, and his
uncle, Cornelis Jansz. van Yk. During the
six or seven years he spent at the yard he
made 'many observations of things I saw and
which I felt worthy of note.' On his uncle's
death he acquired his numerous notes and
'all his writings on shipbuilding.' After he
had abandoned his trade he used this wealth
of material to write his *De Nederlandsche
scheeps-bouw-konst open gestelt* (Dutch shipbuilding unveiled).

121-132

JAN VAN ALMELOVEEN after **HERMAN SAFTLEVEN**

Series of twelve inland vessels, with views of towns and villages

Etchings. Bartsch, Hollstein 1-12. First state of two. In the second state the prints are numbered *1-12*.

Almost all the towns and villages in this series are on the banks of the River Lek, between Vianen and Rotterdam, following the Lek downstream and making a small detour up the IJssel. However, the sequence of the numbered second states is: Lecxmond (11), Jaarsveld (2), Loopick (6), Thienhoven by Ameyde (7), Langerack (3), Schoonhoven (9), Groot Ammers (8), De Hoeck van Kleyn Ammers (5), Streeskerck (12), Lekkerkerck (10), Krimpen (4), Capel (1). The publisher of the numbered series evidently attached little importance to geographical consistency.

121

JAN VAN ALMELOVEEN after **HERMAN SAFTLEVEN**

'Capel'

Below the border at bottom left are the artist's initials, *HSL. invent.*, and at bottom right the name of the etcher, *J. Almeloveen fec.* Numbered *1* in the second state. Capelle aan de IJssel is northeast of Rotterdam.

122

JAN VAN ALMELOVEEN after **HERMAN SAFTLEVEN**

'Jaarsveld'

Numbered *2* in the second state.

123

JAN VAN ALMELOVEEN after **HERMAN SAFTLEVEN**

'Langerack'

Numbered *3* in the second state.

Capel

121

Jaarsveld.

122

Langerack

123

124

JAN VAN ALMELOVEEN after **HERMAN SAFTLEVEN**

'Krimpen'

Numbered *4* in the second state.

The title could refer to two places, either Krimpen aan de Lek or Krimpen aan de IJssel. As with the other prints in the series, the village view, consisting of nothing more than a church, is too sketchy for identification purposes.

125

JAN VAN ALMELOVEEN after **HERMAN SAFTLEVEN**

'De Hoeck van Kleyn Ammers'

Numbered *5* in the second state.

'Hoeck' is the name of a stretch of land on the Lek, southwest of the town of Bergambacht.

126

JAN VAN ALMELOVEEN after **HERMAN SAFTLEVEN**

'Loopick'

Numbered *6* in the second state.

Saftleven's drawing (98 x 78 mm.) for this print is in the Pushkin Museum, Moscow. Van Almeloveen followed the drawing very closely, but left out approximately 1 cm. all round. As a result of the printing process, the print itself is a reverse image of the drawing.

Krimpen

124

De Hoeck van kleyn Ammers.

125

Loopick.

126

127

JAN ALMELOVEEN after HERMAN SAFTLEVEN

'*Tienhoven by Ameyde*'

Numbered *7* in the second state.

128

JAN VAN ALMELOVEEN after HERMAN SAFTLEVEN

'*Groot Ammers*'

Numbered *8* in the second state.

129

JAN VAN ALMELOVEEN after HERMAN SAFTLEVEN

'*Schoonhoven*'

Numbered *9* in the second state.

130

JAN VAN ALMELOVEEN after HERMAN SAFTLEVEN

'*Lekkerkerck*'

Numbered *10* in the second state.

131

JAN VAN ALMELOVEEN after HERMAN SAFTLEVEN

'*Lecxmond*'

Numbered *11* in the second state.

132

JAN VAN ALMELOVEEN after HERMAN SAFTLEVEN

'*Streeskerck*'

Numbered *12* in the second state.
 The name of the village is actually Streef-kerk. Van Almeloveen probably read the *f* as a long *s*.

Thienhoven by Ameyde.

127

Groot Ammers

128

Schoonhoven.

129

Lekker kerck.

130

Lecxmond

131

Streeskerck

132

1.2. Eerste hoofd van Hellevoetsluys naar de zyde van het
   Oude Hoornze Veer.
3. Zyn K. H. nevens Schomberg, Solms, Herbert, Benting, etc.
   zyn afscheid neemende van de aanzienlykste Leeden des Staats.

4. de Pink van zyn K. H. leggende aan de wal.
5. 't Schip van de Lt. Adm. Generaal Herbert.
6. De Arriergarde der oorlogs schepen.
7. Branders.

The key beneath the scene reads as follows:

3. Het Middel corps van Fluyten, Pinasjen etc.
9. Pinken en kleen vaar tuy g.
10. Evertsen de rechter vleugel } *gebiedende.*
11. Almonde de slinker vleugel

12. Het schip van zyn K.H. den Briel genaamt.
13. Avantguarde. 14. Adys jachten.
15. Staande op de scheepen de vlag met het opschrift:
Pro Libertate et Religione: je Maintiendray.

'Departure from Holland of His Royal Highness, the Prince of Orange, on November 11, 1688'

Etching. Muller 2692. On the pier on the right is the address, C. *Allard Excudit.*

In 1688 Stadholder William III (1650–1702) sailed from Hellevoetsluis on the island of Voorn, southwest of Rotterdam, in response to an appeal by the English Protestants that he come to England to displace his unpopular father-in-law, King James II, who had become a convert to Catholicism.

This and the following print are from a series of twenty depicting English history and the doings of William III between 1688 and 1691.

The key beneath the scene reads as follows:

1. 2. The main pier at Hellevoetsluis, seen from the side of the Old Hoorn Ferry.

3. His Royal Highness, with Schomberg, Solms, Herbert, Benting and others, taking leave of the leading members of the States.

4. His Royal Highness's pink lying alongside the pier.

5. The ship of Lieutenant Admiral-General Herbert.

6. Warships forming the rearguard.

7. Fireships.

8. The main body of flutes, pinnaces, etc.

9. Pinks and small vessels.

10. Evertsen commanding the right wing.

11. Almonde commanding the left wing.

12. Den Briel, His Royal Highness's ship.

13. Vanguard.

14. Dispatch vessels.

15. Flag with the inscription: *Pro Libertate et Religione: je Maintiendray.*

Vertrek van haar Konin
PRINSES YA
uit Holland. den

Carolus Allard Excudit Cum Privilegie.

1. Haar K. H. in het Staate jagt, van eenige Leeden van onzen Staat afscheid neemende. 4. Herbert op het oorlogs schip staande
2. Obdam, Alewyn Valkenier, en Steenhuysen, uitgezonderd, om met haar K. H. over te steken. 5. Des Konings afgezondene scheepen a
3. Het Koninglyke schip bezet met boots volk, vol verlangen, om haar K. H. te ontfangen. 6. Scheepen van den Staat tot het wele

*'Departure from Holland of Her Royal
Highness, the Princess of Orange, on February
20, 1689'*

Etching. Muller 2692. In the water at bottom
left is the address and statement: *Carolus Allard Excudit Cum Privilegie*. See also nr. 133.

Mary Stuart, Princess of Orange (1662–
94), sailed from the Netherlands in February
1689 to join her husband, William III, in
England. In April of that year they were
crowned King and Queen of England.

The print shows the princess taking leave
of members of the States-General on the
States yacht, which is alongside the royal
yacht. In the background, beyound the masts
of the massed ships, is the town of Brill.

The key beneath the scene reads as follows:

1. Her Royal Highness in the States yacht,
taking leave of various members of the
States-General.

2. Obdam, Alewyn, Valkenier and Steenhuysen, chosen to accompany Her Royal
Highness on the voyage.

3. The royal vessel, with its crew eager to
receive Her Royal Highness.

4. Herbert standing on the warship ready to
help Her Royal Highness aboard.

5. Ships sent by the King as escorts.

6. Ships of the state to serve the same
purpose.

7. Diverse pleasure boats with people de-
sirous of seeing Her Royal Highness before
she departs.

8. A pleasing prospect of the town of Brill,
seen between the masts and rigging.

Fig. 135a Caspar Luyken, Pamphlet entitled 'Description of the maritime display…,' for which print nr. 135 was originally made. 1697. Etching and letterpress, ca. 44 x 30 cm.

Beschrijving van het Watervermaak, door order der Ed. Magiſtraat van de Stad Amſterdam, ter eere van het Groot Muskoviſch Gezantſchap, aangeſteld op den eerſten September 1697.

Het eerſte Eſquadre was verdeelt onder den Admiraal met de Vlag &c. de Wimpel van booven.

Tot Amſterdam by CAREL ALLARD op den Dam, met Privilegie van de Ed. Gr. Mog. Heeren Staaten van Holland en Weſt-friesland.

Vlagman de Vlag van booven.

Het tweede Eſquadre gerangeert onder den Admiraal met de Vlag van booven.

Admiraal met de Wimpel booven de Vlag.

Seynen en Rangeering.

A mock sea battle held in honor of the Muscovite Legation

Etching. Muller 2986. Van Eeghen 1670. At bottom center, below the border, is the address and statement: *C. Allard excudit cum Privilegio.* Numbered *1* (?) at bottom right, which has been converted into *12* by pen.

Although this print is occasionally found as a separate sheet, it was originally executed for a pamphlet entitled *Beschrijving van het Watervermaak, door order der Ed. Magistraat van de Stad Amsterdam, ter eere van het Groot Muskovisch Gezantschap, aangesteld op den eersten September 1697* (Description of the maritime display held on September 1, 1697, by order of the Noble Magistrate of the City of Amsterdam, in honor of the Great Muscovite Legation; fig. 135a). Part of that title was printed in the margin of the print.

Tsar Peter the Great and the Great Muscovite Legation visited Amsterdam in 1697, and on September 1 the city authorities organised a mock battle on the River IJ to mark the occasion. Forty-six vessels took part, including thirty-six pleasure craft and four ferries (numbered 5, 6, 7 and 8 on the print), manned by the scions of leading burgher families, the yacht of the West India Company (nr. 3), the yacht of Friesland (nr. 4), and the small and large yachts of the East India Company (nrs. 1 and 2), which acted as the flagships of the two sides. Overall supervision of the battle was in the hands of Vice-Admiral Gillis Schey. In order to ensure that the display went smoothly, the participants were issued with a signal code, with instructions for various manoeuvres to be carried out in concert. The battle commenced at 2.30 in the afternoon, and ended as evening fell.

The print shows the two flagships engaging each other. The large yacht of the East India Company is on the left, and the small yacht, with its mainsail brailed up, is on the right. Both ships are also being attacked by two ferry boats.

The illustration is slightly reduced; the actual size of the print is 23 x 28 cm.

135a

E. Allard excudit cum Privilegio.

12.4

135

The jetty

Etching. Bartsch 5. Weigel, p. 224 (as Bargas). Hollstein 5. First state of two. The border at top and bottom was completed in the second state. Weigel considers that the print was made by A. F. Bargas after a painting or drawing by Bout, who was probably his teacher.

137

Twee Steyger Schuyten,

137a

NAVIGIORUM
ÆDIFICATIO.

'tSchips kiel gelegt en steven opgerecht. ‖ Navis carina ponitur, proraque erigitur.

P. Schenk exc. Amst. C.P.

1

138

137
ISAAK VAN DE VINNE

Vignette with a steigerschuit

Woodcut. Enschedé, p. 148, nr. 3057. The printer's mark in the sky at top right has not been identified.

Enschedé states that this woodcut was one of the vignettes from the collection of initials, vignettes, ornamental borders and the like assembled by the Enschedé printing firm from the eighteenth century onwards. The reproduction in his book is after a late impression, when the woodblock had begun to split, and lacked part of the border. The woodcut was much favored by book printers in the late seventeenth century and in the eighteenth century, since it could be used repeatedly. Etchings were preferred for smaller editions.

Van de Vinne took as the model for this vessel a print entitled '*Two steigerschuits*' from the series *Diverse ships and views of Amsterdam* by Reinier Nooms (fig. 137a).

Fig. 137a   Reinier Nooms, 'Two steiger-schuits,' ca. 1655. Etching, 13.7 x 25.1 cm.

138-153
SIEUWERT VAN DER MEULEN

A series of sixteen prints depicting the construction, career and ultimate fate of a ship under the general title of *Navigiorum aedificatio.*

Etchings. Muller 3013A. Wurzbach 1. Beneath each print in the series there is an inscription in Dutch and Latin, and the address *P. Schenk exc. Amst. C. P.* It is not clear why Muller also associated the etcher de Winter with this unique series. All the prints are signed by van der Meulen.

Although the prints make no pretense of being topographically accurate, there are certain details which clearly refer to Amsterdam. Some of the ships fly an Amsterdam flag, with a broad white field in the middle; the tower in nr. 143 is similar to Weepers' Tower; the large, heavy-duty crane stood in the IJ opposite that tower; and the figure of Atlas on the stern of the ship in nrs. 144 and 148 is distinctly reminiscent of the same figure on the roof of Amsterdam Town Hall (now the Royal Palace on Dam Square).

138
SIEUWERT VAN DER MEULEN

'The ship's keel is laid and the stem erected'

Signed *SVM* in the dark area at bottom right. Numbered *1* below the border at bottom right. This first sheet also bears the title of the series: '*Navigiorum aedificatio.*'

139
SIEUWERT VAN DER MEULEN

'A start is made with the ship's planking'

Signed *SV. M* in the water at bottom center. Numbered *2* below the border at bottom right.

Het Schip werd begonnen met boeyen en optimmeren.   Navis locantur fundamenta, prora puppisque eriguntur.

P. Schenk exc. Amst. CP.

'*The planks rise all round the ship*'

Signed *SVM* in the water at bottom right.
Numbered *3* below the border at bottom
right.

Het schip word aan alle kanten opgetimmerd.   ‖Navis contexitur costis; firmatur, vestitur, munitur.

P. Schenk exc. Amst. C.P.   3

'The ship is butted and forced to slip into the water'

Signed *SV Meulen* on the planks in the water at bottom left. Numbered *4* below the border at bottom right.

Het schip word gerammeyd en gedwongen om af te loopen. Navis, arietando et crebris pulsibus in aquas propellitur.

P. Schenk exc. Amst. CP.

4

'*The ship slides into the water*'

Signed *SVM* at bottom left. Numbered *5*
below the border at bottom right.

Het schip, in het sakken en afloopen, in het water. ‖ Navis, repetitis pulsibus adacta, in aquas proruens.

P. Schenk. exc. Amst. C.P.

5

'The masts are stepped'

Signed *SVM* at bottom left. Numbered *6* below the border at bottom right.

Het schip ontfangt syn masten.   Navi fabricatæ maior minorque malus infigitur.

P. Schenk exc. Amst. CP.   6

'The ship is rigged and its yards hoisted'

Signed *SVM* at bottom right. Numbered *7*
below the border at bottom right.

Het schip word toegetaakeld, en haare marssen opgehyst. | *Navis funibus ac rudentibus armatur, eisque galeæ adhibentur*

P. Schenk exc. Amst. C.P.

7

'The ship is careened…'

Signed *SVM* at bottom right. Numbered *8* below the border at bottom right.

Het schip word gekielhaald en op zy gekrengt, om te verhuyden, te breuwen of te harpuysen. ‖ Navis in latus propellitur, ei cortex obducitur, rimæ filis ac cera stipantur.

P. Schenk exc. Amst. C.P.

8

'The ship is careened on the other side'

Signed *SVM* in the water at bottom right.
Numbered *9* below the border at bottom
right.

'The ship being provisioned with good victuals'

Signed *SVM* in the water at bottom right.
Numbered *10* below the border at bottom
right.

Het schip word op de andere zy-de gekielhaald. — Navis in latus alterum propulsa, firmatur.

P. Schenk exc. Amst. C.P.

Het schip word met behoorlyke victalie versien.   'Navi victus atque amictus cœteraque adduntur necessaria.

P. Schenk exc: Amst. C.P.   10

'Ships putting to sea'

Signed *SV Meulen* on the parapet at bottom
right. Numbered *11* below the border at bottom right.

Het uitloopen der Schepen, in Zee.   Naves, à statione recedentes, mare petunt.

P. Schenk exc. Amst. C.P.   11

'*The ship out on the open sea, after leaving the
yard*'

Signed *SVM* on a flag by the large ship.
Numbered *12* below the border at bottom
right.

Schip in volle Zee, van de werf synde afgeloopen. ‖ Navis, iam perfecta et absoluta, aperto mari dans vela ventis.

P. Schenk exc. Amst. C.P.

12

'*Ships ravaged by a sea battle*'

Signed *SV.M* on the flag flying from the
stern of the ship on the left. Numbered *13*
below the border at bottom right.

Schepen, door een zeeslagh geruineerd. ‖Naves, maritimo prælio perforatæ, diffractæ, crematæ.

P. Schenk exc. Amst. C.P.

SIEUWERT VAN DER MEULEN

'*A ship caught in a storm and dashed to pieces on the rocks*'

Signed *SVM* on the rock to the right of the ship. Numbered *14* below the border at bottom right.

EenSchip door storm overvallen, en tusschen de klippen ‖ Navis, tempestate oppressa, scopulis allisa.
aan stukken geslagen.

P. Schenk exc. Amst. C.P.

14

'*A ship cast ashore in a storm*'

Signed *SV Meulen* at bottom left. Numbered *15* below the border at bottom right.

'*An old and worn-out ship at the breaker's yard*'

Signed *SVM* in the water at bottom left. Numbered *16* below the border at bottom right.

Een Schip, door een storm op strand gesmeeten.　Navis, procellis in littus ejecta et arenis immersa.

P. Schenk exc. Amst. C.P.

15

Een oud en afgefleeten Schip word gefloopt. ‖ Annofa et emerita Navis iterum in partes confcinditur.

P. Schenk exc. Amft. C.P.

16

Ships at sea

Etching. Nagler 1. Second state of two.
Signed *A. Silo inv: et fect* below the border at
bottom center. In the first state there is less
hatching in the ships, and the signature is
lacking.
    This and the following two prints come
from a series of six depicting ships at sea.

Roadstead with a fishing boat and other vessels

Etching. Nagler 4. Second state of two.
Signed *A: Silo inv: et fect* below the border
at bottom center. In the first state state there
is less hatching in the sky and ships, and the
signature is lacking. See also nr. 154.

156

ADAM SILO

Shipwreck

Etching. Nagler 5. Second state of two (?).
Signed *A: Silo inv: et fect* below the border
at bottom center. See also nr. 154.

157

ADOLF VAN DER LAAN after SIEUWERT VAN
DER MEULEN

'Damschuit'

Etching. Thieme-Becker, vol. 22, p. 160
(fourteen sheets). Below the border at bottom
left is the name of the artist, *S.Vdr Meulen
Delineavit*, and at bottom right the name of
the etcher, *A. Vander Laan Fecit*. In the center, above the title, is the address, *P. Schenk
Iun: Excudit Amst: cum Priv:*. This information is only to be found on this print, which is
one of an untitled and unnumbered series of
sixteen (?) prints of Dutch and foreign vessels, to which the following three prints also
belong. It therefore seems probable that this
was the first print of the series.

The shaded areas of these prints have been
reinforced with the burin at various points.

Damschuits were ferries plying between
Amsterdam and the neighbouring villages.
The *damschuit* was about six feet shorter than
the *damloper*, which generally had a length of
around fifty-two feet. According to Nicolaas
Witsen the *damschuit* was related to the *smalschip*, and this is borne out by another print in
van der Laan's series entitled '*Smalship or
damschuit with a peaked taffrail.*'

This reproduction is after a print in the possession of the Netherlands National Maritime
Museum, Amsterdam.

A: Silo inv: et fect

S. V.dr Meulen Delineavit.   P. Schenk Iun: Excudit Amst: cum Priv: A. Vander Laan Fecit.

Dam-Schuyt.

ADOLF VAN DER LAAN after SIEUWERT VAN
DER MEULEN

'Steigerschuit, kop boat or yacht'

Etching. Thieme-Becker, vol. 22, p. 160
(fourteen sheets). See also nr. 157.

Kop yacht and *steigerschuit* were two names
for the same type of vessel. The *kop* yacht got
its name from the fore part, or head ('kop' in
Dutch) of the craft, which had a greater vertical depth compared to a boeier yacht of the
same length and beam. The name *steigerschuit*
was derived from the landing stage ('steiger')
where the passage boats and ferries lay. Nicolaas Witsen records that the *steigerschuit* was
used 'to carry people across the inland sea and
lakes.' It was also hired out as a pleasure craft.

Styger-schuyt, of Kop-boot, of Jagt.

'A common Dutch hooker'

Etching. Thieme–Becker, vol. 22, p. 160
(fourteen sheets). See also nr. 157.

Een ordinaere Hollandse Hoeker.

ADOLF VAN DER LAAN after SIEUWERT VAN
DER MEULEN

'*A States or burgher yacht, with a transom*'

Etching. Thieme-Becker, vol. 22, p. 160
(fourteen sheets). See also nr. 157.

A States yacht was a yacht owned by the
States-General or the Provincial States. The
same type of vessel was known as a burgher
yacht when it belonged to a prosperous citizen, or burgher.

This reproduction is after a print in the
possession of the Netherlands National Maritime Museum, Amsterdam.

ADOLF VAN DER LAAN after SIEUWERT VAN
DER MEULEN

'*An hulk or great Hoy upon Herring Fishing
place*'

Etching. Muller 3013C. Wurzbach 5 (twelve
sheets). Numbered *8* below the border at
bottom right.

This and the following two prints are from
a series of sixteen depicting the catching,
processing, sale, etc. of herring. All the prints
have an English inscription, in addition to
the Dutch, probably to give them a more international appeal.

Van der Laan executed a similar series of
sixteen prints on whaling. The two series
were combined, and a first sheet with a title
print, *The great fishery*, was added. That title
print bore the names of van der Meulen as
the designer, van der Laan as the etcher, and
Petrus Schenk as the publisher. The smud-
ges in the English inscription were caused by
dirt on the plate.

Staaten of Heere Jagt, met een spiegel.

Een Hoeker op de Neeringh. ‖ *An Hulk or great Hoy upon Herring Fishing place.*

ADOLF VAN DER LAAN after SIEUWERT VAN
DER MEULEN

*'A Double Shore or Sea Boar upon the Herring
Fishing place'*

Etching. Muller 3013C. Wurzbach 5 (twelve
sheets). Numbered 9 below the border at
bottom right. See also nr. 161.

A pink about twice the size of a normal
pink was known as a 'double shore or sea
boat.' (The word 'boar' in the English inscription is almost certainly a misreading of
the word 'boat.') It is believed that the
nineteenth-century *bomschip* developed from
this type of vessel. The etching shows the
boat lying to its nets with its mast lowered
and resting in a large crutch on the starboard
quarter. To the right is another double shore
boat with a Dutch gaff sail.

The normal way of hauling in a fishing net,
as done on a buss for example, was to bring
the net in over the side through a roller fairlead, and to haul the net warp in over the
bows. Here the process has been reversed.

Een dubbelde strandt of Zee Schuyt op de Neeringh.‖ a Double Shore or Sea Boar upon the Herring Fishing place.

ADOLF VAN DER LAAN after SIEUWERT VAN
DER MEULEN

'The Herring Busse put out to Sea'

Etching. Muller 3013C. Wurzbach 5 (twelve
sheets). Numbered *11* below the border at
bottom right. See also nr. 161.

De Buyssen Loopen in Zee ‖ *The Herring Busse put out to Sea*

'The Dutch floods of 1740 and 1741'

Etching, with engraving in the shaded areas. Muller 3780a. First state of two. Signed and dated *J.C.Philips inv. et fecit, 1741* at bottom center, below a banderole with the address *t' Amsterdam by Kornelis de Wit* (Cornelis de Wit, at Amsterdam). The six river gods around the scene are named as *Donauw* (Danube), *Main*, *Maas*, *Rhyn* (Rhine), *Seine* and *Tiber*.

This was the title print of the *Historisch verhaal van de waternood in 1740 en 1741* (An account of the inundations of 1740 and 1741). In December and January of those years large areas of Gelderland and Brabant were flooded. The town in the background of this print could be Nijmegen.

In the second state (Muller 3780b and 4015A), which was published by T.Crajenschot, the title was changed to *Nederlands water-nood en verscheide bezoekingen* (The Dutch floods and other visitations). Five medallions were also added in that state, depicting such visitations and disasters as teredo worms, a harsh winter, cattle plague, etc. The print was used in this form to illustrate a pamphlet of 1751 entitled *Representation of God's visitations on the Netherlands; on the occasion of the breaching of the dike at Jaarsveld. In the year MDCCLI* and again to illustrate the inundations of 1775 (Muller 4301)!

165

SIMON FOKKE after L. LOOSJES

'Dutch ice-boats…'

Etching. Muller 4003. Second state of two. The first state lacked all text. The name of the designer, *L. Loosjes, inv.*, appears below the border at bottom left, and at bottom right is the name of the etcher, *S. Fokke fec*. Numbered *Pl. IX.* above the border at top right. The print was published facing page 1378 of J.le Francq van Berkhey's *Natuurlyke historie van Holland* (Natural history of Holland), vol. 3, Amsterdam 1776.

At this point in the book there is a passage describing how swiftly these boats sailed over the ice with a two-man crew. On occasion they could apparently cover in two minutes 'a distance which would take quarter of an hour to walk on foot.'

The inscription states that the boats are sailing on the Zaan. This is borne out by the view of Zaandam in the background, and by the windmills on the river bank. A great deal of timber was transported along the Zaan, and from the sixteenth century onwards numerous *paltrok* and capwinder (the mills in this print) sawmills were built along the banks of the river.

Pl. IX.

De Hollandſche Yſſchuitjes, in verſchillende ſtanden, zeilende op de Zaan, benevens eenige Hollandſche Yſſleden enz.

'View near the Old Yacht Basin…'

Etching. Wurzbach 12. First state of three.
Signed *S. Fokke ad viv. del. et fec.* below the
border at bottom left. Beneath the inscription
is the address, *Te Amsterdam by P. Fouquet
junior.* (P. Fouquet junior, at Amsterdam). In
the right half of the margin there is a simpli-
fied form of the inscription, together with the
address, both in French. In the second state
the print was numbered *41*, and in the third
state the address was changed to that of Maaskamp. These states may have been preceded
by a proof impression without the inscription.
The impression reproduced here, without a
fold and unnumbered, would have been sold
as a single sheet.

Despite being numbered *41*, this was one of
the first sheets of the first part of the *Nieuwe
atlas van de voornaamste gebouwen en gezigten
der stad Amsterdam* (New atlas of the principal buildings and views of the city of Amsterdam), published in 1783 by D. J. Changuion
and P. den Hengst. This two-volume '*Fouquet Atlas,*' as it came to be known, was an
annotated edition of the *Afbeeldingen van de
wyd-vermaarde koopstad Amsterdam…*
(Views of the far-famed mercantile city of
Amsterdam…), which consisted of one hundred prints commissioned by Pierre Fouquet
(1729-1800) and published by him around
1780 (see also nr. 177). Fouquet was a dealer
in prints, drawings and paintings. He was
not, however, a bookseller, and when it became clear that there was a demand for an
explanatory text to accompany his *Views* he
was consequently barred from publishing the
edition himself. It seems likely that he then
commissioned Changuion and den Hengst to
produce it for him.

After Fouquet's death the plates passed to
Charles Hodges, a leading portrait painter
and art dealer. In 1805 Evert Maaskamp published another edition of the atlas, by which
time the plates had become extremely worn.
Many of them were reworked, the dates were
removed, and Fouquet's address replaced by
Maaskamp's.

Fokke's drawing for this print (formerly in
the C. van Eeghen collection) is dated 1762.
This was probably one of the first prints produced for Fouquet's edition of around 1780.

The print shows the western section of the
palisade of mooring posts in the IJ before
Amsterdam. This double row of posts was a
continuation of the city walls, joining up with
Funen and Blauwhoofd bastions to the east
and west. The artist chose a viewpoint between the twin palisade opposite the harbor
office of the Old Yacht Basin. Built in 1622-
23, this was the first basin ever to be specifically designed for pleasure craft. It provided
berths for thirty-two large vessels and seven
smaller ones. The basin was administered by

S. Fokke ad viv. del. et fec.

GEZICHT by de OUDE JAGTHAVEN
naar 't Blaauwhoofd te zien.

Te Amsteldam by P. Fouquet junior.

VUE du Y devant Amſterdam.

A Amſterdam chez P. Fouquet junior.

four supervisors, with an assistant for the day-to-day operation. The berths, like the yachts, were privately owned. In 1629 a terrace was built on the IJ side of the basin, giving a magnificent view of the ships moored along the palisade. In 1644 a small house was built on the harbor side of the terrace, and it was here that the supervisors met once a month. The Old Yacht Basin was not the only berthing place for pleasure craft in Amsterdam; there was another one on the River Amstel, the earliest notice of which is in the third edition of the street plan of the city by Balthasar Florisz. van Berckenrode, which was published in 1647. The Amstel Yacht Basin was demolished in 1657 as a result of a city extension program, and a new basin was built at the end of Kattenburg Island. To the west of the Old Yacht Basin was the Nieuwe Waal, an inner harbor where merchantmen could overwinter. The print reproduced here shows a number of three-masters in the Nieuwe Waal harbor. In the background are the buildings on Realen Island and the Bok windmill on Blauwhoofd bastion. To the right of the outer palisade are the house and wheel of a dredging mill, and the masts of several ships at anchor.

167 ▶

ISAAC LODEWIJK LA FARGUE VAN
NIEUWLAND

'View of the Berebijt on the Outer Amstel'

Etching. Previously unpublished. Signed *Nuwland ad viv. et Fec.* below the border at bottom left, and with the address *te Amsterdam by P. Fouquet Junior* at bottom center.

The Berebijt inn, near Utrecht Gate on what is now Amsteldijk, was a terminus for ferry services to towns to the south and east, like Gouda, Leiden and Weesp. The inn was demolished around 1880, and the site is now occupied by a garage of the same name, at the point where the Tweede Jan van der Heijdenstraat comes out onto the Amstel. The name Berebijt is derived from fights, which were held well into the seventeenth century, between bull mastiffs, also known as 'bear-biters' (*berebijters*), and bears or bulls. This form of public entertainment evidently took place at the inn on the right.

Nieuwland ad riv. et Fec.

GEZIGT van de BEEREBEYDT o

te Amsterdam by P. Fou

de BUYTEN AMSTEL .

Junior.

Prospect of the French Frigat la Félicité, Capt. Denel, GEZIGT van't Fransch
chased upon the Shore, at the Height of 's Gravez and by ter Hoogte van 's GRAVE
an English Frigat, the Richmond, Capt. Elphinston. Engelsch Fregat THE RIC

P. C. la Fargue ad viv. del. 25 J

168

'Prospect of the French Frigate la Felicité...'

Etching. Muller 4117. Beneath the inscription, which is in English, Dutch and French, there is the signature and date *P.C. la Fargue ad viv. del. 25 Jan. 1761, Hora 4½ Vespert., & sculps. Hagae Comit.* In other words, la Fargue made a drawing of the stranded frigate at 4:30 in the afternoon of January 25, 1761, and then returned to his home in The Hague, where he prepared the plate.

The print depicts the final phase of a sea battle described by Jan Wagenaar in vol. 23 of his *Vaderlandsche historie* (History of the fatherland). He relates how the French frigate, *La Felicité*, laden with wine, provisions and war supplies, sailed from Dunkirk on January 9, 1761, bound for San Domingo in the West Indies. The following day *La Felicité* was engaged by an English frigate and four smaller vessels, but managed to escape and return to Dunkirk. After the damage had been repaired the frigate put to sea again, and in its turn captured an English ship which was freed after a sizable ransom had been paid. 'Then, upon the following day, an English frigate of thirty-two guns appeared, under the command of Captain Elphiston, in company with another English vessel and a bomb ketch, all of which gave chase. The French captain ordered the hands to the oars, but to no avail. The English frigate, the *Richmond*, had the advantage of the wind, and approached to within musket shot, whereupon a bitter battle ensued. Denel [the captain of *La Felicité*], who was outgunned, sought to retreat to a harbor, and approached our coast near 's Gravenzand. The ship went aground, the captain was hit by a cannonball, and many were killed or wounded by the ceaseless hail of fire poured into the frigate by the three enemy ships. As the tide fell the crew brought the wounded ashore, seeing that their ship was beyond saving. The English captain demanded the surrender of the frigate, threatening that if this was not done immediately he would give no quarter and would fire the stranded vessel. This so terrified the defenseless men that they all resolved to flee ashore, abandoning ship, and taking with them no more than a modicum of clothing. Destitute, these hapless mariners landed on our shores near 's Gravenzand, leaving the French flag flying on the stranded frigate. As the tide began to flood the English approached, replaced the French flag with that of England, and removed as many provisions and other goods as possible from a rich cargo, which the English themselves estimated at thirty thousand pounds sterling, before setting fire to the wreck.'

Zie nu, in deeze print, den Zeeslag voor 'slands eer',
Hoe hier held ZOUTMAN, ginds KINSBERGEN, in 't geweer,
Den weiffelenden stryd, in 't end, deedt overhellen,
En joeg den Brit voor uit, met Hollands Zee korellen.

HAC
HANC

NITIMUR

TUEMUR

Ja zie, hoe 't Britſche volk, hoe PARKER beeft en zucht,
Zyn uitkomst zoekt in een hem ſchandelyke vlugt.
Zoo gaat het, als men, door het traitren en het marren,
Den Nederlandſchen Leeuw, op zyne Zee, durft ſarren. J.L.F.V.B.

The Battle of Dogger Bank

Etching, with engraving in the shaded areas.
Muller 4435a. Third state of four. Signed
K.F.Bendorp.del.et.sculp. in the fourth state.
In the first state the scene was a straightforward
etching. In the second state numerous
engraved lines were added, together with the
signature. The signature was then removed,
and the inscription, the coat of arms and the
letters and the figures in the scene added.
The letters and figures referred to a key
which accompanied the print when it was reproduced
in J. le Francq van Berkhey's *Zee-triumf…* (Triumph at sea…). The signature,
written in a different form, was restored in
the fourth state.

At bottom center, between the two halves
of van Berkhey's poem, are the words *Hac nitimur
hanc tuemur* (On this we rely, and this
we cherish), the device of the Republic of the
United Provinces. The drawing for this print
is in the printroom of the Rijksmuseum, Amsterdam
(Frederik Muller collection).

The poem beneath the print reads as follows:
'Behold, in this print, a sea battle for
our country's honor; | See here how brave
Zoutman, and there Kinsbergen, standing to
arms, | Turned the changing fortunes of the
battle to their advantage | And drove the
British before them, with the aid of Holland's
sea-colonels. || Yes, behold how the British,
behold how Parker quakes and sighs, | And
seeks salvation in shameful flight, | Let this be
a lesson to those who, by abuse and obstruction,
| Dare to twist the tail of the Dutch lion
on his home sea.'

It is clear from this jubilant poem that the
Dutch regarded the Battle of Dogger Bank
of August 5, 1781, as a famous victory. In
reality it was an indecisive encounter, but the
fact that the more heavily gunned English
were the first to break line was regarded as
flight on their part. The officers mentioned,
Rear-Admiral Zoutman and Captain van
Kinsbergen, with seven men-of-war, were
convoying seventy merchantmen en route to
the Baltic when they fell in with an English
convoy escorted by seven warships under the
command of Sir Hyde Parker. A fierce battle
broke out, with the outcome mentioned
above. This was the only 'victory' the Dutch
were to enjoy in the otherwise ill-starred
Fourth Anglo-Dutch War (1780-84).

'T VERZEILEN VAN 'S LANDS SCHIP PRINS WII

EM, OP DE ZUIDER-HAAKS, den 14.ᵉ Sept.ʳ 1781.

170-173
CAREL FREDERIK BENDORP

A series of four prints, sold in a portfolio with the inscription: *Tweede en laatste stel van vier Kunstplaaten, verbeeldende Vaderlandsche Historien ter Zee* (Second and final set of four art plates, depicting the actions of the fatherland at sea).

Muller 4458 II, 1-4. The blue cover of the portfolio bears the names of publishers Harmanus Keyzer and Jan Barend Elwe, who issued the prints in 1784, as well as a list of the contents. The first portfolio contained prints of two events from 1782, and one each from 1783 and 1784. The prints reproduced here deal with events of 1781 and 1784.

170

CAREL FREDERIK BENDORP

'*The Dutch warship, the Prins Willem, runs aground on the Southern Haaks, September 14, 1781*'

Etching. Muller 4471 and 4458 II, 2. Second state of two. Signed *K.F.B. del. et sculp.* in the water at bottom left. The first state lacked the inscription.

The *Prins Willem*, commanded by Captain A. de Bruyn, proceeded to sea on September 10, 1781, to escort a homeward-bound East Indiaman and seven merchantmen. Although the Southern Haaks sandbank was clearly visible from the water breaking over it, and despite the fact that several anchored warships signalled that the *Prins Willem* was standing into danger, the ship ran onto the sandbank and was lost. The wreck caused a considerable stir, partly because the fleet was already way below strength. The Supreme Maritime Court Martial held that the captain had been 'imprudent, careless and confused,' and he was dismissed from the service. The pilot, who was censured for his 'indescribable carelessness and inexcusable disregard for the ship's safety,' was sentenced to be 'dropped thrice from the yardarm, and then, strictly at the discretion of the Commissioners of this Supreme Maritime Court Martial, lashed.' In those days flogging was done with a rope's end covered in felt.

'S LANDS SCHIP DE VRYHEID, BY MINORCA OP LAAGER-WA

VERVALLEN, IN DEN STORM, tusschen den 3ᵉ en 4ᵉ Febrᵣ 1784.

'*The Dutch warship, De Vrijheid, on a lee shore in a storm off Minorca, between February 3 and 4, 1784*'

Etching. Muller 4538a and 4458 II, 4.
Second state of two. The first state lacked the inscription.

In 1783 the States-General decided to dispatch a squadron to the Mediterranean in order to patch up differences thad had arisen between Venice and the Dutch Republic. The squadron, consisting of the *Vrijheid, Noordholland, Hercules, Drenthe, Prins Willem* and *Harlingen*, under the overall command of Vice-Admiral P. H. Reijnst, weighed anchor on December 13 and sailed from the Texel channel for Malaga, which it reached on January 11, 1784. On January 22 the squadron set course for Toulon, but by February 2 it had got no further than the island of Minorca, due to the mild weather and light airs. During the night the wind shifted to the northwest and a storm blew up, and before long a number of the ships were in serious difficulties.

On February 18 Reijnst informed the Amsterdam Admiralty of the events of that night. 'Then, some hours before dawn, we were overwhelmed by a storm of such ferocity as neither I, with all my years of service, nor any of our company can ever recall having experienced. It lasted fully forty-eight hours, and although we were a good twenty miles from the island of Minorca when it blew up, by the forenoon of the second day we were in danger of being driven onto the rocks surrounding that island, and it was only by setting the heaviest press of sail that we were able to avoid them. We found ourselves in this hazardous position for some considerable time, and we sailed so close to the last rocks that the water cast back from them fell over the ship several times. We owe our preservation chiefly to the foresail, which had been newly bent on after the previous one had been blown away at the beginning of the storm, as were most of our sails.'

The print shows the ship on the port tack, clawing its way off the rocks with its foresail, main topmast staysail and mizzen set. The main yard has been lowered to the deck, and the topsails have been torn to shreds.

'T VERGAAN VAN 'S LANDS SCHIP DRENTHE, BY HET EILAN

MINORCA, IN DEN STORM, tusschen den 3⁵ en 4⁵ Febr⁵ 1784.

'*The loss of the Dutch warship Drenthe off the island of Minorca in the storm, between February 3 and 4, 1784*'

Etching. Muller 4539a and 4458 11, 3. Second state of two. The first state lacked the inscription.

The commentary to the preceding print described how the Mediterranean squadron under Vice-Admiral Reijnst got into difficulties in a violent storm in the night of February 3–4, 1784. Lieutenant N. A. van Rijneveld, on board the *Noordholland*, gave the following account of the loss of the *Drenthe*. 'Meanwhile, we saw astern of us a vessel which we had until then taken to be the *Medea*, but was now revealed as the *Drenthe*. She was in a terrible condition, cast on her side, and then a moment later she lay over with her topsail yards in the water, her main topmast gone by the board. The next moment she and everything in and on her disappeared before our eyes. This spectacle, so fearful to us, for we expected no other fate ourselves and were staring death in the face, made the hair rise on our heads in fear and anguish, seeing three hundred and fifty souls being overwhelmed by the raging sea in a second and disappear before our eyes, without being able to save a man of them.'

'T REDDEN VAN DE EQUIPAGIE VAN 'S LANDS SCHIP HOLLAND, gezonk

,,NA DEN SLAG OP DOGGERS·BANK, in den Nacht van den 5.ᵉ Aug.ˢ 1781.

CAREL FREDERIK BENDORP

'The rescue of the crew of the Dutch warship Holland, sunk after the Battle of Dogger Bank, in the night of August 5, 1781'

Etching. Muller 4446a and 4458 II, I. Second state of two. The first state lacked the inscription. Signed *K. F. Bendorp del. et sculp.* in the water at bottom left.

In the Battle of Dogger Bank the *Holland* brought up the rear of the line of battle, and in this position it had to engage two enemy ships. There was so much damage to its masts and rigging, and to the hull below the waterline, that it was decided to abandon the ship. The event was reported as follows in the continuation to Jan Wagenaar's *Vaderlandsche historie* (History of the fatherland). 'Despite having plugged one hundred holes, both above and below the waterline, there were forty inches of water in the well, and even with hard pumping the level continued to rise. During the night it was decided to cast the guns overboard, but this did not avail, and the ship was in imminent danger of sinking. The ship had to be abandoned, and the crew was ferried across to the *Spion*, a dispatch vessel, in a small gig, since the larger gig and the longboat had been shot through and were no longer serviceable. This transfer of so many men to a small ship was carried out with great difficulty at two o'clock at night in the midst of a storm, with thunder and lightning. A number of the wounded and dying had to be left to meet their pitiable fate. The mainmast almost went overboard, and the ship sank into the deeps.'

The Battle of Dogger Bank left both the Dutch and English fleets severely battered (see also nr. 169).

N. v.d. Meer, jun. ad Vir. del. & fec.

GEZICHT IN DE KOEKOEK, BY KAMPEN, I

DE OVERSTROOMING, DEN 15^{DEN}. NOVEMB. 1775.

De Wed. Loveringh en Allart, Excud.

Proefdruk.

'*View of Koekoek, near Kampen, during the floods of November 15, 1775*'

Etching, with engraving in the shaded areas. Muller 4302a(7). First state of three. Signed *N.v.d.Meer, Jun. ad Viv. del. & fec.* below the border at bottom left, and with the address *De Wed. Loveringh en Allart, Excud.* at bottom right. At bottom right, below the inscription, is the annotation *Proefdruk* (Proof impression). This was removed in the second state. In the second state the print was published facing p. 243 of J. H. Hering's *Bespiegeling over Neêrlandsch waternood, tusschen den 14.den en 15.den Nov: MDCCLXXV* (Consideration of the floods in the Netherlands, between November 14 and 15, 1775), vol. 1, Amsterdam 1776. In the third state the address was replaced by that of P. Conradi and V. v. d. Plaats, 1787.

Koekoek was a hamlet near Kampen. It was almost totally destroyed by the storm, and the land reverted to bog.

YGEZICHT, NAAR 'T BLAAUW HOOFD, VOOR AM

ELDAM, IN DEN STORM, DEN 21STEN NOVEMB. 1776.

Proefdruk.

NOACH VAN DER MEER after HENDRIK
KOBELL

'*View of the IJ at Amsterdam, looking towards
Blauwhoofd, during the storm of November 21,
1776*'

Etching, with engraving in the shaded areas.
Muller 4314(1). First state of three. Below
the border at bottom left is the name of the
designer, *H. Kobell, ad Viv. del.*, in the center
the address *De Wed. Loveringh en Allart, Excud.*, and at bottom right the name of the
etcher, *N.v.d. Meer, Jun. sculps.* Below this is
the annotation *Proefdruk* (Proof impression).
This was removed in the second state. In the
third state the title was changed to '*View of
Blauwhoofd, seen from the IJ...,*' and the
names below the border were removed. The
publishers of the third state were P. Conradi
and V. v.d. Plaats, 1787. The print appeared
in the second state in 1778 as one of the five
prints depicting floods in J.H. Hering's *Bespiegeling over Neêrlandsch waternood, tusschen den XXIsten and XXIIsten November,
MDCCLXXVI* (Consideration of the floods
in the Netherlands, between November 21
and 22, 1776; facing p. 12). Unlike the proof
impressions, which were sold loose, the prints
from the book are always folded.

Blauwhoofd was originally called
Leeuwenburg, but it soon acquired its popular name from the blue freestone of which it
was built. The De Bok windmill can be seen
on the bastion. Today this site is occupied by
Barentszplein.

HET SPRINGEN VAN 'S LANDS OORLOGSC

P. Conrad

P ALPHEN, IN DE HAVEN VAN CURAÇAO.

.Plaats excud.1787.

JAN PUNT after HENDRIK KOBELL

'The Dutch warship Alphen destroyed by an explosion in Curaçao harbor'

Etching, with engraving in the shaded areas. Muller 4332b. Third state of three.

In the center, below the title, is the address and date *P. Conradi en v.d. Plaats excud. 1787*. The first state had only the name of Sallieth [!] below the scene. The title, the names of Kobell, the designer, and Punt, the etcher, were added in the second state, together with the address of J. Allart and the date *1779*. The print, in the state reproduced here, was included in the continuation of J. Wagenaar's *Amsterdam, in zyne opkomst, aanwas…* (Amsterdam, its rise, growth…), part 4, Amsterdam 1788 (between pp. 320 and 321).

The *Alphen* had a crew of two hundred and eighty, and was commanded by Captain van der Feltz. On September 15, 1778, it blew up, killing more than two hundred people and causing extensive damage. The cause of the explosion was never discovered. On the right is an English brig, and on the left the flagship of Rear-Admiral van Bijlandt, who had been stationed with a squadron in the West Indies for about a year in order to protect Dutch merchantmen from English privateers.

A drawing of this event by Kobell is in the van Stolk Atlas, Rotterdam. It may have served as a model for this print, although numerous changes were made.

GEZICHT van het ZEEREGT aan den Kamper-Steiger.
tot Amsterdam.

te Amsterdam by P. Fouquet junior.

VUE de l'EDIFICE, nommée ZEEREGT, au Côté du Ty.
à Amsterdam.

à Amsterdam chez P. Fouquet junior.

'*View of the Zeeregt building on Kamper Wharf, Amsterdam*'

Etching. Previously unpublished. First state of three. Signed *H.Schoute, del. ad viv. & fecit.* below the border at bottom left. Below the title at bottom left is the address *te Amsterdam by P. Fouquet junior*. (P. Fouquet junior, at Amsterdam). The title and the address are repeated, in French, in the right half of the print.

The second state, to which the number *40* was added, was published in the *Nieuwe atlas… der stad Amsterdam* (New atlas of the city of Amsterdam), 1783. The third state bears the address of E. Maaskamp. See also nr. 166.

The 'Zeeregt' (Maritime Court) was built in 1618 as a guardhouse. It got its name from the court of Admiralty Commissioners, which was held in the building between 1641 and 1655. The building was demolished in 1878, having served the last ten years of its life as the offices of the Municipal Water Board. It stood on Prins Hendrikkade, near the Damrak.

H. Kobell junior del.   C. S. Roos

Het Stranden der Kaag v

Op Woensdag, den 2^{den} December 1778, is onder de Vlieter, by Texel voor z

grond geslagen, de Kaag van Klaas Ringels, voor het Schip van Jan R

den Ligter behoorende, zyn gered, door den Amelander Schipper Ha

MATTHIAS DE SALLIETH after HENDRIK KOBELL

'The wreck of the kaag belonging to skipper Klaas Ringels'

Etching. Muller 4336a. Second state of two. Below the border at bottom left is the name of the designer, *H.Kobell junior del.*, in the center the address *C.S.Roos, excud.*, and at bottom right the name of the etcher, *M: de Saillieth sculps.* The first state lacked the address, the title, and the explanatory text below the title. Moreover, the inscriptions were formulated differently and written in freehand: at left *Desine par H: Kobell.*, and at right *Grave, par Sallieth. a Rotterdam 1779.*

The explanatory text reads as follows: 'On Wednesday, December 2, 1778, the *kaag* belonging to Klaas Ringels, ferrying out to Jan Rousman's ship bound for Essequibo, was lying at anchor below the Vlieter off Texel when a storm blew up out of the southeast and drove it ashore on the west coast of the island. Two passengers and three of the lighter's crew were rescued by Harmen Pieters, a skipper from Ameland, after they had spent ten hours clinging to the mast.'

M: de Saillieth sculps.

Schipper Klaas Ringels,

nker, door een Storm uit den Zuid-Oosten, op de West-Kust in den

an naar Esfequebo, twee Pasfagiers benevens drie Menfchen aan

Pieters, na dat ze tien uuren in de mast gezeeten hadden.

H. Kobell Jr. del. 1778.

DE HARING

ISSCHERY.

MATTHIAS DE SALLIETH after HENDRIK
KOBELL

'*The herring fishery*'

Etching, with engraving in the shaded areas.
Muller 179a (under the year 1295, when herring fishing was first mentioned) and 5107A
(under 1788!). Third state of three. Below
the border at bottom left are the name of the
designer and the date *H. Kobell Jr. del. 1778.*,
and at bottom right the name of the etcher
and the date *M. Sallieth sculps. 1781*. In the
first state (Muller 179b) only the etched lines
were incised in the plate, and the signature,
etc. were written freehand below the border
at bottom right: *M:d. Sallieth sculp: a Rotterdam 1780*. There was no text at all in the
second state.

The print shows a fleet of herring boats. In
the left foreground a buss is lying to its nets,
which are being hauled in. The herring drift
net, or fleet, consists of a series of separate
nets joined together. Each net is approximately fifteen meters high and thirty meters
wide. The total length of the fleet comes to
some four kilometers. Each net is attached
to the horizontal net warp by long lines
known as seizings. The fleet is kept afloat by
barrels, which are attached to the warp by
buoy ropes. In this print the net warp has
been detached from the net and is being
winched in over the bows of the buss with the
aid of a capstan, which is before the aftermost
mast. The fleet itself is being manhandled
aboard through a net port. In the right foreground is another buss, probably a fast herring carrier, which collected the catch from
the other boats and brought it ashore as fast
as possible. The man-of-war in the center is
convoying the fishing fleet.

H. Kobell J.r del. 1778.

DE WALVI

C H V A N G S T.

M. Sallieth sculps. 1781.

MATTHIAS DE SALLIETH after HENDRIK
KOBELL

'The whale fishery'

Etching, with engraving in the shaded areas.
Muller 5107A (under 1788). Third state of
three. Below the border at bottom left are the
name of the designer and the date *H. Kobell
Jr. del. 1778.*, and at bottom right the name
of the etcher and the date *M. Sallieth sculps.
1781*. This state was also published in the
book *De walvischvangst, met veele byzonder-
heden daartoe betrekkelijk* (Whaling, with
many relevant particulars), Amsterdam and
Harlingen 1784.

In the eighteenth century whaling was
done from *bootschips*, which were specially
equipped for hunting and processing whales
at sea. A distinctive feature of this type of
ship was the heavy beam laid across the top
of the after cabin, from which two longboats
were slung, one either side of the ship, ready
for immediate launching when a whale was
sighted.

The print shows a fleet of *bootschips* at anchor off the ice-pack. In the right foreground
two longboats are approaching a whale which
has betrayed its presence by spouting. A har-
pooner is on the point of hurling his weapon
into the whale. The man in the bows of the
second boat is holding a line which will keep
the longboats in contact with the harpooned
whale. In the middle of the bay a captured
whale is being towed back to the mother ship.
On the starboard side of that ship men are at
work flensing another whale. A large piece of
blubber is being hoisted aboard to be rendered down in the vat, the chimney of which
can be seen belching smoke abaft the mainmast.

Dk de Jong ad vivum delin 1780.

ROTTERDAM van de MAAS te zien.

TE AMSTERDAM by P. YVER, J. SMIT en Zoon, en F. W. GREEBE.

ROTTERDAM vûe du coté de la MEUSE.

À AMSTERDAM chez P.YVER, J.SMIT & Fils, & F.W.GREEBE.

181

MATTHIAS DE SALLIETH after DIRK DE JONG

'*Rotterdam seen from the Maas*'

Etching, with engraving in the shaded areas. Thieme-Becker, vol. 19, p. 129 (under de Jong). Second state of three. Below the border at bottom left are the name of the designer and the date *Dk. de Jong, ad vivum delin 1780*, and at bottom right the name of the etcher, *M. Sallieth, sculp*. Numbered *1* above the border at top right. Below the title is the address *Te Amsterdam by P. Yver, J. Smit en Zoon, en F.W. Greebe* (Amsterdam, at the premises of P. Yver, J. Smit and Son, and F.W. Greebe). There was no text at all in the first state. In the third state the address was altered to that of E. Maaskamp. Between the Dutch and French inscriptions are the arms of Rotterdam. The viewpoint is almost identical to that used by Groenewegen, seventeen years later (see nr. 205).

This and the following print appeared in the *Atlas van alle de zeehavens der Bataafsche Republiek* (Atlas of all the seaports of the Batavian Republic), described by Cornelis van der Aa. The atlas was published in several editions, notably those of 1802, by J. Allart, and 1805, by E. Maaskamp. The drawing which de Jong made for this print in 1780 is now in the Rotterdam City Archives.

The ships depicted are, from left to right, a hooker, the Rotterdam-Katendrecht ferry (foreground), a three-masted galliot, a two-masted sloop going about, a *paviljoenjacht* on the starboard tack, a frigate heeling over on the port tack, and an unknown type running before the wind.

The landmarks in the background are, from left to right, the turret on Schiedam Gate, the Oranjeboom and Pelikaan windmills, the turret of White Gate (in the gap between the sprit and the sail of the ferry), the entrance to Leuvehaven Docks, the East Nieuwehoofd Gate, also known as Shipwrights' Gate, the Church of St. Lawrence, the tower of the Town Hall (to the right of the galliot's main-mast), the roof of the East India Company depot, and, to the right of the frigate, the entrance to Oude Haven Docks, East Oude-hoofd Gate, and the Admiralty depot.

DE NIEUWE HAVEN VAN TEXEL,

met het Dorp 't Schilt in 't verschiet.

TE AMSTERDAM by P.YVER, J.SMIT en Zoon, en F.W.GREEBE.

LE NOUVEAU PORT DE TEXEL,

avec le Village 't Schilt dans le lointain.

À AMSTERDAM chez P. YVER, J. SMIT & Fils, & F. W. GREEBE.

MATTHIAS DE SALLIETH after DIRK DE JONG

'*The new harbor at Texel, with the village of 't Schilt in the background*'

Etching, with engraving in the shaded areas. Thieme-Becker, vol. 19, p. 129 (under de Jong). Second state of three. Below the border at bottom left are the name of the designer and the date *Dk. de Jong, ad vivum delin 1781.*, and at bottom right the name of the etcher, *M. Sallieth, sculp.* Numbered *11* above the border at top right. Below the title is the address *Te Amsterdam by P. Yver, J. Smit en Zoon, en F. W. Greebe* (Amsterdam, at the premises of P. Yver, J. Smit and Son, and F. W. Greebe). The title and the address are repeated, in French, in the right half of the print.

Between the Dutch and French inscriptions are the arms of Texel. See also nr. 181.

Before the North Holland Canal was opened in 1824, Dutch warships and merchantmen anchored in the sheltered roads off Texel. The last stage of the passage to Amsterdam was considered too hazardous, due to sandbanks in the Zuider Zee, the Pampus shallows, and increasing silting of the River IJ.

Geteekend en gegraveerd door D.' de Jong 1781.

Het springen van den Hollandsche Haagsche Kaaper den Dappere Patriot welke op een Roemwaardige wyze
vegtenderhand is opgevloogen met zyne geheele moedige Equipagie op dingsdag morgen den 14 Augusty 1781.
Opgedraagen aan den WelEd. Heer en M.' JAQUES BERGEON Banquier en Advocaat in 's Hage en aan alle de verdere Nederlansche
Gëeerde Patriotten.   Door haar WelEd. onderdanige dienaar D.' de Jong.

DIRK DE JONG

'The Dappere Patriot, a Dutch privateer of The Hague, destroyed by an explosion…

Etching. Muller 4460. Signed and dated, be-low the border in the center: *Geteekend en gegraveerd door Dk. de Jong 1781* (Drawn and engraved by Dk. de Jong 1781).

The remainder of the inscription reads as follows: '…blown up in glory with all its brave crew on the morning of Tuesday, August 14, 1781, having fought a famous battle. Dedicated to the honorable Jacques Bergeon, banker and lawyer of The Hague, and to all honored Dutch patriots by their honors' humble servant, Dk. de Jong.'

In 1781, during the Fourth Anglo-Dutch War, the *Dappere Patriot* was fitted out as a privateer by the Vaderlandsche Reederij at The Hague. The ship undoubtedly owed its name (The Brave Patriot) to the fact that the owners belonged to the anti-Orangist Patriot faction. The ship was commanded by Daniël Verbaan and had a crew of fifty-four. The privateer sailed from Brill on August 13, 1781, and the following morning fell in with the British frigate *Cameleon*, six miles south-east of Texel. The *Cameleon* gave chase, over-hauled the Dutch privateer, and demanded that the captain strike his colors.

Verbaan refused, and opened fire on the frig-ate with his fourteen guns. The frigate re-turned the fire, and half an hour later the bat-tle ended when the *Dappere Patriot* blew up.

The illustration is slightly reduced; the ac-tual size of the print is 20 x 28 cm.

HENDRIK KOBELL

'Confluence of the Krabbe and the Mallegat'

Etching. Wurzbach 10. Second state of two. Signed *H. Kobell f:* below the border at bot-tom right, with the address *Ad. Walpot Exc=* at bottom left. The first state lacked the address.

The Mallegat, a man-made channel below Dordrecht, and the Krabbe, a waterway lead-ing off the River Maas, flow together in the Dordtsche Kil.

185
HENDRIK KOBELL

'Diligente, labore' (Toiling and scrupulous)

Etching. Wurzbach 6. Signed and dated *Kobell. f 1774* below the border at bottom left.

In addition to this print of 1774, Wurzbach mentions another five, dated 1777, with similar brief Latin inscriptions. One of those prints, of a horseman on a beach, is signed as a joint work, *'per experimentum,'* by Kobell and Dirk Langendijk. Although it is clear from the dating that these etchings are not early works, Kobell evidently regarded them as experiments.

186
HENDRIK KOBELL

'Elucro, damnum' (Damage attends pursuit of profit)

Etching. Wurzbach 1. Signed and dated *Hf* and *H: Kobell jr. Experimentr = f 1777* below the border at bottom left. See also nr. 185.

The inscription refers to the necessity of building and overhauling ships which are used to earn a profit from trade.

187
HENDRIK KOBELL

'Utiliter et iucunde' (Useful and pleasant)

Etching. Wurzbach 5. Signed and dated *Kobell Expermt. 1777* below the border at bottom left. See also nr. 185.

185

186

187

188
HENDRIK KOBELL

A ship being caulked and a squadron of warships putting to sea

Etching. Wurzbach 11. Signed and dated *Kobell f 1778* below the border at bottom left.

*The entrance to Oude Haven Docks at
Rotterdam*

Etching. Wurzbach 12. Signed, dated and
numbered in pen at top left: *Hendk. Kobell
1768 junior N4.* The thick border around the
scene is in pen.

A hengst is lying alongside the pierhead
with its spritsail brailed up. Out on the river
a gaff-rigged *paviljoenjacht* is sailing close-
hauled.

The Ooster Oudehoofd Gate is on the extreme left, and the entrance to Oude Haven
Docks is in the foreground. In the center and
on the right is the New Maas river, and in the
background are the windmills on Boerengat
and Buizengat.

189

HENDRIK KOBELL

Harbor scene with a ship being careened and a transom yacht

Etching. Wurzbach 8. Signed and dated *H Kobell f 1774. Rotterdam* below the border at bottom left. On the right there are traces of a signature which was evidently bungled and deleted. Wurzbach also mentions an impression of this print on red paper.

190

195
GERRIT GROENEWEGEN

'*A hengst*'

Etching. First state of two. The letter *F*, the inscription and the number *5* were added in the second state.

The print shows a small Zeeland hengst in light airs. It has a spritsail, topsail, and a small jib. One of the crew is poling the laden vessel along.

196
GERRIT GROENEWEGEN

'*A snik*'

Etching. First state of two. The letter *F*, the inscription and the number *6* were added in the second state.

P. le Comte, in his book of prints, *Afbeeldingen van schepen en vaartuigen* (Illustrations of ships and other craft), states that *sniks* were built at Warmond, near Leiden, and that they were generally used for collecting fresh fish from *bomschips* and carrying it to Brabant and Zeeland. 'They cram on all rags and travel bravely in order to bring the fish to its destination in good condition.' They had excellent sailing qualities, and could sail as close as four-and-a-half points off the wind.

195

196

197

GERRIT GROENEWEGEN

'A peat boat with a lugsail'

Etching. First state of two. The letter *F*, the inscription and the number *7* were added in the second state.

In the eighteenth century *eikers* (see nr. 192) were used for carrying peat from the South Holland peat districts to Amsterdam, Rotterdam and The Hague. In the seventeenth century there is mention of *eikers* serving as ferries between Amsterdam and Gouda. Van Yk refers to 'Zevenhuizen peat *ponts*.' The print shows a clinker-built *eiker* with a lugsail. The main feature of this sail is that it is set on a lug or yard mounted foreand-aft on the mast rather than athwartships.

198

GERRIT GROENEWEGEN

'A schokker'

Etching. First state of two. The letter *F*, the inscription and the number *8* were added in the second state.

The schokker was a fishing vessel used on the Zuider Zee, the North Sea and the coastal mudflat regions. The craft depicted by Groenewegen is a two-masted schokker with a sprit mainsail and a small gaff mizzen.

The fall of the port leeboard has been omitted in this first state, but was inserted in the second state. A distinctive feature of the schokker is the heavy, raked stem, and the curved cutaway in the upper planking of the bows. It is believed that the schokker took its name from the island of Schokland, in the former Zuider Zee.

197

199

GERRIT GROENEWEGEN

'A passage boat'

Etching. Second state of two. Below the border at bottom left is the letter *F*, in the center is the inscription, and on the right the number *9*.

Passage boats were vessels which sailed at stated times and on fixed routes, carrying cargo, passengers or both. Skippers plying these routes had to take their turn in the sailing schedule. In the south of the country the *poon* was the most common type of passage boat.

The vessel shown here is running with the wind on its port quarter. It is a stateroom *poon* with a peaked taffrail, and it carries a spritsail, a square foresail and a square topsail.

This illustration is from a specimen in the library of the Rijksmuseum, Amsterdam.

200

GERRIT GROENEWEGEN

'A Frisian pram'

Etching. First state of two. The letter *F*, the inscription and the number *10* were added in the second state.

Despite its name, the Frisian pram was actually a small *hektjalk*, and not a true pram at all. Prams had no sheer, a wale low down on the hull that curved sharply upwards to the stem, and a tiller which could clear the ship's side. The stern of the Frisian pram had a peaked, decorated taffrail and a decorated rudder head.

een Beurtschip.

199

200

201

GERRIT GROENEWEGEN

'A yacht with a Dutch gaff sail'

Etching. First state of two. The letter *F*, the inscription and the number *11* were added in the second state.

Yachts of the type shown here were known as transom yachts or stateroom yachts, from the shape of the stern and the cabin accommodation aft. They generally had a standing gaff rig, and for that reason were sometimes referred to as gaff yachts. The vessel in this print has the Dutch gaff rig, which was becoming increasingly popular in Groenewegen's day.

202

GERRIT GROENEWEGEN

'A ferry pont'

Etching. First state of two. The letter *F*, the inscription and the number *12* were added in the second state.

The *pont* in this print is ferry-rigged. This was a modified spritsail rig. The sprit is shorter, the sail is almost square, and it could be hoisted or lowered independently, leaving the sprit in position. The mast is stepped at the side of the vessel in order to allow vehicles to pass freely down the length of the craft. The ferry is being steered with a long sweep. The vangs to the outer end of the sprit are missing, but they were added in the second state.

201

202

A brig and other ships in a broad channel

Etching. Previously unpublished. First state
of four. Clouds were added in the second
state, and were further elaborated in the third
state. The fourth state has the signature and
date *G. Groenewegen 1793* and the number *3*
below the scene.

This and the following print are from a
series of six. The dots in the sky are due to
ink being spattered on this particular impression.

The illustration is slightly reduced; the actual size of the print is 18.5 x 27.5 cm.

GERRIT GROENEWEGEN

Ships in the mouth of a river, with travellers in the foreground

Etching. Previously unpublished. Second state of three. The first state lacked the clouds. The signature and date *G. Groene-wegen 1793* and the number *5* were added in the third state. See also nr. 203.

The vessels, from left to right, are a single-masted cargo hooker, an English brig at anchor, and a smack sailing close-hauled.

The illustration is slightly reduced; the actual size of the print is 18.5 x 27.5 cm.

GERRIT GROENEWEGEN

'*Rotterdam seen from the Maas*'

Etching, with engraving in the shaded areas.
Catalogue Rotterdam 1976-77, nr. 47b.
Second state of two. Signed and dated
G:Groenewegen 1797 below the border at bottom left, and numbered *3* at bottom right.
The signature, date and number were only
added in this state, and there is some additional reinforcing with the burin. See also
nr. 181.

This and the following print are from a series of six views of the River Maas. This view,
which is from Katendrecht on the south bank
of the river, shows, from left to right, the Pelikaan windmill, the Ooster Nieuwehoofd Gate
at the end of Leuvehaven Docks, Boompjes
wharf with the tower of the Church of St.
Lawrence behind it, and on the far right the
depot in the Naval Dockyard.

The illustration is slightly reduced; the actual size of the print is 18.5 x 27.5 cm.

G Groenewegen 1797

Rotterdam van de Maas te zien

3

'The central and western pierheads at Delfshaven'

Etching. Catalogue Rotterdam 1976-77, nr. 127b. Second state of two. Signed and dated *G.Groenewegen 1797* below the border at bottom left, and numbered *4* at bottom right. See also nr. 205.

The road on which Groenewegen lived, 'below the high sea dike under Cool' (present-day Westzeedijk), ran from Rotterdam to Delfshaven. Groenewegen, who was lame, fortunately lived within easy walking distance of Delfshaven. His lameness restricted his activities to Rotterdam and the villages around it, such as Delfshaven, Schoonderloo and Overschie. Delfshaven was built on the Delfshavense Schie as the outport for Delft. It belonged to Delft until 1795, when its status became rather uncertain for a while. It became a municipality in its own right in 1811, but at the end of the nineteenth century it was incorporated into Rotterdam.

The central pierhead is in the foreground, with the western pierhead behind it. On the right are some of the buildings on the west side of Voorhaven, and a small summer house in a garden. The New Maas river is on the left. There is a drawing of the same scene in the Rotterdam City Archives, but it is regarded as being a copy by another hand.

The illustration is slightly reduced; the actual size of the print is 18.5 x 27.5 cm.

G.Groenewegen 1797

4

Het middel en westersch hooft van Delfshaven.

G. Groenewegen. 1791

1

5

Yacht off a jetty

Etching and aquatint. Catalogue Rotterdam
1976-77, nr. 46. Second state of two. Signed
and dated *G:Groenewegen. 1794* below the
border at bottom left, and numbered *1* at
bottom right.

This and the following print are from a
series of six aquatints lacking any inscription.
Only the first sheet is dated. The prints were
unnumbered and unsigned in the first state.
The border was also less clearly outlined, and
the plate not so elaborately worked. The
series is described in the catalogue referred to
as being fairly rare, unlike the majority of
Groenewegen's ship prints.

A ship on fire in Rotterdam harbor

Etching and aquatint. Catalogue Rotterdam
1976-77, nr. 46. Second state of two. Traces
of the signature *G.Groenewegen* can be detected below the border at bottom left. Numbered *5* at bottom right. See also nr. 207.

The print presents a mirror-image reversal
of the New Maas seen from the island of
Feijenoord across the river from Rotterdam.
On the left is the depot of the National Dockyard. This large depot, which was built in
1785, was part of the Maas Admiralty Dockyard. In 1795 it was renamed the Naval Dockyard when the country's five Admiralties were
amalgamated. It later became known as the
State Dockyard.

Fishing boats off a jetty

Etching. Catalogue Rotterdam 1976-77, nr.
23. Second state of two. Signed and dated
G:Groenewegen 1807 below the border at bottom left, and numbered *1* at bottom right.
The first state lacked the signature, date and
number.

This and the following two prints are from
a series of six marine and river views which
were later published in a portfolio with the
inscription *Schepen door G.Groenewegen. 1e
zestal. Te Rotterdam bij J.van den Brink.
1829* (Ships by G. Groenewegen. First set of
six. Rotterdam, at the premises of J. van den
Brink.1829).

Various ships on a calm expanse of water

Etching. Catalogue Rotterdam 1976–77, nr.
23. Second state of two. Signed and dated
G:Groenewegen 1807 below the border at bottom left, and numbered *2* at bottom right.
See also nr. 209.

Ships in difficulties off a rocky coast

Etching. Catalogue Rotterdam 1976–77, nr.
23. First state of two. The second state was
signed and dated *G:Groenewegen 1807* below
the border at bottom left, and numbered *6* at
bottom right. See also nr. 209.

211

A cutter and a frigate

Etching and aquatint. Previously unpublished.

The border around the scene was drawn
with pen and ink. The choice of subject and
the combination of etching and aquatint are
sufficient grounds for attributing this and the
following print (also previously unpublished)
to Groenewegen.

The ship on the right is a small twenty-gun
frigate. Above the main topgallant sail it has a
kite, a triangular sail which was hoisted with
a rope passed through a small sheave in the
truck of the flagpole.

GERRIT GROENEWEGEN

Two cutters

Etching and aquatint. Previously unpublished. The border around the scene was drawn with pen and ink. See also nr. 212.

In the last quarter of the eighteenth century the Dutch began using cutters as dispatch vessels for the fleet. They were seaworthy and fast vessels with a raked mast and topmast, and had a large, boomed mainsail set on a gaff.

The cutter in this print has a foresail before the mast, and a jib on the distinctive, long bowsprit. It still has the curved stem, which gave way to the straight stem in the nineteenth century. Right aft, under the boom of the mainsail, is a furled sail. This was the ringtail, a rectangular auxiliary sail carried on a small yard and boom aft of the mainsail.

214

JAN KOBELL

'The exceptional bravery of Captain Jarry, a Flushing privateer…'

Etching. Muller 4492. Signed *J Kobell f [ecit?]* below the border at bottom right. In the center are the arms of Zeeland. The remainder of the inscription reads: '…in overpowering and cutting a collier out of the English convoy, despite the heavy fire of the accompanying warships, on October 24, 1782.'

When the Fourth Anglo-Dutch War broke out in 1780, Zeeland shipowners began fitting out their vessels as privateers. Although the bulk of the crews were made up of local men, the ships were commanded by foreigners. The Frenchman Nicolas Jarry, who had earned his spurs as lieutenant under Pierre le Turc, was appointed captain in the service of Nortier of Flushing. In 1782 he captured a large number of English merchantmen with his swift cutter, *De Vlissinger*. The print reproduced here represents one of his more famous feats, when he sailed into a convoy and cut out a collier.

ONGEMEENE DAPPERHEYT DER VLISSINGER KAPER. KAPT. IARRY.
In het veroveren en uyt het Engelsch Convoy sleepen van een Koolhaalder niet tegenstaande het sterk schieten der Convoyers op den 24. October. 1782.

'Capture of an English packet commanded by Captain Fleyn…'

Etching. Muller 4493. Signed *J Kobell del: et sculp.* below the border at bottom right. In the center are the arms of Zeeland. The remainder of the inscription reads: '…sailing from Hellevoetsluis to Harwich, by the Zierikzee privateer, *De Goede Verwachting*, commanded by Captain I. W. Sextroh, on October 28, 1782. Dedicated to the honorable owners of the aforementioned privateer by their honors' faithful servant, J. Kobell.'

In 1782, during the war with England (see nr. 214), Zeeland privateering concerns suffered a number of damaging losses. Treachery was suspected, and Captain I. W. Sextroh in *De Goede Verwachting* was ordered to intercept the Harwich-Hellevoetsluis packet and search it for incriminating documents. It was a delicate operation, for although the two countries were at war, the packet was immune from seizure. No suspect correspondence was found, and as a result the Dutch delegate to the Paris peace negotiations was forced to apologize for the incident.

HET NEEMEN DER ENGELSCHE   PAKETBOOT VAN KAPT. FLEYN
*van Hellevoetsluis na Harwich, door de Zierikzeese   Kaper de Goede Verwachting, Kapt. I.W. SEXTROH,
op den 28 Octob. A= 1782*
Op gedraagen   aan de Edl: Heeren REEDERS. der Voorn Caper   Door hun Wl: D:W Dienaar J.Kobell.

J C Schotel

Steendy van Steuerwald & Compe te Dordt.

Pinks beached at the foot of a tower

Lithograph. Previously unpublished. Signed *JC Schotel* at bottom left. Below the border at bottom left is the address *Steend rij van Steuerwald & Compie te Dordt*.

The technique of lithography, or printing from stone, was invented in 1796 by Aloys Senefelder. The print was made from a flat surface, and the process was ideal for fast production in large editions. Senefelder's book, *Vollständiges Lehrbuch der Steindruckerey* (Complete manual of lithography), was published in 1818. The first Dutch lithographs appeared around 1820.

C.H.G. Steuerwald was one of the first to adopt the new technique, and he communicated his enthusiasm to his younger brother, Jan Dam Steuerwald. They were active in Dordrecht from 1822 to 1833, when they moved their lithographic studio and printing works to The Hague.

The dating between 1826, when the name Steuerwald & Comp. was first used, and 1833, when the brothers moved to The Hague, would make this the earliest print in this volume to be produced by the lithographic process.

217

Ferryboat on a river

Lithograph in black and yellowish gray.
Signed *A. Schelfhout* at bottom right. There
is a border around the scene which is not
visible in this reproduction. Above it was
printed the name of the artist, *A. Schelfhout*,
repeated at bottom left as the person who
transferred the drawing to the stone,
A. Schelfhout lith., and at bottom right the
address *Steendrukkerij van C. W. Mieling te
's Hage.*

  This lithograph appeared in the second
volume of *Het Hollandsche Schilder en Letterkundig Album* (The Dutch art and literary album), published by Mieling in 1848 as a
successor to *De Hollandsche Schilderschool*
(The Dutch school of painting; see nr. 230
below). In that volume the print was reproduced with far more gray, giving the impression of dusk. It was printed without the border, and a different letter type was used.

  Schelfhout made three colored lithographs
for this periodical at a time when the technique of using a different stone for each tone
was still in its infancy.

  Behind the woman standing on the river
bank is a roller guide post. These posts were
placed at river bends to provide a lead for the
tow line between the horse and the barge.

  The illustration is slightly reduced; the actual size of the print is 20 x 27 cm.

The Maas at Dordrecht

Lithograph. Previously unpublished. Signed
A. Schelfhout at bottom left.

  Cut from a sheet with three sketches. The
entire print, with two small landscapes above
this river view, was numbered *Pl. I* and published by C. W. Mieling. It was probably part
of a portfolio of draftsman's models (cf. nr.
236).

Pl. 15.

P. Le Comte del et lith.

P. Le Comte del et lith.

'A full-rigged merchantman sailing close-hauled'

Lithograph. Printed on paper with an embossed mark. Previously unpublished. Signed *P. Le Comte del et lith.* below the border at bottom left, and numbered *Pl. 15.* above the border at top right.

This and the following seven prints are from le Comte's *Afbeeldingen van schepen en vaartuigen in verschillende bewegingen* (Illustrations of ships and other craft carrying out various evolutions), a series of fifty lithographs published in 1831. The sheets of paper on which the lithographs are printed have an embossed mark with the initials of le Comte's name, *PLC*, the letters *RMWO*, and the ribbon and decoration which le Comte was entitled to wear as a Knight of the Military Order of Willem (Ridder in de Militaire Willemsorde, abbreviated to RMWO).

In his commentary on this print the artist states that the full-rigged merchantman putting to sea is sailing one to two points off close-hauled. Studding sails have been set outside the foresail and fore topsail. Generally these sails were only set in a moderate wind coming from abaft the beam.

Le Comte's drawing for this print is in the Netherlands National Maritime Museum, Amsterdam.

'An English channel boat, or lugger'

Lithograph. Printed on paper with an embossed mark. Previously unpublished. Signed *P. LeComte del et lith.* below the border at bottom left, and numbered *Plaat 16.* above the border at top right. See also nr. 219.

The vessel in the foreground is a pilot boat. The sails, from fore to aft, are a jib, two lugsails and a spanker. Le Comte had the following to say about this type of ship in his commentary. 'They run alongside a ship under sail, usually striking their own sails. They catch a rope thrown across to them and transfer a pilot in a twinkling if one is required, pass on news of current interest, and conclude the conversation by begging some rum, genever or the like.'

'A koff'

Lithograph. Printed on paper with an embossed mark. Previously unpublished. Signed *P. LeComte del et lith.* below the border at bottom left, and numbered *Pl. 17.* above the border at top right. See also nr. 219.

The *koff* was a coaster which gradually supplanted the cat and the flute as a freighter in the eighteenth century. Although they were good weather ships they were very wet, hence the saying: 'Smacks and *koffs* are water troughs.'

The print shows the *koff* setting out to sea with all sails set. It has a mainsail, a mizzen, a topsail and topgallant sail, and before the mainmast a fore staysail, an outer jib and a flying jib.

Le Comte's drawing for this print is in the Netherlands National Maritime Museum, Amsterdam.

Pl. 17.

P. LeComte del et lith.

'A smack'

Lithograph. Printed on paper with an embossed mark. Previously unpublished. Signed *P. LeComte del. et lith.* below the border at bottom left, and numbered *Pl. 18* above the border at top right. See also nr. 219.

The smack was a coaster covering the range from Spain to the Baltic. However, its construction also made it suitable for working the coastal mudflat waters and the inland waterways of the northern provinces of the Netherlands.

It had two masts and carried a gaff mainsail and a mizzen. The mizzenmast was stepped hard up against the taffrail, and so a bumpkin was used for working the sheets. Before the mainmast the smack carried a square foresail, square topsail and square topgallant sail, together with a fore-and-aft foresail, jib and flying jib.

Le Comte called the smack 'the sister of the *koffs.*' The *koff*, however, lacked the peaked taffrail.

'A corvette becalmed'

Lithograph. Printed on paper with an embossed mark. Previously unpublished. Signed *P. Le Comte. lith.* below the border at bottom left, with the address *Steend. Desguerrois en Co.* at bottom right, and numbered *Pl. 25* above the border at top right. See also nr. 219.

This well-deck corvette is the *Van Speyk* of the Royal Netherlands Navy. It is shown in the mouth of the River Scheldt off Flushing, and has anchored in order to prevent itself being carried by the tide, since the breeze is too light to provide steerage way. Ship-rigged vessels mounting up to thirty-two guns were known as corvettes. The well-deck corvette had a hold for stores, a middle deck with the crew's quarters, a gundeck or well deck, and an upper deck consisting of a forecastle and a quarterdeck.

'A single-masted merchant hooker'

Lithograph. Printed on paper with an embossed mark. Previously unpublished. Signed *P. Le Comte, lith.* below the border at bottom left, numbered *Pl. 26* above the border at top right. See also nr. 219.

The hooker was originally a fishing vessel, but by the second half of the eighteenth century the larger hookers were being used for carrying cargo. This broadside view shows the characteristic rounded stern, with the tiller mounted so that it could clear the ship's side, and the ketch rig. The mainmast is stepped halfway down the length of the ship, and its shrouds are set way aft, so that the mainsail yards could be braced up sharply, enabling the ship to sail as close as five points off the wind. In the bows is a long jib boom. The hooker is reaching, with the wind abeam, under a mainsail, topsail and jib, with the mizzen brailed up and the foresail lowered.

Pl. 18.

P. LeComte. del. et lith.

Pl. 25.

P. Le Comte lith.   Steend. Desguerrois en Ce

Pl. 26.

P. Le Comte lith.

Pl. 27.

P. LeComte. del.

225

Pl. 30.

P. Lecomte, del et Lith.

226

'*A South American brig*'

Lithograph. Printed on paper with an embossed mark. Previously unpublished. Signed *P. Le Comte. del.* below the border at bottom left, and numbered *Pl. 27* above the border at top right. See also nr. 219.

Brigs had two masts, with a combination of square sails and gaff sails on both. Staysails could be set on the bowsprit and jib boom, and between the masts.

The brig depicted by le Comte is scudding before the wind. It has its fore topmast staysail set in order to drive the ship before the wind, a foresail in order to lift it over the peaks of the waves, and a deeply reefed main topsail in order to maintain way when the ship sinks into the troughs between the waves, where the wind is prevented from reaching the lower courses.

Le Comte's drawing for this print is in the Netherlands National Maritime Museum, Amsterdam.

'*The Urania training corvette*'

Lithograph. Printed on paper with an embossed mark. Previously unpublished. Signed *P. Le Comte, del et Lith.* below the border at bottom left, and numbered *Pl. 30* above the border at top right. See also nr. 219.

The *Urania* is lying at anchor off the entrance to Medemblik harbor. This flush-decked, ten-gun corvette was used for training young officers at the Royal Naval Institute at Medemblik, which was founded in 1829. The *Urania* went on training voyages in the Zuider Zee in order to give the young officers practical experience of seamanship.

Le Comte has allowed himself a certain amount of artistic license in this print. His album of illustrations appeared in 1831, whereas the *Urania*, whose keel was laid in 1830 at the State Dockyard in Amsterdam, was only launched in 1832.

Le Comte's drawing for this print is in the Netherlands National Maritime Museum, Amsterdam.

'*A ship of the line scudding before the wind*'

Lithograph. Printed on paper with an embossed mark. Previously unpublished. Signed *P. Lecomte, del.* below the border at bottom left, with the address *Steend. Desguerrois en Co.* at bottom right, and numbered *Pl. 50* above the border at top right. See also nr. 219.

In le Comte's day a full-rigged warship mounting seventy-four or eighty-four guns was referred to as a ship of the line, to distinguish it from full-rigged frigates, which were more lightly armed with between thirty-two and sixty guns.

The illustration is after a print in the Netherlands National Maritime Museum, Amsterdam.

P. le Comte R.M.W.O. fecit.

Den
De Nederlandsche Vlag
aan Boord Z. M.

b 1831
J. C. J. van Speyk in gevaar;
nonneerboot N°.2.

Steend. v. Daiwaille en Veldhuijsen.

Uitgegeven by F. Kaal, Blaauwburgwal. N°. 15.

'*February 5, 1831. The Dutch flag at hazard on board HNLM Gunboat Nr. 2, commanded by J.C.J. van Speyk*'

Lithograph. Printed on paper with an embossed mark. Muller 6607. Signed *P. le Comte R.M.W.O. fecit.* below the border at bottom left, and with the addresses of the printer and the publisher at bottom right: *Steend. v. Daiwaille en Veldhuijsen.* and *Uitgegeven by F. Kaal, Blaauwburgwal, No. 15.*

In August 1830 civil disorder broke out in the southern provinces of the Kingdom of the Netherlands (which at the time embraced present-day Belgium), and it was decided to send a number of warships to Antwerp. The citadel was secure in the hands of General Chassé, but shipping in the port was being hindered by the rebels.

The city was heavily shelled on October 27, and on November 5 a cease-fire was arranged, as result of which the naval force was reduced to a small flotilla of gunboats. On January 30, 1831, gunboats nrs. 2 and 4 were ordered to anchor off Vlaamse Hoofd near the citadel, since floating ice was forming on the river. On February 5 the ships were ordered to return to their previous station on the river. Gunboat nr. 2, commanded by Lieutenant J.C.J. van Speyk, started dragging its anchor and was unable to carry out the manoeuvre. The ship was driven towards the quay by a northwest wind, and appeared to be in imminent danger of being captured by the Belgians, who managed to seize hold of the Dutch flag. Van Speyk set a spark to the ship's store of gunpowder, blowing up friend and foe alike.

This heroic deed ensured van Speyk's fame. Artists were commissioned to depict the event, statues were erected, and van Speyk's cry of 'Better to be blown up than surrender' has passed into the popular vocabulary.

Le Comte's drawing for this print is in the Netherlands National Maritime Museum, Amsterdam.

P. le Comte R.M.W.O. fecit.

De eer der Nederl...
J. C. J. van Speyk geha...

che Vlag door
afd 5 february 1831.

Steend. v. Daiwaille en Veldhuijzen.

Uitgegeven bij F. Kaal, Blaauwburgwal, No 15. Amsterdam.

'*The honor of the Dutch flag upheld by
J.C.J. van Speyk, February 5, 1831*'

Lithograph. Printed on paper with an embossed mark. Muller 6618. Signed *P. le Comte
R.M.W.O.fecit* below the border at bottom
left, with the word *Gedeponeerd* (Registered)
below the signature. At bottom right are the
addresses of the printer and the publisher:
Steend. v. Daiwaille en Veldhuijsen. and *Uitgegeven bij F. Kaal, Blaauwburgwal, No. 15.
Amsterdam.* See also nr. 228.

A Waldorp lith.

Lithographie v C.W. Mieling te 's Hage

230

ANTONIE WALDORP

A punter and a hektjalk offshore

Lithograph in black and grayish-yellow.
Proof impression. Previously unpublished.
Signed *A: Waldorp* at bottom right. There is
a printed border around the scene. Above it
appears the name of the artist, *A. Waldorp*,
repeated below the border at bottom left as
the person who transferred the drawing to
the stone: *A. Waldorp lith*. At bottom right is
the address *Lithographie .v. C. W. Mieling te
's Hage*.

The print was published with this text and
with the addition of a dark yellow and a
brown stone in 1847 in the first volume of *De
Hollandsche Schilderschool: Teekeningen en
Schetsen van de beroemdste schilders van Nederland, door hun zelven op Steen geteekend...*
(The Dutch school of painting: drawings and
sketches by the most famous artists of the
Netherlands, drawn on the stone by the artists
themselves...). This edition by Mieling contained lithographs by more than thirty artists,
including Bosboom, Leickert, Rochussen
and Schelfhout. Most of the lithographs were
printed in black with a yellowish-gray tone.
In a few cases, including the print reproduced
here, more than one stone was used.

The illustration is slightly reduced; the actual size of the print is 18.5 x 26.5 cm.

231

ANTONIE WALDORP

Ships on the river near Overschie

Lithograph. Previously unpublished. Signed
A. Waldorp (reversed) at bottom right.

In the foreground is a broad towpath with a
horse towing a barge. Horse-drawn barges
were in use in the Netherlands until late in
the nineteenth century. In the background is
the village of Overschie, near Rotterdam.
This was a busy waterway, with ferries serving Rotterdam, Delft and Schiedam. The ornate spire of Overschie church was later destroyed by fire and replaced in 1899.

PETRUS JOHANNES SCHOTEL

A hektjalk leaving harbor

Etching. Printed on chine collé. Previously unpublished.

In the booklet which G. D. J. Schotel wrote on his artist brother he stated that Petrus, who had been living in Düsseldorf for some years, 'published a number of etchings with Reisz & Co. in 1858.' This print may be one of those etchings. Schotel may have taken up etching as a result of the activities of an 'Etching Club' established in The Hague by a group of artists in 1848. In the eighteenth century, etchings were mainly used in the Netherlands for illustrating books. When lithography began to take over that role in the first half of the nineteenth century there was renewed interest in etching as an indepedent means of artistic expression.

232

233

PETRUS PAULUS SCHIEDGES

Fishing boats in a harbor at sunset

Lithograph in black and light brown. Previously unpublished. Signed *Schiedges, del. & lith*. in the margin at bottom left, and with the address *Lithographie v. C.W. Mieling te 's Hage* at bottom right. There are also proof impressions of this print from the black stone alone and before the inscription.

The print appeared in 1848, in these colors but without the inscription, in the first instalment of the second volume of *Het Hollandsche Schilder en Letterkundig Album: Verzameling van oorspronkelijke steenteekeningen en gemengde lektuur in proza en poezij* (The Dutch art and literary album: collection of original lithographs and various works of prose and poetry).

The anchored vessel in the left foreground is a schokker, recognizable from the heavy, raked stem and the egg-shaped hull. Alongside the jetty on the right is a *hektjalk* laden with hay.

234

PETRUS PAULUS SCHIEDGES

A moonlit beach

Lithograph. Proof impression in black. Previously unpublished. Signed *Schiedges, del: & lith:* in the margin at bottom left, and with the address *Kon-ke lith. v. C.W. Mieling* at bottom right.

This print (with the addition of a graygreen stone, mainly for the sky) appeared in 1852 in the sixteenth instalment of *Kunstkronijk* (Art Chronicle), vol. 13. This periodical was the successor to the *Schilder en Letterkundig Album* (see nr. 233).

Schiedges. del. & lith.

Kon.ke lith v C.W.Mieling

Two-master offshore

Lithograph in black and yellow. Previously
unpublished. Signed and dated *F A Br. de
Groot 46* at bottom left. Above the border at
top center is the name of the artist, *F. A. Breuhaus de Groot.*, below the border at bottom
left the words *F. A. Breuhaus de Groot. lith.*,
and at bottom right the address *Steendrukkerij
van C. W. Mieling te 's Hage.* There are also
proof impressions of this print from the black
stone alone.

The print appeared in 1847 in the first instalment of *De Hollandsche Schilderschool*
(see nr. 230).

The illustration is slightly reduced; the actual size of the print is 19.5 x 26 cm.

Sketches of various ships on the water

Lithograph. Previously unpublished. Signed
and dated *F.A. Br. de Groot 46* at bottom
left. Signed *F. A. Breuhaus de Groot del. et
lith.* in the margin at bottom left, and with
the address *Steend. v. C.W. Mieling te 's Hage*
at bottom right.

Sheets of this type served as drawing models for young artists or amateurs, and were
generally available in portfolios in sets of
twelve.

The illustration is slightly reduced; the actual size of the print is 22 x 29 cm.

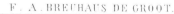

F. A. BREUHAUS DE GROOT.

F. A. Breuhaus de Groot lith.   Steendrukkerij van C. W. Mieling te 's Hage.

F. A. Breuhaus de Groot del et lith.

Rowboats on the banks of the River Waal at Nijmegen

Etching in brown. Previously unpublished. Signed *J.C. Greive Jr.* at bottom right, with the description *De Waal bij Nijmegen* (The Waal at Nijmegen).

This and the following two prints are from a series of six etchings by Greive.

On the river at left there is an anchored *keen*, with another *keen* under sail to the right of it. *Keens* had a very distinctive rudder, with curved arms from the rear of the rudder blade to the tiller.

JOHAN CONRAD GREIVE

Eel boats in calm weather on the Zuider Zee near Spakenburg

Etching in brown. Previously unpublished. Signed *J.C. Greive Jr.* at bottom left, and the location *Spakenburg* at bottom right. See also nr. 237.

Botters in Spakenburg harbor

Etching in brown. Previously unpublished.
Signed *J.C. Greive Jr.* at bottom right, and
with the location *Spakenburg* at bottom left.
See also nr. 237.

7.

BEURTSCHIP (GAFFELSCHIP.)

Uitgegeven door Frans Buffa en Zonen te Amsterdam.

'Passage boat (Gaff ship)'

Lithograph. Previously unpublished. Signed *J.C. Greive Jr=* at bottom left. Numbered *7* in the margin at bottom center, with the address of the publisher, *Uitgegeven door Frans Buffa en Zonen te Amsterdam*, below the title, and the address of the printer, *Steendr van R. de Vries Jr=*, at bottom right. This and the following three prints are from a series of twelve depicting various ship types. They were published in a portfolio on the cover of which was an illustration of a ship with its sail being hoisted, and the title *Studien van Hollandsche Schepen naar de natuur geteekend en op steen gebracht door J.C.: Greive Jr=* (Studies of Dutch ships drawn from life and transferred to the stone by J.C. Greive Jr; fig. 240a).

Kaags, which were spritsail-rigged, were distinguished from gaff-rigged *kaags*, which were called gaff *kaags* or gaff ships. They were generally used as cargo carriers, often transferring cargo to and from seagoing ships anchored in the Texel roads. The gaff ship was also used as a passage boat, as the inscription tells us.

Fig. 240a   Johan Conrad Greive, cover of 'Studies of Dutch ships,' ca. 1860. Lithograph, 28 x 37.5 cm.

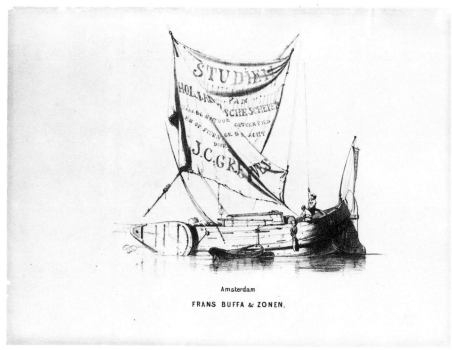

240a

'Shrimper'

Lithograph. Previously unpublished. Signed *J.C. Greive Jr=* at bottom right. In the margin at bottom left is the printer's address, *Steendr. van R.de Vreis Jr=*. Numbered *8.* at bottom center, with the address of the publisher, *Uitgegeven door Frans Buffa en Zonen te Amsterdam*. See also nr. 240.

The shrimper was a fishing boat with an overall length of some seven meters which fished in coastal waters from around 1800 up to the Second World War. It was clinker-built, like the *bomschuit*, but it differed in the construction of the stern. In the shrimper the strakes ended in a flat stern, but in the *bomschuit* they extended to the sternpost. Both types were designed to work from the beach, since there were few harbors on the Dutch North Sea coast until the end of the nineteenth century.

The preliminary drawing for this print is in the Netherlands National Maritime Museum, Amsterdam.

8.

GARNALEN BOOT.

Uitgegeven door Frans Buffa en Zonen te Amsterdam.

10.

BOK.

Uitgegeven door Frans Buffa en Zonen te Amsterdam.

JOHAN CONRAD GREIVE

'Bok'

Lithograph. Previously unpublished. Signed *J.C. Greive Jr=* at bottom left. Numbered *10.* in the margin at bottom center, together with the address of the publisher, *Uitgegeven door Frans Buffa en Zonen te Amsterdam.,* and with the address of the printer, *Steendr. van R. de Vries Jr=* at bottom right. See also nr. 240.

Boks were used for carrying peat to the large towns from the peat workings in the northwest of Utrecht province. In the course of the nineteenth century the *bok* evolved from a small, clinker-built vessel without a deckhouse to a carvel built with a deckhouse. It shared the straight, raked stem and the protruding bolt heads either side of it with ships built in the west of the Netherlands, such as the *snik* and the *westlander*.

JOHAN CONRAD GREIVE

'Peat boat'

Lithograph. Previously unpublished. Signed *J.C. Greive Jr=* at bottom left. Numbered *12.* in the margin at bottom center, together with the address of the publisher, *Uitgegeven door Frans Buffa en Zonen te Amsterdam.,* and with the address of the printer, *Steendr. van R. de Vries Jr=* at bottom right. See also nr. 240.

In the commentary to nr. 197 it was explained that *eikers* were used in the eighteenth century for carrying peat to the large towns from the South Holland peat workings. They continued to fill this role in the nineteenth century. P. le Comte states in his *Afbeeldingen van schepen en vaartuigen* (Illustrations of ships and other craft) that *eikers* were mainly built at Zevenhuizen, Waddinxveen and Nieuwerkerk. They were long, narrow boats, since they had to navigate the narrow polder channels. Petrejus and Crone point to the similarity in construction to river boats like the 's-Gravenmoer *aak*, in which the strakes came together in the bows not in a stem but in a solid block of wood.

The vessel shown here is sailing before the wind with its mainsail to port and its foresail to starboard.

12.

TURFSCHIP.

Uitgegeven door Frans Buffa en Zonen te Amsterdam.

Fig. 244a   Johan Barthold Jongkind, title print of the 'Cahier de Six Eaux forte,' 1862. Etching, 13.8 x 21.8 cm.

244a

244

A hektjalk by a river bank

Etching. Delteil 6. Hefting 258. First state of
three. Signed and dated *Jongkind fecit 1862*
(reversed) at bottom right. In the second
state a line was drawn in the sky by accident.
This was removed in the third state, and
Delâtre's address added below the scene.

This and the following print come from a
series of six etchings. Together with the title
sheet, which was also etched by Jongkind,
they were printed by Delâtre in Paris in 1862
and published by Cadart et Chevalier (fig.
244a). This publishing house was also the seat
of the newly-formed Société des Aquafortistes, whose aim was to revitalize the art of
etching in France. Although Jongkind had
never before made a print, he joined the society very early on, and found himself in the
company of such artists as Bracquemond,
Daubigny and Méryon. Philippe Burty, the
well-known art critic, wrote a very favorable
article in the *Gazette des Beaux-Arts* of
March 23, 1862, immediately after Jongkind's
series was published.

Two sailing ships

Etching. Delteil 7. Hefting 259. Second state
of two. Signed and dated *Jongkind 1862* (reversed) at bottom right. Below the border at
bottom right is the address *Impe. A. Delâtre
Rue St. Jacques 265 Paris*. The first state
lacked this address. See also nr. 244.

As was the case with Jongkind's other
prints, the plate surface, with the exception
of the incised lines, was not wiped clean, but
had a layer of tone, or 'sauce,' added. This
was to prevent the print from looking too
dry, and was a technique Delâtre applied a
great deal (to excess, in the opinion of some).

JOHAN BARTHOLD JONGKIND

Dutch windmills

Etching. Delteil 14. Hefting 444. Second state of three. At bottom right are the location, date and signature: *Rotterdam 1867 Jongkind*. The scratch to the right of the rider on the towpath does not appear in the first state. Various inscriptions were added in the third state, including the title, *Moulins en Hollande*, and the address of the publisher, Cadart's widow. There are also a few rare proof impressions from before the state mentioned in the most generally consulted literature as being the first (see, for example, catalogue nr. 5 of the Weston Gallery, 1979). Those proof impressions were made from the plate before it was steeled, and they have a dark patch at bottom right where the acid penetrated too far into the ground, roughening the plate so that it caught the ink.

In 1867 Jongkind paid one of his visits to the Netherlands, and it was probably on that trip that he executed this etching. There is a painting of the same scene, also dated 1867, in a private collection (Hefting 418).

JOHAN BARTHOLD JONGKIND

'Soleil couchant – Port d'Anvers' (Sunset in the port of Antwerp)

Etching. Delteil 15. Hefting 492. Second state of four. At bottom right are the location, signature and date: *Anvers Jongkind 1868*. Below the scene, from left to right, are the address of the publishers, *Cadart & Luce, Editeurs, Rue Nve des Mathurins, 58.*, the title, and the address of the printer, *Imp. Delâtre, Paris*. Numbered *14* at top right. This state was published in 1868 in the *Illustration Nouvelle*. The first state lacked the addresses and the number, and in the subsequent states they were removed again or altered.

L'Illustration Nouvelle was the successor to the publications of the Société des Aquafortistes, which was disbanded in 1867. Jongkind spent some time in Antwerp in 1866 and 1867, on his way to the Netherlands, and made numerous studies along the River Scheldt and in the port area.

This print has been compared to the famous painting, *L'Impression*, which Monet painted in 1874, and which gave Impressionism its name.

CADART & LUCE, Editeurs, Rue N°. des Mathurins, 58.

SOLEIL COUCHANT ___ PORT D'ANVERS

Imp Delâtre Paris

Jongkind 1863

Jongkind sculp

Paris, Publié par A. CADART & LUQUET, Éditeurs, 79, Rue Richelieu.

ENTRÉE DU PO

DE HONFLEUR.   Imp. Delâtre, Rue St Jacques, 303, Paris.

'Entrée du port de Honfleur' (Entrance to Honfleur harbor)

Etching. Delteil 10. Hefting 283. Third state of three. Signed and dated *Jongkind 1863* at bottom left. Signed *Jongkind sculpt.* below the border at bottom left, together with the address *Paris, Publié par A. Cadart & Luquet, Editeurs, 79, Rue Richelieu*. At bottom center is the title, and at bottom right the address of the printer, *Imp. Delâtre, Rue St. Jacques, 303, Paris*. Numbered *85* above the border at top right. In the first state the border was some 3 mm. lower at the bottom, so that all of the *g* in Jongkind's name was visible. This was altered in the second state to the dimensions reproduced here. The third state was published in January 1864 by the Société des Aquafortistes in the fifth instalment of the second volume.

Between 1862 and 1866 Jongkind regularly stayed for months at a time in the Channel fishing port of Honfleur, on the left bank of the mouth of the Seine. He made many paintings, drawings and etchings of Honfleur, always with a different staffage. The painting which is closest to this etching is in the Art Institute, Chicago (Hefting 297).

Jongkind 1864

DE HONFLEUR.

JOHAN BARTHOLD JONGKIND

'Sortie du port de Honfleur' (Exit of Honfleur harbor)

Etching. Delteil 11. Hefting 319. Fourth state of four. Signed and dated *Jongkind 1864* at bottom left, and with the title below the border at bottom center. In the first state the border was set slightly lower (see also nr. 248). The scene was reduced in size in the second state, and in the third state the addresses of publishers Cadart & Luquet and printer Delâtre were printed below the scene. The print was published in that state, numbered *143*, in January 1865 by the Société des Aquafortistes. In the fourth state, reproduced here, the number was removed and the addresses were embossed, because although they were in the plate they were not inked.

There is a painting of 1864 of the same scene in a private collection (Hefting 295). The watercolor (reversed left for right) which Jongkind probably used as a model for this print is in the Louvre (Hefting 318).

Jong Kind 1865

Jong Kind. sculp.   Paris, Publié par CADART & LUQUET, Editeurs, 79, Rue Richelieu.   JETÉE EN BOIS DANS

PORT DE HONFLEUR.

Imp. Delâtre, Rue St Jacques, 303, Paris.

'Jetée en bois dans le port de Honfleur'
(Pierhead at Honfleur)

Etching. Delteil 12. Hefting 368. Second
state of three. Signed and dated *Jongkind
1865* at bottom left, and numbered *202* at top
right. *Jong Kind sculp.* is printed in letterpress below the border at bottom right, with
the address *Paris, Publié par Cadart &
Luquet, Editeurs, 79, Rue Richelieu.* At bottom center is the title, and at bottom right the
address of the printer, *Imp. Delâtre, Rue
St. Jacques, 303, Paris.* The first state lacked
the number and the inscriptions below the
border. In the third state only the title remained. The print was published in the state
reproduced here in January 1866 by the
Société des Aquafortistes in the fifth instalment of the fourth volume. Jongkind executed five of the three hundred prints published by the society between 1862 and 1867
(see also nr. 248 and 249).

There is a painting of the same scene, executed in 1866, in a private collection (Hefting
386).

Biographies

AB, Monogrammist

Etcher. Active around 1650. AB was at one time thought to be Abraham Casembrot, but Nagler later attributed the monogram to Arnold Blom; Hollstein attributed it to Abraham van den Bergh.

ABk, Monogrammist

Painter and etcher. Active around 1650 or in the second half of the seventeenth century, probably in Amsterdam. The monogram has been attributed at various times to Abraham Casembrot or Abraham Bloteling. Nagler mentions six etchings with marine subjects by this artist.

ADAM, RICHARD

Painter, etcher and die-cutter. Born around 1644-45, year of death unknown. Mentioned in Amsterdam in 1669, and in The Hague and Middelburg in 1672. His signature has also been regarded as that of Philipp Adam, a Tyrolean artist of the second half of the seventeenth century. Only two series of six prints each are known: one with a foreground figure and peasant dwellings, the other with river views.

ALDEWERELT, HERMAN VAN

Painter. Born in 1629, died after 1662 or in 1669 (?) in Amsterdam (?). He painted chiefly portraits and history pieces.

ALLARD[T], CAREL

Publisher and etcher. Born in 1648 in Amsterdam, where he died in 1709. Active in Amsterdam from 1673.

ALLART, JOHANNES

Publisher. Active in Amsterdam between 1773 and 1811, and in The Hague between 1812 and 1816.

ALLARTSZ., HERMAN

Publisher, bookbinder and bookseller. Born in Warmenhuizen in 1572, died in or after 1652 in Amsterdam. He called himself Coster after becoming sexton (koster) of the New Church in Amsterdam in 1603. Active in Amsterdam between 1597 and 1618.

ALMELOVEEN, JAN VAN

Etcher. Born in Mijdrecht around 1652, died after 1683. He was probably in Utrecht between 1678 and 1683, where he was influenced by the work of Herman Saftleven, who was active there at that time. He spent some time in Germany around 1680. He made 38 etchings, almost all of them landscapes. Approximately half are of localities along the

River Rhine, and are after his own designs. The remainder are after designs by Saftleven, and are views of the Rhine and Dutch rivers.

AVEELE, JOHAN VAN DE[N]

Etcher. Born in Amsterdam around 1655, died in Stockholm in 1727. He was active in Amsterdam between 1678 and 1681. He then probably moved to Utrecht, and from 1696 was in Leiden. In 1698 he left for Stockholm, where, after the death of Willem Swiddes, he made 160 prints for the album Suecia antiqua et hodierna, 1716. He produced numerous book illustrations, as well as a number of views on the estates of Sorghvliet, near The Hague, and Enghien. He also etched The rigged ship, which appeared in 1678 in Jacobus Robijn's De Hollandsche Scheepsbouw (Dutch shipbuilding).

BACKHUIZEN, LUDOLF

Painter, etcher and calligrapher. Born in Emden in 1630, died in Amsterdam in 1708. He arrived in Amsterdam in 1649 and began drawing, inspired by the busy shipping in the port. He studied under Allaert van Everdingen and Hendrik Dubbels, and became one of the most respected and productive marine painters of his day. Numerous prints were made after his work in the eighteenth century. It was only in 1701, towards the end of his life, that he himself took up the etching needle, producing a series of ten prints of ships off the coasts of the North Sea and Zuider Zee. A few other etchings of ships and a portrait have been attributed to him, with varying degrees of certainty.

BARGAS, A.F.

Etcher. Active in Brussels at the end of the seventeenth century. He was probably a pupil of Pieter Bout. The majority of his nine etchings were made after his own designs, and a few after designs by Bout.

BASSE, WILLEM

Etcher. Born in Amsterdam around 1613-14, and died there in 1672. Active in Amsterdam. His work was heavily influenced by Rembrandt. He made some 70 prints, of landscapes and of religious, mythological and genre subjects. The prints are dated between 1628 and 1648.

BAST, PIETER

Cartographer, engraver and publisher. Born in Antwerp around 1570, died in 1605 in Leiden. After leaving Antwerp, probably to escape the Spanish domination of the city, he is known to have been in Middelburg in

1594. He lived in Leiden from 1601. He travelled throughout the northern Netherlands and made ground plans and profiles of various towns, including Amsterdam, Franeker and Dordrecht, amounting to some twenty in all. He was the leading figure in the development of cartography in Amsterdam at the beginning of the seventeenth century.

BAUDOUS, ROBERT DE

Engraver and publisher. Born in Brussels around 1575, died after 1659 in Wassenaar (?). Active in Amsterdam between ca. 1590 and 1644, in Leiden between 1646 and 1648, in Rijnsburg between 1653 and 1654, and in Wassenaar in 1659. The prints from his hand, some 120 in all, have dates between 1605 and 1628. Some are after his own designs, while others are after Lucas van Leyden, Goltzius and van Wieringen. In addition to religious scenes there are studies of men fencing, and of horses. His publications included many of Goltzius's prints, as well as Jacob de Gheyn's Wapenhandelinghe (The use of arms), 1608.

BENDORP, CAREL FREDERIK

Painter, etcher and publisher. Born in Sas van Gent in 1763, died in Dordrecht in 1814. In 1769 he left Dordrecht and lived in Rotterdam for several years, where he worked as a glass-blower. Increasingly, though, he turned to painting and drawing. On his return to Dordrecht he devoted himself entirely to art. He made numerous prints, some of them after designs by others. He particularly favored seventeenth-century artists like Albert Cuyp and Ludolf Backhuizen. The prints after his own designs consist mainly of views in Rotterdam and Dordrecht, and sea battles.

BLAEU, WILLEM JANSZ.: see JANSEN

BOL, CORNELIS

Painter (?) and etcher. The data on Bol's life are somewhat contradictory. According to Waller he was born in Veere around 1650, or a little earlier, and was active in Brill. Hollstein places him in London in 1666, the year of the Great Fire, which he supposedly recorded in a painting. The oeuvre attributed to him consists of approximately ten Dutch and Italian town views and landscapes, and a series of five Italian ports and ships which he etched after Abraham Casembrot.

BORCHT IV, PIETER VAN DER

Engraver and etcher. Born in Mechelen in 1545, died in Antwerp in 1608. In 1572 he fled from Mechelen to Antwerp to avoid the Spanish forces. His activities in Antwerp in-

cluded work for Christopher Plantin's printing and publishing house, 'De Gouden Passer.' He made approximately 600 prints, the majority of which appeared in books. One-third are of religious subjects. The remainder include designs of gardens after Vredeman de Vries, the months of the year, and the investiture of Albert and Isabella in Antwerp in 1599.

BORMEESTER, JOCHEM

Publisher. Active in Amsterdam between ca. 1677 and 1690.

BOUT, PIETER

Painter and etcher. Born in Brussels in 1658, and died there in 1719. Between 1675 and 1677 he was active in Paris, and possibly in Italy. Only four prints have been attributed to him.

BRAY, DIRCK DE

Painter, etcher and maker of woodcuts. Born in Haarlem around 1620, died before 1702, probably in a monastery in Brabant. He was the son of Salomon de Bray, and was thus brought up in one of Haarlem's leading artist families. He started out as a bookbinder, and in 1658 wrote an illustrated description of what he had learned of the craft entitled Kort onderweys van het boeckenbinden (Brief instruction in bookbinding). He made only a few paintings, but produced 146 woodcuts and 29 etchings of biblical, allegorical and topographical subjects, and portraits. The prints are dated between 1658 and 1676.

BREUHAUS DE GROOT, FRANS ARNOLD

Painter and lithographer. Born in Leiden in 1824, died in Brussels in 1872. Studied at the Drawing Academy in The Hague from 1839 to 1847. He worked from 1850 to 1861 in Amsterdam, in The Hague in 1861, and from then on in Brussels. As a painter he specialized in landscapes, like his father before him, Frans Breuhaus de Groot. His lithographs are chiefly of shipwrecks and stormy seas.

BRINK, J. VAN DEN

Publisher. Active in Rotterdam at the beginning of the nineteenth century.

BROEN, WILLEM DE

Publisher, etcher and calligrapher. Born in Amsterdam around 1686-87, died in Leiden in 1748. Active in Amsterdam from ca. 1705.

BRUEGEL, PIETER

Painter and etcher. Possibly born in Bruegel (near Breda?) around 1525, died in Brussels in 1569. He was a pupil of Pieter Coecke van Aelst, and was admitted to the Antwerp painters' guild as a master in 1551. In 1551-54 he made a journey across the Alps and travelled in Italy. In 1563 he married in Brussels. Although he only made one etching himself (*The rabbit hunt*), numerous prints were made after his drawings. Many of those prints were commissioned by Hieronymus Cock from such artists as Pieter van der Heyden, Frans Huys and Philips Galle for distribution through Cock's publishing house, 'Aux quatre Vents.' They include the series of large landscapes of ca. 1555, in which Bruegel recorded his impressions of his Italian journey, the allegorical series with the Virtues and the Vices, and the series of ship prints.

BUFFA AND SONS, FRANS
Publishers. Active in Amsterdam from 1824.

CADART, ALFRED
Publisher. Born in Saint-Omer in 1828, died in Paris in 1875. He settled in Paris in 1859 as a publisher and dealer in prints. From 1861 he published albums of original etchings, and was later responsible for the publications of the Société des Aquafortistes. He was successively associated with Chevalier, Luquet and Luce.

CADART ET CHEVALIER
Publishers. Active in Paris between 1861 and 1863.

CADART ET LUCE
Publishers. Active in Paris from late 1867 to ca. 1871.

CADART ET LUQUET
Publishers. Active in Paris between 1863 and 1867.

CASEMBROT, ABRAHAM
Painter and etcher. Born in Flanders. He moved to Messina, probably for religious reasons, and was active there between ca. 1650 and 1675. His etchings, amounting to some twenty in all, are chiefly of Mediterranean ports and ship types.

CHANGUION, DANIEL JEAN
Publisher. Active in Amsterdam between 1772 and 1778.

CHEVALIER: see CADART ET CHEVALIER

CLEYNHENS, BERNARDUS
Publisher and painter (?). Active in Haarlem between 1735 and 1779.

COCK, HIERONYMUS
Publisher, painter and etcher. Born in Antwerp around 1510, died in Rome (?) in 1570. His publishing house, 'Aux quatre Vents,' was

the largest concern of its kind in the Low Countries around 1550. He commissioned drawings from Bruegel and prints from other artists, which were made either after their own designs or after those by prominent foreign artists, such as Raphael and Michelangelo. He made some fourteen etchings of his own.

COLLAERT I, HANS
Engraver. Born in Antwerp in 1566, died there in 1628. Three engravers of this name worked in Antwerp, and for a long time it was difficult to distinguish between the oeuvre of Hans Collaert the Elder and that of his son, Hans Collaert, the artist represented in this book. At present there are some 220 prints attributed to the latter, many of them religious scenes after Maarten de Vos and others. He also executed various series, such as the '*Nova reperta,*' yachts after Stradanus and four ornament series, with designs for jewellery.

COMTE, PIETER LE
Naval officer, painter and lithographer. Knight of the Military Order of Willem. Born in Amsterdam in 1802, died there in 1849. From 1828 to 1837 he was Commodore in charge of the School of Seamanship and Navigation. His *Afbeeldingen van schepen en vaartuigen, in verschillende bewegingen* (Illustrations of ships and other craft carrying out various evolutions) was published in 1831. It included a large number of lithographs, which give us a clear picture of the ship types and evolutions of the day. In 1842 he published *Praktikale zeevaartkunde en theoretische kennis voor handel en scheepvaart* (Practical navigation and theoretical knowledge for commerce and shipping).

CONRADI, PETRUS
Publisher. Active in Amsterdam between 1740 and 1792.

CORNELISZ., LAMBERT
Engraver. Active in Amsterdam between 1593 and 1621. He made some fifteen prints, the majority of them portraits.

CRAJENSCHOT, THEODORUS
Publisher. Active in Amsterdam between 1746 and 1801.

DAIWAILLE AND VELDHUYSEN
Publishers. Active in Amsterdam in the years 1831-32.

DANCKERTS, CORNELIS
Publisher and etcher. Born in Amsterdam in 1603, died there in 1656. Active in Amsterdam between 1630 and 1656.

DANCKERTS, DANCKER
Publisher and etcher. Born in Amsterdam in 1634, died there in 1666.

DELATRE, AUGUSTE
Printer. Born in Paris in 1822, died there in 1907. He printed numerous etchings by Méryon, Millet and others, and was the printer for the group of young etchers who formed themselves into the Société des Aquafortistes in 1862.

DESGUERROIS & CO.
Printers of lithographs. Active in Amsterdam from 1827.

ELSHEIMER, ADAM
Painter and etcher. Born in Frankfurt in 1578 (?), died in Rome in 1610. He lived for some time in Venice, and moved to Rome in 1600. Painted mainly history pieces and landscapes.

ELWE, JAN BAREND
Publisher. Active in Amsterdam between 1777 and 1815.

FARGUE, ISAAC LODEWIJK LA
Painter and etcher. Born in The Hague in 1726, died there in 1805. He called himself van Nieuwland after his mother. His name is recorded in The Hague up to 1768. His works include a few history prints depicting events from the life of William the Silent, and a series of thirteen village views. He and his brother, P. C. la Fargue, executed the series of artists' portraits for the *Toneel der uitmuntende schilders van Europa* (Showcase of the leading painters of Europe), 1752.

FARGUE, PAULUS CONSTANTIJN LA
Painter and etcher. Born in The Hague in 1729, died there in 1782. His work, including some ten prints, consists chiefly of views in and around The Hague.

FOKKE, SIMON
Engraver, etcher and publisher. Born in Amsterdam in 1712, died there in 1784. For some time he earned his living as an actor. He was a pupil of J. C. Philips and a prolific printmaker. The majority of his prints were for book illustrations, consisting of portraits, title prints, vignettes, etc. He also made reproductions after Avercamp, Berchem and Pronk, and Dutch views after Jan de Beyer.

FOUQUET, PIERRE
Publisher. Born in Amsterdam in 1729, died there in 1800 (?). Active in Amsterdam between 1759 and 1800. He was also a painter, being a member of the Guild of St. Luke from 1753, but no paintings by him are known. He was an art dealer, and soon began publishing prints. He is chiefly known for his publication of city views of Amsterdam, which were gathered together in the so-called Fouquet *Atlas.*

FRISIUS, SIMON
Painter, engraver, etcher and calligrapher. Born in Harlingen around 1580, died in The Hague in 1629. Lived in The Hague from 1614. He was a dealer in silk and arms, in addition to being a graphic artist. He travelled a great deal, and visited Paris (1598-99), Russia, Spain and other countries. He made more than 230 prints, including works after Lucas van Leyden and David Vinckboons. His calligraphy in the *Spiegel der schrijfconste* (Model of the art of writing), 1605, was after a design by Jan van de Velde.

GALLE, PHILIPS
Publisher and engraver. Born in Haarlem in 1537, died in Antwerp in 1612. He settled in Antwerp in 1564, becoming the leading publisher in the city after the death of Hieronymus Cock in 1570. There are some 800 prints from his hand, after designs by Maarten van Heemskerk, Pieter Bruegel, Johannes Stradanus and others.

GALLE, THEODOOR
Publisher and engraver. Born in Antwerp around 1570, died there in 1633. After working for his father, Philips Galle, he moved to the Plantin publishing house, which was being continued by Plantin's son-in-law, Jan Moretus. He made more than 430 prints, including numerous religious scenes and landscapes.

GEEL, JOOST VAN
Painter and etcher. Born in Rotterdam in 1631 (?), died there in 1698. He was trained for a life of trade, and after 1670 had a vinegar brewery. Little is known of his work as a painter and etcher. His paintings are predominantly genre pieces in the style of Gabriel Metsu, who may well have been his teacher. His painted views of Rotterdam are now lost. It only became known in this century that he had also made prints, these being the Postal Map and chart of the River Maas of 1665, both of which were commissioned by Jacob Quack.

GOLE, JACOB
Mezzotint engraver, etcher and publisher. Born in Amsterdam, and died there in 1724. Worked in Paris in 1680, and in Amsterdam from 1681. He made more than 425 prints, the majority of them mezzotints. The bulk of his output consisted of portraits and genre scenes.

GOLTZIUS, HENDRICK
Painter, engraver and maker of woodcuts (?). Born in Mühlbracht (near Venlo) in 1558, died in Haarlem in 1617. He came to Haarlem in 1577, where he got to know Carel van Mander and Bartholomeus Spranger. In 1590-91 he travelled in Italy. The prints attributed to him, the majority of which were made be-

fore 1600, comprise some 360 engravings and 24 woodcuts. Most of the woodcuts are printed in chiaroscuro. (This technique involves printing the paper with a number of wood blocks: a line block for the outlines, and tone blocks for the large areas of color. Goltzius probably copied this technique from Venetian woodcuts.)

GOOS, ABRAHAM

Engraver and publisher. Died before 1643. Active in Amsterdam from 1610 to after 1630. In 1616 he published the *Nieuw Nederlandtsch caertboeck* (New book of maps of the Netherlands), one of the first Dutch atlases.

GOOS, PIETER

Publisher. Born in Amsterdam around 1616, died there in 1675. Active in Amsterdam from 1642.

GOUDT, HENDRICK

Painter (?) and engraver. Born in Utrecht in 1582 (?), died there in 1648. From 1608 to 1611 he was in Rome, where he got to know Adam Elsheimer, after whose paintings he etched seven prints.

GREEBE, FREDERIK WILLEM

Publisher. Active in Amsterdam between 1758 and 1788.

GREIVE, JOHAN CONRAD

Painter, etcher and lithographer. Born in Amsterdam in 1837, died there in 1891. He was a pupil of his uncle, Petrus Franciscus Greive, and of Cornelis Springer. Almost all his prints are town and river views.

GROENEWEGEN, GERRIT

Painter and etcher. Born in Rotterdam in 1754, died there in 1826. He spent his entire life in Rotterdam, living just outside the town on the Westzeedijk. He was a ship's carpenter, like his father. However, he lost part of his right leg in an accident when still a young man, and he had to abandon his calling, taking up art instead. Only seven paintings by Groenewegen are known, but he was a prolific draftsman and etcher. His earliest drawings date from 1779, the last from 1826. Hundreds of his drawings and watercolors are of a topographical nature, depicting Rotterdam and its environs, with the emphasis on the docks and the River Maas. In addition to topography, he specialized in the portrayal of ships, in both drawings and prints. Between 1786 and 1801 he etched 84 illustrations of ship types. He also executed a number of other series, almost all consisting of six prints.

HENGST, PETRUS DEN

Publisher. Active in Amsterdam between 1778 and 1804.

HONDIUS, HENDRICK

Publisher and etcher. Born in Duffel in 1573, died in The Hague in 1650. Worked in The Hague from 1597, with a brief interruption in Amsterdam before 1606. He made some 250 prints, chiefly portraits and allegorical scenes. Not to be confused with Henricus Hondius, who lived from 1596-97 to 1651, and who worked in Amsterdam exclusively as a publisher.

HOORN, JAN TEN

Publisher. Active in Amsterdam between 1673 and 1711.

HUBERTI, A.: *see* HUYBRECHTS

HUYBRECHTS, ADRIAEN

Engraver and publisher. Born before 1573, died after 1614. Active in Antwerp.

HUYS, FRANS

Engraver and etcher. Born in Antwerp around 1522, died there before April 1562. He was admitted to the Guild of St. Luke as a master before 1546. No paintings or drawings by him are known. The majority of his 117 prints were published by Hieronymus Cock and his brother-in-law, Hans Liefrinck. They include portraits and religious, mythological, historical, topographical and genre scenes after Pieter Bruegel, Frans Floris and others, as well as ornament prints after Cornelis Floris and Hans Vredeman de Vries.

JANSEN, WILLEM

Publisher. Also known as Willem Jansz. Blaeu. Active in Amsterdam between 1598 and 1638. He was a publisher of guides for seamen and loose geographical maps. After ca. 1630 his publishing house became famous for its atlases of the world.

JANSSONIUS, JOHANNES

Publisher. Active in Amsterdam between 1614 and 1664.

JANSZ., JAN: *see* JANSSONIUS

JANSZ., JOOST

Sculptor, architect, engraver, land surveyor and publisher. Born in Amsterdam before or in 1541, died there in 1590.

JANSZ., WILLEM: *see* JANSEN

JONG, DIRK DE

Publisher and engraver. Active in Rotterdam between 1779 and 1802 (?). He worked both from his own drawings and from those of other artists, such as Cornelis Pronk. He was the designer of the series of Dutch seaports of which de Sallieth made prints.

JONG[H]E, CLEMENT DE

Publisher. Active in Amsterdam between 1649 and 1679.

JONGKIND, JOHAN BARTHOLD

Painter and etcher. Born in Lattrop (near Denekamp) in 1819, died in La Côte-Saint-André in 1891. He studied at the Drawing Academy in The Hague, and was a pupil of A. Schelfhout. From 1846 he lived and worked chiefly in France. His only lengthy stay in the Netherlands thereafter was from 1855-60, which was a period of acute depression. He then returned to Paris, where he came under the protection of Madame Fesser. He made many excursions to Normandy and Brittany, and passed the summers of 1867-69 in the Netherlands. He made some twenty etchings between 1862 and 1878. They are all of his only theme: landscape.

KAAL, F.

Publisher. Active in Amsterdam between 1823 and 1841.

KEERE, PIETER VAN DER

Also known as Kaerius. Publisher and etcher. Born in Ghent around 1571, died after 1630 in Amsterdam (?). Active in Amsterdam between 1593 and 1630.

KEYZER, HARMANUS

Publisher. Active in Amsterdam between 1772 and 1798.

KOBELL, HENDRIK

Painter and etcher. Born in Rotterdam in 1751, died there in 1779. He was originally destined for a life in business. He got his training as an artist during a business stay in England, 1770-71, and in Amsterdam. He travelled throughout France. In 1773 he returned to Rotterdam, and between 1774 and 1778 lived in Delfshaven. His drawings and watercolors were much sought after, and served as models for prints by such artists as de Sallieth and Simon Fokke. He made only a few paintings, and approximately twenty etchings.

KOBELL, JAN

Painter and engraver. Born in Rotterdam in 1756, died there in 1833. He was a brother of Hendrik Kobell, and worked mainly in Rotterdam, with a brief interruption in Gouda, 1793-95. He made two etchings of events at sea, a series of portraits after designs by other artists, and a few history prints.

LAAN, ADOLF VAN DER

Born in Amsterdam (or Utrecht?) around 1690 (or in 1684?), died in Amsterdam in 1742. He worked for many years in Paris. He made a large number of prints, including portraits, landscapes after Johannes Glauber, and scenes with ship types and fishery after Sieuwert van der Meulen.

LANGENDIJK, DIRK

Painter and etcher. Born in Rotterdam in 1748, died there in 1805. He is known chiefly for his drawings, which were initially of marine views, and later of scenes with soldiers. He made only a few prints, the first of which dates from 1769. In 1774 he etched a print jointly with Hendrik Kobell.

LAURENS, HENDRIK

Publisher. Active in Amsterdam between 1609 and 1649.

LETH, HENDRIK DE

Engraver, etcher and publisher. Born in Amsterdam in 1703, died there in 1766.

LIEFRINCK II, CORNELIS

Painter and etcher. Born in Leiden after 1574 (?), died there around 1640. Bailiff of Rijnsburg and Boskoop. Worked in Leiden between 1619 and 1626, and in Rijnsburg between 1626 and 1635. The only prints known to be by him are the three depicting the journey of the Leiden militia to the town of Grave.

LIEVENS, JAN

Painter, etcher and maker of woodcuts. Born in Leiden in 1607, died in Amsterdam in 1674. From 1619 to 1621 he was a pupil of Pieter Lastman in Amsterdam. He then returned to Leiden, where he worked with Rembrandt until 1631. Between 1638 and 1643 he worked in Antwerp, where he was heavily influenced by van Dyck. He painted mainly portraits and historical and allegorical scenes. His prints consist almost entirely of portraits and figure studies.

LODEWYCKSZ., LODEWYCK

Publisher. Active in Amsterdam between 1654 and 1658.

LONS, DIRCK EVERSEN

Etcher and publisher. Born in Amsterdam around 1599, died after 1666 (?). Active in Amsterdam between ca. 1615 and 1631. He made 28 prints, some after his own designs, and the remainder after designs by such artists as Abraham Bloemaert and Esaias van de Velde. He was also the publisher of some of those prints, among them a series of landscapes with large foreground figures. Claes Jansz. Visscher later became the publisher of Lons's prints, such as the four windmill types issued in 1631. The series of ship types published by Pieter Goos in 1642, most of which bear Lons's name, is probably based on a series which was originally etched by Lons, and published by Visscher in 1629.

LOOSJES, L.

No mention found in the literature.

LOVERINGH, WED. H.

Publisher. Active in Amsterdam between 1775 and 1778.

LUCE: *see* CADART

LUQUET: *see* CADART

LUYKEN, CASPAR
Etcher. Born in Amsterdam (?) in 1672, died there in 1708. Worked in Amsterdam, apart from a break between 1698 and 1705 in Nuremberg. As was the case with his father, Jan Luyken, his print output consists of numerous book illustrations, the majority after his own drawings. In addition to many religious scenes, he made a large number of illustrations for literary works.

LUYKEN, JAN
Etcher, publisher and poet. Born in Amsterdam in 1649, died there in 1712. He made some 3,300 prints, the majority after his own drawings. They include dozens of series of book illustrations to accompany biblical stories, travel accounts, historical works, etc. Some of the best-known series are the *Story of the Old and New Testaments*, published around 1700 by P. Mortier, and the *Cabinet of occupations*, 1694.

MAASKAMP, EVERT
Painter and publisher. Born in Vollenhoven in 1769, died in Amsterdam in 1834. Worked in Amsterdam from 1794.

MEER, NOACH VAN DER
Etcher and publisher. Born in Leiden in 1741 (?), died in Amsterdam in 1822. Worked in Leiden until 1768, then in Amsterdam. He produced more than 150 book illustrations and some ten loose prints, including *The Amsterdam Theatre*, and *The concert hall of Felix Meritis*.

MEULEN, SIEUWERT VAN DER
Painter and etcher. Died in Alkmaar in 1730. He was admitted to the Alkmaar Guild of St. Luke in 1700, and was working in Haarlem around 1706. In addition to the series of ship prints he made garden views and a series of bird prints. There are some 40 prints from his hand.

MEYSENS, JOHANNES
Painter, engraver and publisher. Born in Antwerp (?) in 1602 (?), died in Antwerp in 1670. He was the founder of one of the largest publishing houses in Antwerp.

MIELING, C. W.
Lithographic printer and publisher. Worked in Rotterdam from 1839 to 1845, and in The Hague from 1845 to 1848. The Koninklijke Steendrukkerij C. W. Mieling existed in The Hague from 1848 to 1868.

MONTAIGNE: *see* PLATTENBERG

MORIN, JEAN
Painter, etcher and publisher. Born in Paris around 1605, died there in 1650.

MOUSIJN, MICHIEL
Etcher. Active in Amsterdam ca. 1640-55. Little is known of his life. He produced 96 prints, half of them being decorative ornament prints after G. van den Eeckhout and Jacob van Campen. Several other prints are portraits of admirals.

NIEUWLAND: *see* LA FARGUE

NOOMS, REINIER
Signed himself ZEEMAN (Seaman). Painter and etcher. Born in Amsterdam around 1623, died there in 1664. His year of death was only established in 1968. Beyond this virtually nothing is known of his life or training as an artist. The alias, 'Zeeman,' and a number of scenes of foreign towns and ship types, have led to the assumption that he probably spent some time at sea as a sailor, or at any rate travelled to Paris, London and North Africa. He made more than 160 etchings, the bulk of them being topographical views and ship scenes.

PASSE II, CRISPIJN DE
Engraver. Born in Cologne in 1597, died in Amsterdam (?) around 1670. At first (from 1612) he worked with his father, Crispijn de Passe the Elder, in Utrecht. Between 1617 and 1630 he spent some time in Paris. He then worked again in Utrecht, before moving to Amsterdam in 1640. His brothers, Simon and Willem, and his sister Magdalena also worked as engravers.

PEETERS, BONAVENTURA
Painter and etcher. Born in Antwerp in 1614, died in 1652. Van der Kellen mentions thirteen etchings from his hand, nine of which depict ships at sea.

PEETERS, JAN
Painter. Born in Antwerp in 1624, died after 1677. Like his brother, Bonaventura Peeters, he painted mostly sea pieces and topographical works.

PHILIPS, JAN CASPAR
Engraver. Born in Amsterdam around 1700, died there around 1765. Simon Fokke was one of his pupils. He was a prolific printmaker, producing numerous portraits, title prints, etc. after his own designs and those of others, such as Jan de Beijer and Cornelis Pronk.

PLAATS, VOLKERT VAN DER
Publisher. Active in Harlingen between 1728 and 1801.

PLANTIN, CHRISTOPHER
Printer and publisher. Born in St. Avertin in 1514, died in Antwerp in 1589. Worked in Antwerp as a printer from 1550.

PLATTENBERG, MATTHIJS VAN
Also known as van Platten, Platte-Montaigne, or Montaigne. Painter and etcher. Born in Antwerp around 1608, died in Paris in 1660. After a period in Italy he married, in 1630, a sister of painter Jean Morin, settled in Paris and adopted the French form of his name. He made 29 etchings, the majority of them of ports and river banks, somewhat in the style of Claude Lorrain.

PORCELLIS, JAN
Painter and etcher. Born in Ghent before 1584, died in Zoeterwoude in 1632. In 1585-86 his parents moved to Rotterdam. He travelled to various countries, including England, and after 1615 spent some years in Antwerp. In 1622 he was living in Haarlem. In 1624 he moved to Amsterdam, in 1626 to Voorburg, and finally, around 1627-29, to Zoeterwoude. According to Houbraken he was a pupil of Hendrik Vroom. He specialized in marine paintings. He was known chiefly for his monochrome technique, which superseded his earlier colorful and illustrative marine pieces. He made some twenty etchings, including eighteen of '*Diverse beaches and water views.*'

PUNT, JAN
Painter, etcher and publisher. Born in Amsterdam in 1711, died there in 1779. He worked in Amsterdam, with the exception of a period in Rotterdam from 1773 to 1777. He was a pupil of Adolf van der Laan, and later taught Reinier Vinkeles. He was also an actor for a while. The majority of his 150 prints are after designs by others.

RAM, JOHANNES DE
Publisher and etcher. Born in Amsterdam in 1648, died there in 1693.

REMBRANDT
Painter and etcher. Born in Leiden in 1606, died in Amsterdam in 1669. He was a pupil of Jacob van Swanenburg in Leiden, and of Pieter Lastman in Amsterdam. He worked in Amsterdam from 1631. He became a much sought-after portrait painter, but his popularity declined from around 1650. He got into financial difficulties, and in 1656 petitioned to be declared a bankrupt. He made 290 prints, the majority of them etchings, but he also used the burin and dry-point. The earliest dated prints are from 1628, and the last from 1661. The prints cover virtually every subject: portraits, biblical scenes, figure studies, genre scenes, landscapes, etc. Only a few of his prints were made for books.

ROGHMAN, ROELANT
Painter and etcher. Born in Amsterdam in 1627, died there in 1692. His paintings and his approximately 40 prints are mainly of landscape and Dutch topography.

ROGUIÉ
Publisher (?). No details known.

ROOS, CORNELIS SEBILLE
Publisher. Active in Amsterdam between 1779 and 1820.

ROY, H. LE
Publisher. No details known.

SAFTLEVEN, HERMAN
Painter and etcher. Born in Rotterdam around 1609-10, died in Utrecht in 1685. Worked in Utrecht from 1632. He worked in the style of such Haarlem masters as Buytewech, Jan van de Velde and Pieter Molijn until around 1640, when his work began to display the influence of the Italianate painters, notably Both and Breenbergh. He specialized in mountain and river landscapes and topography. He made some 35 etchings.

SALLIETH, MATTHIAS DE
Engraver, etcher and publisher. Born in Prague in 1749, died in Rotterdam in 1791. After studying in Vienna and Paris he settled in Rotterdam in 1779. He worked chiefly to the designs of other artists, producing some 25 portraits and 33 sheets of Dutch costumes after Perkois and Prins. The majority of his marine and river views are after drawings by Hendrik Kobell and Dirk de Jong.

SCHELFHOUT, ANDREAS
Painter, lithographer and etcher. Born in The Hague in 1787, died there in 1870. He worked in his father's picture framing shop until around 1810. His paintings brought him great success, particularly those of winter scenes. His prints consist of fifteen lithographs, three of which are in color.

SCHENCK, PETRUS
Engraver, etcher and publisher. Born in Eberfeld in 1660, died in Amsterdam around 1718-19. Active in Amsterdam between 1684 and 1718.

SCHENCK JUNIOR, PETRUS
Publisher. Active in Amsterdam between 1769 and 1784. He was the son and successor of Petrus II.

SCHIEDGES, PETRUS PAULUS
Painter, etcher and lithographer. Born in The Hague in 1813, died there in 1876. He studied at the Academy of Fine Arts in The Hague. His work consists in the main of marine and river views.

SCHOTEL, JOHANNES CHRISTIAAN

Painter, etcher and lithographer. Born in Dordrecht in 1787, died there around 1838-39. He made several journeys to France and Germany with his son, P. J. Schotel, and did a great deal of his work in the province of Zeeland. Almost all his paintings, drawings, watercolors and the few prints are marine and river views.

SCHOTEL, PETRUS JOHANNES

Painter, etcher and lithographer. Born in Dordrecht in 1808, died in Dresden in 1865. He was a pupil of his father, J.C. Schotel. He travelled in various countries, including France, Belgium and Germany. In 1840 he crossed the North Sea in a warship, and in 1843 he was with a training squadron in the Mediterranean. Between 1830 and 1850 he taught drawing at the Royal Naval Institute at Medemblik. He then moved to Kampen, and around 1855 to Düsseldorf. In 1864 he finally settled in Dresden. His output consisted chiefly of paintings and drawings, and he made only a few lithographs and etchings. His main theme was the marine view with ships.

SCHOUTE[N], HERMANUS PETRUS

Born in Amsterdam in 1747, died in Haarlem in 1822. He was the pupil of his father, Johannes Schoute(n), Paul van Liender, and Cornelis Ploos van Amstel. He worked in Haarlem from 1792. Around 1770 Pierre Fouquet commissioned 59 drawings from Schoute(n), many of which Schoute(n) also engraved for Fouquet's *Atlas*. Schoute(n) generally followed this method. He would make a sketch on the spot and then return to his studio, where he worked the sketch into a detailed drawing which then served as the model for the print.

SEGERS, HERCULES

Painter and etcher. Born in Haarlem around 1589-90, died in The Hague between 1633 and 1638. Until 1606 he studied at Amsterdam under Gillis van Coninxloo. In 1612 he became a member of the Guild of St. Luke in Haarlem, where he remained until 1614. He then lived in Amsterdam, Utrecht (from 1629 to 1631) and The Hague. His paintings had a certain influence on the landscapes of Rembrandt and Philips Koninck. His prints, too, are mainly of landscapes, only two being marine views. There are only 183 surviving impressions of the 54 prints currently given to Segers. Almost all the impressions of any one print differ from each other, since Segers continually used different types of paper, or even canvas, printed in different colored inks, and often worked up the impressions with the brush.

SERWOUTER, PIETER

Engraver. Born in Antwerp in 1586, died in Amsterdam in 1657. He is recorded in Amsterdam from 1622 onwards. The earliest date on his prints is 1607. Many of his prints are book illustrations, after such artists as Adriaan van de Venne and David Vinckboons.

SIBRANTSZ., PIETER

Painter. He became a citizen of Amsterdam in 1599. Serwouter took his models on several occasions from the works of this marine painter, notably for the ships in his large profile of Rotterdam.

SILO, ADAM

Painter and etcher. Born in Amsterdam in 1674, died there in 1760 (?). He also modelled in wax, built optical instruments, and was a shipbuilder. He only took up painting around 1700. Works from his hand include *Afteekeningen van verscheide soorten en charters van scheepen en andere vaartuigen* (Drawings of various types and designs of ships and other craft), 1757. Nagler mentions nine prints, all with marine views, while Thieme-Becker lists more than twenty.

SMIT AND SON, JOHANNES

Publishers. Active in Amsterdam between 1778 and 1782.

STEUERWALD & COMPIE

Lithographic printers. Based in Dordrecht between 1826 and 1833. After 1833 the J.D. Steuerwald lithographic works was in The Hague. It was the continuation of one of the first Dutch lithographic printers, which had been established in 1822 in Dordrecht by two brothers, Christiaan Heinrich Gottlieb Steuerwald and Jan Dam Steuerwald. Christiaan was born in Bergen op Zoom in 1802, and died there in 1874. He was a professional army officer and an amateur lithographer and lithographic printer. Jan Dam was born in Bergen op Zoom in 1805, and died in The Hague in 1869. He was also a lithographer and lithographic printer, and managed the printing works.

STRAAT, JAN VAN DER

Also known as Stradanus. Born in Bruges in 1523, died in Florence in 1605. He was a pupil of Pieter Aertsen in Antwerp. He travelled a great deal, and spent much of his life in Florence. He made numerous designs for frescos, tapestries and prints, including a series of yachts.

STRADANUS: *see* STRAAT

SWANENBURGH, WILLEM

Painter and engraver. Born in Leiden in 1581, died there in 1612. The approximately 40 prints attached to his name, which include portraits, are chiefly after designs by others.

VALCK, GERARD

Publisher, engraver and etcher. Born in Amsterdam, died there in 1726. He worked in Amsterdam between 1670 and 1726, with a break in London between 1672 and 1675 or 1678.

VELDE, JAN VAN DE

Engraver and etcher. Born in Rotterdam around 1593, died in Enkhuizen in 1641. He worked in Haarlem from 1614, when he was admitted to the Guild of St. Luke as a master, until 1636, when he moved to Enkhuizen. The majority of his approximately 490 prints were made between 1615 and 1633. Many of them are series, of which half are of landscapes and river views, as well as numerous portraits. Until around 1618 he worked from his own drawings, but later he also made prints after designs by Molijn, van Wieringen, Buytewech and others. In his observation of nature he was greatly influenced by Claes Jansz. Visscher. His 'night scenes' were influenced by Hendrick Goudt's prints after Elsheimer.

VELDHUIJSEN: *see* DAIWAILLE

VINNE, ISAAK VAN DE

Etcher, maker of woodcuts and publisher. Born in Haarlem in 1665, died there in 1740. He was born into a Haarlem artist family, and was a pupil of his father, Vincent Laurens van de Vinne. He was a prolific printmaker. The exact number of his prints has not yet been established, since many are variously attributed to other members of the family.

VISSCHER, CLAES JANSZ.

Publisher and etcher. Born in Amsterdam around 1587, died there in 1652. In 1608 he is recorded in Amsterdam as being an engraver. He was one of the first artists, at the beginning of the seventeenth century, to depict the Dutch landscape as faithfully as possible. His prints, numbering at least 200, were initially made after the designs of other artists, among them David Vinckboons and Cornelis Claesz. van Wieringen. Later he began producing his own spontaneous and 'realistic' etchings, which included landscapes. However, his work as an etcher is overshadowed by the important role he played as a publisher of prints by his contemporaries and predecessors. It is often difficult to determine whether some prints were not worked up, copied or even added to by Visscher.

VISSCHER, N.

Publisher. One of the two successors to Claes Jansz. Visscher with the same name. One was Nicolaes Visscher, who lived from 1618 to 1679 and worked in Amsterdam between 1652 and 1679. The other was Nicolaus Visscher, who lived from 1650 to 1702 and was working in Amsterdam in 1679-80.

VOSKUYL, DIRCK PIETERSZ.

Publisher. Active in Amsterdam between 1612 and 1623.

VRIES, RUURT DE

Lithographic printer, publisher and lithographer. Active in Monnickendam between 1835 and 1840, and then in Amsterdam.

VROOM, HENDRIK

Painter. Born in Haarlem around 1566 (?), died there in 1640. After an eventful youth, which included travels in Spain and Italy as a faïence painter, he finally returned to Haarlem. It was there, around 1596, that he produced the first of the ship portraits, sea battles and marine views that were to become his specialty.

WALDORP, ANTONIE

Painter and lithographer. Born in The Hague in 1803, died in Amsterdam in 1866. He worked at first in The Hague, but moved to Amsterdam in 1857. He and Wijnand Nuyen travelled through France, Germany and Belgium. He started out as a stage designer, and only later began painting landscapes, townscapes and river views.

WALPOT, ADRIAAN

Publisher. Active in Dordrecht between 1754 and 1780.

WIERINGEN, CORNELIS CLAESZ. VAN

Painter and maker of woodcuts (?). Born in Haarlem (?) around 1580, died in Haarlem in 1633. Like his teacher, Hendrik Vroom, he specialized in marine views. It is not certain whether he also made prints. Wurzbach mentions six etchings from his hand, while other authors attribute a few woodcuts to him. Various artists made prints after his drawings, among them Claes Jansz. Visscher, in the series 'Amoeniores aliquot regiunculae' of 1613, and Hendrick Goltzius (?).

WINTER, ANTONIE DE

Engraver, etcher and art dealer. Worked in Utrecht around 1670, and in Amsterdam between 1679 and 1700.

WIT, FREDERICK DE

Publisher. There were three members of the same family with this name, father, son and grandson, who worked in Amsterdam between 1648 and 1712.

WIT, KORNELIS DE

Publisher. Active in Amsterdam between 1735 and 1763.

YVER, PIETER

Writer, engraver, etcher and publisher. Born in Amsterdam in 1712, died there in 1787. Author of the supplement to Gersaint's catalogue of Rembrandt's etchings.

Literature

Aa, A. J. van der, *Aardrijkskundig woordenboek der Nederlanden*, 13 vols., Gorinchem 1838-51

Ailly, A. E. d', *Repertorium van de profielen der stad Amsterdam en van de plattegronden der schutterswijken* [Amsterdam 1953]

Amsterdam, Amsterdam Historical Museum, exhibition catalogue *The Dutch cityscape in the seventeenth century and its sources*, 1977

—, exhibition catalogue *The world on paper: cartography in Amsterdam in the seventeenth century*, 1967

Anderson, R. and R.C., *The sailing-ship*, London etc. [1926]

Asart, G., P.M. Bosscher, J.R. Bruyn and W.J. van Hoboken, *Maritieme geschiedenis der Nederlanden*, 4 vols., Bussum 1976-78

Bailly-Herzberg, J., *L'Eau-forte de peintre au dix-neuvième siècle: La Société des Aquafortistes 1862-1867*, Paris 1972

Bakker, B., *Amsterdam getekend: tekeningen en aquarellen uit vier eeuwen in de historisch-topografische atlas van het Gemeentearchief*, The Hague 1978

Bartsch, A., *Le peintre-graveur*, 21 vols., Vienna 1803-21

Bastelaer, R. van, *Les estampes de Peter Bruegel l'Ancien*, Brussels 1908

Beets, N., 'Aanwinsten van zestiende-eeuwsche houtsneden in het Rijks-prentenkabinet te Amsterdam,' *Het Boek* 21 (1932-33), pp. 177-208

Berk, G.L., 'Vragen rond de rollepaal,' *Spiegel der Zeilvaart* 2 (1978), nr. 1, p. 17

Beylen, J. van, *Schepen van de Nederlanden, van de late middeleeuwen tot het einde van de zeventiende eeuw*, Amsterdam 1970

—, 'De uitbeelding en de dokumentaire waarde van schepen bij enkele oude meesters,' *Bulletin van de Koninklijke Musea voor Schone Kunsten* [Antwerp] 10 (1961), pp. 123-50

Bom Hgz., G.D., 'D'Vrijheid,' *1781-1797: geschiedenis van een vlaggeschip*, Amsterdam and London 1897

Bonnefoux, [P.M.J.] de, *Compleet handboek der manoeuvres met zeilschepen*, Flushing 1856

Bruggen, B.E. van, 'Gedachten over de ontwikkeling van het uiterlijk van de romp bij de noordelijke zeegaande handel- en oorlogsschepen in de zestiende eeuw,' *Mededelingen van de Nederlandse Vereniging voor Zeegeschiedenis* (1975), nr. 31, p. 33

Burchard, L., *Die Holländischen Radierer vor Rembrandt*, Berlin 1917

Burger Jr., C.P., 'Amsterdam in het einde der zestiende eeuw: studie bij de uitgaaf van den grooten plattegrond van 1597,'

Jaarboek Amstelodamum (1918), pp. 1-101

—, 'Nederlandsche houtsneden 1500-1550: Het schip van Sinte Reynuut,' *Het Boek* 20 (1931), pp. 209-21

Buyssens, O., 'De schepen bij Pieter Bruegel de Oude: proeve van identificatiën,' *Mededelingen [van de] Academie van Marine van België* (1954), p. 159

Colnaghi, P. & D., *Exhibition of fine prints by old masters*, nr. 19, London 1963

Comte, P. le, *Afbeeldingen van schepen en vaartuigen, in verschillende bewegingen*, Amsterdam 1831

—, *Praktikale zeevaartkunde en theoretische kennis voor handel en scheepvaart*, Amsterdam 1842

Cornaz, G. and J. Derville, 'Livardes et balestrons,' *Le Petit Perroquet* (1975-76), nr. 18, p. 37

Cornelissen, J.D.M., 'Twee allegorische etsen van Rembrandt: 1. Het Scheepje van Fortuin,' *Oud-Holland* 58 (1941), pp. 111-26

Craddock & Barnard, *Engravings and etchings (fifteenth to eighteenth centuries)*, nr. 111, London 1966, nr. 51

Crone, E., *Bladzijden uit de geschiedenis der jachthavens en van de zeilsport te Amsterdam*, Amsterdam 1925

Crone, G.C.E., *Nederlandse jachten, binnenschepen, visschersvaartuigen en daarmee verwante kleine zeeschepen, 1650-1900*, Amsterdam 1926

Dekker, P., *De laatste bloeiperiode van de Nederlandse arctische walvis- en robbevangst*, Zaltbommel (Cultuurgeschiedenis der Lage Landen, vol. 8) 1971

Delteil, L., Le peintre-graveur illustré, vol. 1, Paris 1906

Dodgson, C., 'Deux estampes d'après P. Bruegel,' *Mélanges Hulin de Loo*, Brussels and Paris 1931, pp. 81-82

Dutuit, E., *Manuel de l'amateur d'estampes*, 6 vols., Paris and London 1884-88

Eeghen, I.H. van, 'De Atlas Fouquet,' *Maandblad Amstelodamum* 47 (1960), pp. 49-59

—, 'De Berebijt,' *Maandblad Amstelodamum* 39 (1952), p. 144

—, 'De kunstenaarsfamilie Schoute(n),' *Maandblad Amstelodamum* 47 (1960), pp. 129-36

Eeghen, P. van, *Het werk van Jan en Caspar Luyken*, Amsterdam 1905

Enschedé, C., *Fonderies de caractères et leur matériel dans les Pays-Bas du XVe au XIXe siècle*, Haarlem 1908

Franken Dz., D., *L'Oeuvre gravé des Van de Passe*, Amsterdam and Paris 1881

Franken, D. and J.P. van der Kellen, *L'Oeuvre de Jan van de Velde*, Amsterdam and Paris 1883

Haverkamp Begemann, E., *Hercules Segers: the complete etchings*, Amsterdam and The Hague 1973

Hazewinkel, H.C., 'De Postkaart van Quack en haar auteur,' *Rotterdamsch Jaarboekje* (1931), pp. 9-15

Hefting, V., *Jongkind, sa vie, son oeuvre, son époque*, Paris 1975

Hirschmann, O., *Verzeichnis des graphischen Werks von Hendrick Goltzius*, Leipzig 1921

Hoff, B. van 't, 'Grote stadspanorama's, gegraveerd in Amsterdam sedert 1609,' *Jaarboek Amstelodamum* (1955), pp. 81-131

—, *Jacob Quack Postmeester van Rotterdam en de door hem uitgegeven Maaskaart en Postkaart*, Rotterdam and The Hague 1965

Hollstein, F.W.H., *Dutch and Flemish etchings, engravings and woodcuts, ca. 1450-1700*, vols. 1-20, Amsterdam 1949-

Houten, W. van, *De scheepvaart*, Breda 1833

Huitema, T. (ed.), *Ronde en platbodemjachten*, Amsterdam 1962

Jonge, J.C. de, *Geschiedenis van het Nederlandsche zeewezen*, 6 vols., Haarlem 1858-62

Jongh, E. de, *Zinne- en minnebeelden in de schilderkunst van de zeventiende eeuw*, [n.p.] 1967

Kampen, H.C.A. van, and H. Kersken Hzn., *Schepen die voorbijgaan*, 2nd edition [n.p. 1927]

Keble Chatterton, E., *Sailing ships and their story*, Londen [1923]

Kellen, J.P. van der, *Le peintre-graveur hollandais et flamand, ou catalogue raisonné des estampes gravées par les peintres de l'école hollandaise et flamande. Ouvrage faisant suite au Peintre-graveur de Bartsch*, Utrecht [1866]

Keyes, G.S., 'Cornelis Claesz. van Wieringen,' *Oud-Holland* 93 (1979), pp. 1-46

Knipping, B., O.F.M., *De iconografie van de Contra-Reformatie in de Nederlanden*, 2 vols., Hilversum 1939-40 (English translation: *Iconography of the Counter Reformation in the Netherlands: heaven on earth*, 2 vols., Nieuwkoop and Leiden 1974)

Kölker, A.J., *De kaart van Holland door Joost Jansz - 1575 - opnieuw uitgegeven*, Purmerend [1971]

Konijnenburg, E. van, *Shipbuilding from its beginnings*, 3 vols., Brussels [ca. 1905]

Landström, B., *The ship*, London 1969

Lavalleye, J., *Lucas van Leyden, Peter Bruegel l'Ancien: gravures, oeuvre complet* [Paris 1966]

Lebeer, L., *Beredeneerde catalogus van de prenten naar Pieter Bruegel de Oude* [exhibition in the King Albert I Royal Library], Brussels 1969

—, 'Nog enkele wetenswaardigheden in verband met Pieter Bruegel den Oude,' *Gentsche Bijdragen tot de Kunstgeschiedenis* 9 (1943), pp. 217-36

Loon, F.N. van, *Beschouwing van den Nederlandschen scheepsbouw met betrekking tot deszelfs zeilaadje*, Haarlem 1820

—, *Handleiding tot den burgerlijken scheepsbouw*, Leeuwarden 1843

Maritieme encyclopedie, 7 vols., Bussum [1970-73]

Maritieme geschiedenis der Nederlanden, 4 vols., Bussum 1976-78

Meijerman, A.M., *Hollandse winters*, Hilversum and Antwerp 1967

Meyer, J., *Allgemeines Künstler-Lexikon*, vol. 1, Leipzig 1872

Moes, E.W. and C.P. Burger, *De Amsterdamse boekdrukkers en uitgevers in de zestiende eeuw*, 4 vols., Amsterdam and The Hague 1900-15

Mollema, J.C., *Geschiedenis van Nederland ter zee*, 4 vols., Amsterdam 1939-42

Morton Nance, R., 'A sixteenth-century seamonster,' *The Mariner's Mirror* (1912), p. 97

Muller, F., *Beredeneerde beschrijving van Nederlandsche historie-platen, zinneprenten en historische kaarten*, 3 vols. and supplement, Amsterdam 1863-82

—, *Beschrijvende catalogus van 7000 portretten van Nederlanders en van buitenlanders, tot Nederland in betrekking staande*, Amsterdam 1853

Nagler, G.K., *Neues allgemeines Künstler-Lexikon*, 22 vols., Munich 1832-52

—, *Die Monogrammisten*, 5 vols., Munich 1858-79

Nederlandsche Jaerboeken, inhoudende... geschiedenissen... der Vereenigde provintien, Amsterdam 1748-65

Nieuw Nederlandsch biografisch woordenboek, 10 vols., Leiden 1911-37

Nooms, Reinier, alijas Zeeman, *Verscheijde Schepen en Gesichten van Amstelredam, Naert leven afgetekent en opt Cooper gebracht*. Joint publication of the Netherlands Historical Shipping Museum of Amsterdam and the Friends of the Zuider Zee Museum of Enkhuizen, Alphen aan de Rijn 1970

Petrejus, E.W., *De bomschuit, een verdwenen scheepstype* [Rotterdam 1954]
—, *Nederlandse zeilschepen in de negentiende eeuw* [Bussum 1974]
—, *Oude zeilschepen en hun modellen*, Bussum [1971]

Ramaix, I. de, 'Frans Huys: catalogue de l'oeuvre gravé,' *Le Livre et l'Estampe* 55-56 (1968), pp. 258-93, and 57-58 (1969), pp. 23-54
Ratsma, P., 'De Rotterdamse tekenaar Gerrit Groenewegen, 1754-1826,' *Rotterdams Jaarboekje* (1977), pp. 153-80
—, 'Het topografische tekenwerk van Gerrit Groenewegen (1754-1826),' *Holland* (February 1978), pp. 17-31
Rees, P.A. van, and P.M. Brutel de la Rivière, *Memorandum voor den jeugdigen zeeofficier*, Nieuwediep 1859
Register met de namen, de afmetingen en het bouwjaar van Nederlandsche oorlogsschepen, 1557-1840 (manuscript, ca. 1850)
Robert-Dumesnil, A.-P.-F., *Le peintre-graveur français*, vol. 5, Paris 1841
Rotterdam, City Archives: P. Ratsma, *Gerrit Groenewegen, tekenaar van Rotterdam, 1754-1826*. Catalogue of the exhibition held in the Rotterdam City Archives, 1976-77
Rotterdam, Boymans-van Beuningen Museum and the printroom of the Rijksmuseum, Amsterdam, exhibition catalogue *150 tekeningen uit vier eeuwen uit de verzameling van Sir Bruce and Lady Ingram, 1961-1962*
Ryneveld, N.A. van, *Reize naar de Middelandsche Zee en, door den Archipel, naar Constantinopolen, gedaan in de jaaren 1783 tot 1786 met 's Lands schip Noordholland*, 2 vols., Amsterdam 1803

Schotel, C.D.J., *De zeeschilder P.J. Schotel*, Utrecht 1866
Simon, M., *Claes Jansz. Visscher* (reproduced from typescript), dissertation Freiburg i.B. 1958
Slooten, H. van der, 'De Dappere Patriot,' *Ons Zeewezen* (1931), p. 12
Smekens, F., 'Het schip bij Pieter Bruegel de Oude: een authenticiteitscriterium?,' *Jaarboek [van het] Koninklijk Museum voor Schone Kunsten* [Antwerp] (1961), pp. 5-57
Soeteboom, H., *Saanlandse Arcadia*, Amsterdam 1702
Sopers, P.J.V.M., *Schepen die verdwijnen*, Amsterdam [ca. 1971]
Sotheby & Co., *Catalogue of important old master engravings, etchings and woodcuts*, auction catalogue March 17, 1963, nr. 52
Springer, J., *Die Radierungen der Herkules Seghers*, Berlin (Graphische Gesellschaft) 1910-12 and 1916
Stridbeck, C.G., *Bruegelstudien*, Stockholm 1956
Strauss, W.L., *Hendrik Goltzius, 1558-1617: the complete engravings and woodcuts*, 2 vols., New York 1977
Swillens, P.T.A., *Nederland in de prentkunst*, Amsterdam 1944

Tervarent, G. de, *Attributs et symboles dans l'art profane, 1450-1600*, Geneva 1958
Thiel, P.J.J. van, 'Houtsneden van Werner van der Valckert en Mozes van Uyttenbroeck: de Hollandse houtsnede in het eerste kwart van de zeventiende eeuw,' *Oud-Holland* 92 (1978), pp. 7-42
Thieme, U. and F. Becker, *Allgemeines Lexikon der bildenden Künstler*, 37 vols., Leipzig 1907-50

Velius, D., *Chronyke van de stadt van Hoorn*, Hoorn 1604
Verscheide soorten van Hollandse vaartuigen geteekend en gesneden door Gerrit Groenewegen, with commentary by P. Dekker, Zaltbommel 1967
Voort, J.P. van de, *Vissers van de Noordzee*, The Hague (Triangel series) 1975
Vries, A.G.C. de, *De Nederlandsche emblemata: geschiedenis en bibliographie tot de achttiende eeuw*, Amsterdam 1899
Vries, R.W.P. de, *Amsterdamsche stadsgezichten*, Amsterdam 1913

Wagenaar, J., *Amsterdam in zijn opkomst, aanwas, geschiedenissen, voorregten...*, Amsterdam etc. 1760-67
—, *Vaderlandsche historie*, Amsterdam 1749-96
Waller, F.G., *Biographisch woordenboek der Noord-Nederlandsche graveurs*, The Hague 1938
Walsh Jr., J., 'The Dutch marine painters Jan and Julius Porcellis: I. Jan's early career. II. Jan's maturity and "de jonge Porcellis,"' *Burlington Magazine* 860 (1974), pp. 653-62, and 861 (1974), pp. 734-45
Weber, R.E.J., 'De trekschuit,' *Spiegel Historiael* 2 (1967), p. 301
Weigel, R., *Kunstlager-Catalog*, Achtundzwanzigste Abtheilung, Leipzig 1857
—, *Suppléments au Peintre-graveur de Adam Bartsch*, Leipzig 1843
Weston Gallery, *A special selection of fine prints for collectors, 1798-1935*, catalogue nr. 5, Annual summer exhibition, London 1979
Wieder, F.C., *Merkwaardigheden der oude cartographie van Noord-Holland*, Leiden (Koninklijk Nederlandsch Aardrijkskundig Genootschap) 1918
—, 'Nederlandsche historisch-geographische dokumenten in Spanje,' *Tijdschrift van het Koninklijk Nederlandsch Aardrijkskundig Genootschap*, extra publication, Leiden 1915
Wijnman, H.F., *D'Ailly's historische gids van Amsterdam*, Amsterdam 1963
Winschooten, W. à, *Seeman, behelsende een grondige uitlegging van de Nederlandse konst, en spreekwoorden, voor soo veel die uit de seevaart sijn ontleend, en bij de beste schrijvers deeser eeuw gevonden werden*, Leiden 1681
Witsen, N., *Aeloude en hedendaegsche scheepsbouw en bestier*, Amsterdam 1671

Wurzbach, A. von, *Niederländisches Künstler-Lexikon*, 3 vols., Leipzig 1906-11

Yk, C. van, *De Nederlandsche scheepsbouwkonst open gestelt*, Delft 1697

Glossary

The purpose of this glossary is, first and foremost, to provide a description of certain Dutch types of vessel which are not treated at length in the main body of the book. In certain instances, where a type is mentioned several times in the commentaries to different prints, reference is made to the commentary containing the full description. Some maritime terms are also explained, but here the reader is referred to the introduction on 'The ships' (pp. 17-23), where a full description is given of the principal components of a ship's hull and rigging, and of certain common manoeuvres. The numbers given at the end of glossary entries refer to the clearest illustrations of the type discussed.

The following works were consulted for the compilation of this glossary, although it should be noted that the various authorities are not always in full agreement on the features and evolution of certain types of vessel.

Beylen, J. van, et al., *Maritieme encyclopedie*, 7 vols., Bussum 1970-73

Crone, G.C.E., *Nederlandse jachten, binnenschepen, visschersvaartuigen en daarmee verwante kleine zeeschepen, 1650-1900*, Amsterdam 1926

Kemp, P. (ed.), *The Oxford companion to ships and the sea*, London, New York and Melbourne 1976

Kerchove, R. de, *International maritime dictionary* (2nd edition), Princeton and New York 1961

Landström, B., *Sailing ships*, London 1969

The Glossary was compiled by Michael Hoyle.

AAK

Generic name for a wide variety of flat-bottomed river craft used for bulk transport of cargo. Their most distinctive feature is that they have no stem, the bottom planking being extended upwards to form a flat bow. They are usually clinker-built, with a broad, shallow rudder and leeboards. They originally carried only a single mast, rigged with a square sail or spritsail. The numerous types are named according to their place of origin or use, or after the shape of the hull (see *beitelaak*).

ADMIRALTIES

From 1597 to 1795 the maritime affairs of the Netherlands were regulated by five Boards of Admiralty: one for the region around the River Maas, based at Rotterdam; one at Amsterdam; one in the North Quarter, the headquarters alternating every three months between Hoorn and Enkhuizen; one in Zeeland, at Middelburg; and one in Friesland, based at Dokkum until 1645, thereafter at Harlingen.

BAARDZE

Originally a rowed warship of the fourteenth to the sixteenth centuries, but sailing versions had appeared by 1438 as a development of the cog (q.v.). They had fore and after castles, and from one to three spritsail-rigged masts. The *baardze* depicted by the Monogrammist WA is a three-master with fore and after castles, and is carvel-built with wales.

BAGGYWRINKLE

A bushy material designed to prevent chafing between ropes and sails, consisting of short strands of rope wound around two lengths of marline.

BEITELAAK

Literally: chisel *aak*, from the shape of the bows. See nr. 47.

BOEIER

The boeier was originally a large, seagoing tjalk (q.v.) used in the coastal trade. This type disappeared towards the end of the seventeenth century, but the name lived on in smaller, inland vessels. They have very round bows and stern, and very broad leeboards, but the individual shapes vary, depending on where the boeier was built and used. They lasted into the present century as the most common type of pleasure craft with stateroom accommodation. See nr. 52.

BOK

A small, inland cargo vessel, generally used for carrying peat. Has a raked stem and sternpost, with a deck forward and a raised after deck. See nr. 242.

BOMSCHIP [BOM, BOMSCHUIT]

A fishing boat used on the North Sea. It evolved from the 'double shore boat' (see nr. 162), a larger version of the pink. It was clinker-built, with square ends and a U-shaped hull section. Designed as a beach boat, it had a shallow draft and a very heavy keel. Its beam was generally about half its length. It was fully decked, and had a fish tank for keeping the catch fresh. The rig was a mainsail, main topsail, fore staysail and jib. *Boms* survived until the beginning of the present century, and were remarkable in that they were the only type of Dutch fishing boat to be extensively decorated. They were also used on occasion as merchantmen and warships.

BONNET

An additional strip of canvas laced to the foot of a sail to increase the sail area.

BOOTSCHIP

A merchantman, which was also used as a whaler from the second half of the seventeenth century. It was a specifically North European type, being halfway between a flute (q.v.) and a galliot (q.v.). It had a galliot hull and a flute's upper planking. The hull curved round to meet the sternpost, above which was a broad taffrail with windows. It was a three-master, originally with lower courses and topsails only, but topgallant sails were added on the foremast and mainmast in the eighteenth century, and the lateen mizzen was replaced by a gaff sail. See ill. 26, nr. 180.

BOTTER

A Zuider Zee fishing boat some 45 feet long and with a beam of 13 feet. The botter evolved from the *tochtschuit* (q.v.), and is flat-bottomed with curved sides, a high, curved stem and a low, narrow stern. The leeboards are long and narrow. The fish were kept fresh in a free-flooding fish well amidships. The single mast is rigged with a narrow, Dutch gaff sail, and a broad foresail. They are swift sailers, and were one of the most elegant, and seaworthy, of Dutch fishing boats. Many have been converted into yachts, being exceptionally roomy inside. See nr. 239.

BRIG

A merchantman and warship developed in the eighteenth century. The true brig has two masts and is square-rigged on both. The hermaphrodite brig is square-rigged on the foremast, has a fore-and-aft mainsail and square topsails. See nrs. 204, 225.

BUMPKIN

Originally a short spar either side of the bows for extending the clew (lower aftermost corner) of the foresail to windward. Nowadays the term is used for a short spar extending over the stern for sheeting the mizzen when the mizzenmast is stepped so far aft that the sheets cannot be worked inboard.

BUSS

For centuries the herring buss was the commonest Dutch fishing boat. It was from 50 to 70 tons burthen, and was from 60 to 90 feet long. Busses were solidly built, with a keel and a high, curved stem. The stern was originally square, but later became rounded. They had three masts, square-rigged on each. When the buss was lying to its nets the foremast and mainmast were lowered to reduce the strain on the hull. The buss became extinct in 1886. See nrs. 23, 36, 77, 163, 179.

CAPWINDER MILL

A windmill whose cap, or top, is wound round to set the sails to the wind, as opposed to the *paltrok* mill (q.v.).

CARAVEL

A Mediterranean merchantman from the fourteenth to the seventeenth centuries, which was also used by the Spanish and the Portuguese on their voyages of exploration (Columbus's *Santa Maria* was a caravel). They had three, or even four masts, square-rigged on the foremast and mainmast, and with lateen mizzens. Their average length was 75-80 feet, but some were as long as 100 feet. See nr. 4.

Caravel was also the name of a large class of Dutch inland vessel which later evolved into the *smalschip* and the *wijdschip* (qq.v.). See nr. 18.

CAREEN, TO

To heave a ship down onto one side, thus exposing the other side so that it can be cleaned, repaired and caulked.

CARRACK

Large merchantman of northern and southern Europe from the fourteenth to the seventeenth centuries. It had a similar rig to the later three-masted caravel, but was larger, beamier and stronger, and had very high fore and after castles. It was the forerunner of the large three-masted seagoing ship, which survived until the introduction of steam in the nineteenth century. The carrack was superseded in the seventeenth century by the galleon (q.v.), in which the high fore castle was eliminated, making for far better sailing qualities when heading near the wind. See ill. 3, fig. 4a.

CAT

A merchantman in Holland, England and Scandinavia in the seventeenth and eighteenth centuries. According to Nicolaas Witsen, it was a cross between a boeier and a flute, and not a variant of either type. It was flat-bottomed, with straight sides. It originally had three short pole masts, square-rigged on the foremast and mainmast, and with a boomless mizzen. By the end of the eighteenth century it had topsails and topgallant sails. See ill. 28.

COG

The oldest (first mentioned around 1000) and most important of Dutch merchantmen. It had a clinker-built, round hull, with a round bow and stern. It was heavy and beamy, and had fore and after castles. It had one massive mast amidships, on which it carried a square sail. It was gradually supplanted by the hulk and the caravel (qq.v.), and finally vanished around 1500.

CORVETTE

Warship of the seventeenth and eighteenth centuries, generally flush-decked and with a single tier of guns. It was smaller than a frigate, but was ship-rigged on three masts. Corvettes were very fast sailers, and could steer close to the wind. See nrs. 223, 226.

CUTTER

Small, single-masted vessel with a long bowsprit. They were very fast on the wind, and were generally used as fleet auxiliaries and to combat smugglers. See nrs. 212, 213.

DAMLOPER

An inland vessel whose name (literally dam-runner) was derived from the fact that it could be hauled over dams and dikes. See nr. 25.

DAMSCHUIT [also DAMSOUT]

Related to the *damloper*, but smaller. See nrs. 80, 157.

DIJNOP

An inland vessel, 55-60 feet long, used for transporting peat, sand and ballast. Despite considerable research in the past ten years, little is known about the *dijnop*. It has, however, been established that Aalsmeer, in a fen-land region, was one place where the *dijnop* was built. See nr. 84.

DOGGER

The name is first mentioned in 1404, and is derived from an old word for cod. *Doggers* were small fishing boats of varying shapes and sizes that worked the North Sea fishing grounds. They had a mainmast abaft the middle of the boat and a foremast stepped close to the stem. Both masts were square-rigged. The Dutch *dogger* gave its name to the Dogger Bank in the North Sea, which in turn gave it to the English dogger, a short, beamy fishing boat which trawled or lined on the Dogger Bank. The English type was square-rigged on the mainmast, had a lugsail on the mizzenmast, and carried two jibs on a long bowsprit. See nr. 27.

DRIJVER

Another name for a *tochtschuit* (q.v.). See nr. 78.

EIKER

A lighter, generally used for carrying peat. See nr. 192.

FLUTE

One of the foremost Dutch trading vessels. The first flute was built in 1595 at Hoorn, on the Zuider Zee. Flutes had a length-to-beam ratio of four or even five to one. They had a straight stem, broad bows, a round stern, and sides which narrowed sharply at the stern. The foremast and mainmast were square-rigged with lower courses and topsails, while a lateen was carried on the mizzenmast. There was also a bowsprit with a spritsail. Flutes brought corn from the Baltic, timber from Norway, and various products from the Mediterranean. They were also used as whalers. See ill. 4, nrs. 81, 98, 100, 101.

FRIGATE

A three-masted warship, fully rigged on each mast, with between 24 and 38 guns on a single gundeck. They were used as squadron lookouts and signal repeaters, and often acted on detached service against pirates or as convoy escorts. They were originally classified as 5th or 6th rates, and so were not ships of the line. Later, 44-gun, frigates were classified as 4th rates. See ills. 24, 31, nrs. 76, 81, 94, 168, 212, 227.

GALLEON

A seventeenth-century development of the carrack (q.v.), in which the high fore castle was eliminated, enabling the ship to sail closer to the wind. The original design was produced in England by Sir John Hawkins in 1570. The idea was adopted in Spain seventeen years later, originally for use as a warship, but later superseding the carrack as the principle type of merchantman. See fig. 4a.

GALLEY

An oared Mediterranean warship from ca. 3000 BC to the eighteenth century. The original single bank of oars evolved into banks at different levels, producing biremes (two banks), triremes (three banks), and so on. Galleys were originally armed with a ram, but in the sixteenth and seventeenth century they mounted a battery of guns on a platform in the bows. These guns could not be trained individually, so the entire ship had to be pointed at the target. Galleys could also be sailed, carrying one or two lateen-rigged masts which were lowered during battle to provide greater manoeuvrability. See nrs. 5, 104, 105.

GALLIOT

A small, flat-bottomed coaster, originally with leeboards, and later with a fixed keel. In the eighteenth century a larger type of galliot appeared, carrying three masts. The galliot was very similar to the koff (q.v.), the main difference being that it was narrower and faster. See nrs. 58, 181.

GOOSEWING, TO

A term applied in a fore-and-aft rigged ship when the headsail is boomed out on the opposite side to the mainsail to make the most of a following wind.

HEKTJALK

A small cargo boat with a round hull and curved hatches. The word *hek* refers to the triangular opening in the upper planking at the stern through which the tiller passed. *Hektjalks* were originally rigged with a sprit-sail and bonnet, but in the eighteenth century the standing gaff rig was adopted. In the nineteenth century this gave way to the ordinary gaff sail. The rudder head was often decorated with a figure. See further under tjalk. See nrs. 200, 230, 232, 233, 244.

HENGST

A small cargo vessel and fishing boat. It had a low, rounded stern, narrow leeboards, and a straight stem raked at an angle of around 45°. See nr. 195.

HOOKER

A short, tubby vessel, developed from the ketch. Hookers were used for two distinct purposes: as merchantmen and as fishing vessels. Initially the rig was almost the same in each type, but by the seventeenth century the merchant version had two, or even three masts. The long bowsprit for the foresails was added later. The fishing version often had a tank extending over the width of the boat abaft the mast. Perforations in the tank kept the water fresh. See ill. 25, nrs. 71, 159, 224.

HOY

The name is mentioned around 1500 as a freighter plying in the Maas and Scheldt estuaries, but there was also a larger type that crossed to England. Hoys were also used as coastal and inland ferries. See nrs. 29, 161.

HULK

Hulks are first mentioned around 1000. By the fifteenth century they had grown considerably in size and had fore and after castles, rounded bows and stern, and three masts, square-rigged on the foremast and the mainmast, and with a lateen mizzen. As a seagoing merchantman it had supplanted the cog by the beginning of the sixteenth century. See nr. 1.

KAAG

A type of cargo vessel and passenger ferry of which there were scores of variants. It was a flat-bottomed vessel, clinker-built, with a straight, raked stem and sternpost, and had a pronounced sheer. The original spritsail later gave way to a gaff rig, and in the seventeenth century the clinker construction was abandoned in favor of a carvel build. See nrs. 28, 74, 83.

KEEN

A class of river craft of German origin used for trading on the Rhine between the Netherlands and Germany. *Keens* were light, clinker-built boats, with a length-to-beam ratio of seven to one. They were flat-bottomed, and had neither stem nor sternpost. They carried a mainmast, which could be lowered, and a mizzenmast. See nr. 237.

KETCH RIG

A two-masted rig in which the mizzenmast is stepped forward of the rudder head rather than abaft it, as in the yawl rig.

KEULENAAR

Type of *aak* (q.v.) used on the Rhine. The name is derived from the Dutch word for Cologne. See nr. 193.

KOFF

A small coaster of the eighteenth and nineteenth centuries. Koffs were of a heavy build and had a fairly pronounced sheer, which was greater aft than forward. The length-to-beam ratio was three to one. The bows and stern were round and full. See nr. 221.

KOP YACHT

A yacht dating from the mid-seventeenth century built along boeier lines, i.e. with rounded bows and stern and rigged as a boeier. See nr. 158.

LAST

A measure of weight equivalent to 2 metric tons burthen; or 2,000 Amsterdam pounds (1,976 kg.).

LATEEN SAIL

Narrow, triangular sail on a very long yard. It is believed to be pre-Christian in origin.

MARTNETS

System of ropes from the main top opening out into crowfeet around the leeches (outer edges) of square sails and used for gathering the sail together when reducing sail. Later replaced by leech lines. See nr. 1.

PALTROK MILL

A windmill peculiar to the Zaan district, near Amsterdam. It was mounted on a ring of rollers on a brick base, the entire mill being turned into the wind. See also capwinder mill.

PUNTER

A small, flat-bottomed craft with sharp bows and stern which could be sailed, rowed or poled along. The stem and sternpost were straight, and raked at a sharp angle. See nr. 230.

SAMOREUS

A large *aak* used on the Rivers Sambre (hence the name) and Maas.

SHEER

The upward curve of the deck towards the bows and stern.

SMALSCHIP

See commentary to nr. 53.

SNOW

A two-masted merchantman of the sixteenth to the nineteenth centuries. It was the largest two-master of its period, ranging up to 1,000 tons. It was rigged as a brig, with square sails on both masts, but had a small trysail mast immediately abaft the mainmast for a boomed trysail, or alternatively a horse on the mainmast to which the luff (leading edge) of the trysail was attached. See ill. 30.

STEIGERSCHUIT

See commentary to nr. 158.

TJALK

A name not for a distinct class, but for a group of broad, barge-type vessels used for carrying cargo. Tjalks originated in Friesland around the end of the seventeenth century as successors to the *smalschip* and *wijdschip* (qq.v.). They are flat-bottomed, and have either a heavy, flat keel plank or a shallow vertical keel. The bows and stern are bluff and square. The spritsail or ferry rig with a foresail gave way to the gaff rig in the nineteenth century.

TOCHTSCHUIT

Fishing boat, smaller and lighter than the *waterschip* (q.v.), and assumed to be the forefather of the botter (q.v.). It had a curved stem and a straight sternpost, with round bows and stern. Open abaft the mast. *Tochtschuits* carried a spritsail, a fore staysail and a square foresail. See nr. 78.

WATERSCHIP

The type was first mentioned in the sixteenth century, being used as a fishing vessel and for towing larger ships over the mudbanks in the waterway between the Zuider Zee and Amsterdam. The *waterschip* had a full, high bow with a straight stem. The cut of the hull was such that leeboards were unnecessary. See nr. 19.

WESTLANDER

A narrow, flat type of craft used for carrying agricultural produce from the growing regions in the west of the country to the large towns. See further the commentary to nr. 242.

WIJDSCHIP

See commentary to nr. 53.

Aa, Cornelis van der p. 13, nr. 181
aak nrs. 47, 181
AB, Monogrammist p. 16, nrs. 58, 59
ABk, Monogrammist nrs. 96, 97
Actium, Battle of nr. 63
Adam, Philipp nrs. 116-18
Adam, Richard nrs. 116-18
Admiralties *see under* Amsterdam, England, Maas
Aemilia p. 10
Africa nr. 21
Aldewerelt, Herman van nr. 95
Alexander the Great nr. 21
Alkmaar nr. 30
Allard, Carel nrs. 40, 52, 91, 92, 96, 133, 134, 135
Allart, Hugo fig. 71a
Allart, Johannes nrs. 174, 175, 176, 181
Allartsz., Herman nrs. 20, 33
Almeloveen, Jan van p. 13, nrs. 121-32
Alphen nr. 176
Alva, duke of nr. 33
Alvarez d'Avila, don Juan nr. 62
Ameiden nr. 127
Ameland nr. 127
Ampzing, Samuel p. 13
Amsterdam nr. 110
Amsterdam passim
  Achtergracht nr. 73
  Admiralty of nrs. 71, 81, 97, 110, 171
  Admiralty Commissioners nr. 177
  Amstel, River nrs. 86, 166, 167
  Amsteldijk nr. 167
  Amstel Yacht Basin nr. 166
  Apple Market nr. 74
  arms of nrs. 1, 19, 20, 32, 55, 78, 110, 112, 135, 138-53, 166, 175
  banner of nr. 15
  Barentszplein nr. 175
  Berebijt Inn nr. 167
  Bicker's Island nr. 79
  Blauwhoofd nrs. 79, 166, 175
  Bok Windmill nrs. 166, 175
  Chamber of the Noble Lords of the Water Company nr. 75
  Dam Square nr. 20
  Damrak nrs. 74, 75, 177
  Dutch East India Company nr. 110
  Exchange nrs. 20, 86, 87
  flag of nrs. 19, 21, 32, 97, 138-53
  Funen nr. 166
  Gasthuismolensteeg nr. 73
  Haarlem Gate nr. 19
  Heiligeweg nr. 74
  Herring Packers' Tower nr. 20
  IJ River nrs. 11, 19, 20, 55, 78, 110, 112, 135, 138-53, 166, 175
  inland ferry services nrs. 17, 19, 28, 55, 73, 74, 86, 87, 157, 167, 197
  Kalverstraat nr. 74
  Kamper Wharf nr. 177

Amsterdam (cont.)
  Kattenburg Yacht Basin nr. 166
  Kostverlorenvaart nr. 17
  Kruissteeg nr. 73
  Leeuwenburg nr. 175
  Leiden ferryhouse nrs. 17, 74
  Martelaarsgracht nr. 19
  militia nr. 18
  Montelbaan Tower nr. 20
  Municipal Water Board nr. 177
  Netherlands National Maritime Museum ills. 18-33, nrs. 219, 221, 225, 226, 228
  New Church nrs. 19, 20, 33
  Nieuwe Waal nrs. 79, 166
  Nieuwe Zijds Chapel nr. 86
  Northern Market nr. 74
  Old Church nrs. 19, 20
  Old Yacht Basin p. 13, nr. 166
  Oude Waal nr. 19
  Oude Zijds Chapel nr. 19
  Overtoom p. 13, nrs. 17, 74, 88, fig. 17a
  Overtoomse Vaart nr. 17
  palisade of mooring posts nrs. 79, 166
  Pepper Wharf nrs. 19, 20
  personification of nrs. 20, 110
  Prins Hendrikkade nrs. 75, 177
  profile views of pp. 7-8, nrs. 19, 20
  Reguliers Gate nr. 17
  Rijksmuseum, printroom nearly all prints illustrated in the book; drawing fig. 49a
  Rijzenhoofd nr. 20
  Rokin nrs. 86, 87
  St. Anthony's Gate nr. 17
  St. Anthony's Market nr. 74
  Schinkel nr. 17
  Singel nrs. 19, 73, 74
  Sloterkade nr. 88
  Slotervaart nr. 17
  South Church nr. 20
  State Dockyard nr. 226
  Tollhouse p. 21, ill. 24
  Town Hall nrs. 19, 20, 138-53
  Tweede Jan van der Heijdenstraat nr. 167
  University Library fig. 31a
  Utrecht Gate nr. 167
  Valck Inn nr. 88
  Volewijk nr. 19
  Waal nr. 20
  Weepers' Tower nrs. 19, 20, 138-53
  Zeeregt Building p. 13, nr. 177
Anglo-Dutch Wars p. 11
  First nrs. 76, 81, 90
  Second nrs. 81, 98
  Fourth nrs. 169, 183, 214, 215
Anonymous, 'Navire Royale' p. 10, ill. 6
  Defeat of the Spanish Armada p. 10, ill. 9
  'The ship of St. Stony-broke' pp. 7, 14, ill. 1
Anonymous, ca. 1600 p. 10, nrs. 36-40

Anonymous, ca. 1640 p. 10, nrs. 52-56, fig. 52a
Anthonisz., Cornelis pp. 7, 12, ill. 2
Antipodes nr. 11
Antony, Mark nr. 63
Antwerp pp. 7, 12, nrs. 3, 228, 229, 247
  Municipal Printroom p. 12, nr. 4
  Vlaamse Hoofd nr. 228
apostles nrs. 6, 59
Arabia nr. 21
Arion nr. 4
Armada, Spanish p. 10, ill. 9
arms and coats of arms *see under* Amsterdam, Haarlem, Holland, Hoorn, Prince Maurice, Rotterdam, Texel
Asia nr. 21
Aveele, Johan van der p. 11, ill. 11, nr. 134

baardze p. 9
Backhuizen, Ludolf nrs. 110-115
Baltic Sea nrs. 169, 222
Bantam p. 11, nr. 21
Barfleur, Battle of nr. 110
Bargas, A.F. nr. 136
barquentine p. 22, ill. 27
Basse, Willem nr. 62
Bast, Pieter p. 12, nrs. 19, 20
Batavia nr. 21
Baudous, Robert de pp. 11, 14, nrs. 11-17
beach-launched boat nr. 89
Bendorp, Carel Frederik nrs. 169-73
Berckenrode, Balthasar Florisz. nr. 166
Bergen op Zoom nr. 18
Beylen, J. van nr. 52, fig. 52a
Bicker, Jan nr. 79
Bijlandt, Rear-Admiral nr. 176
Blaeu, Willem Jansz. nr. 31
bloody flag nr. 81
boating nr. 70
boeier nrs. 1, 52, 53, 111, 113, 114, 158, 194
boeier yacht nr. 158
bok nr. 242
Bol IV, Cornelis nrs. 107-09
bomschip nrs. 162, 196
bomschuit nr. 241
bootschip pp. 22-23, ill. 26, nr. 180
Borcht, Pieter van der p. 14, nrs. 6, 59
Bormeester, Jochem nr. 24
Bosboom, Johannes nr. 230
botter nr. 239
Bout, Pieter nr. 136
Brabant nrs. 68, 164, 196
Bracquemond, Félix nr. 244
Braun and Hogenberg p. 12, ill. 12
Brave Patriot nr. 183
Bray, Dirck de p. 14, nr. 69, 70
Brazil nr. 57
Breem, Adam van nr. 32

Breuhaus de Groot, Frans Arnold nrs. 235, 236
brig nrs. 176, 203, 204
Brill (Den Briel) nrs. 30, 99, 109, 134, 183
Brink, J. van den nrs. 191-202, 209
Brittenburg near Katwijk nr. 30
Broen, W. de nr. 72
Bruegel, Pieter pp. 7, 9, 10, ill. 8, nrs. 1-5, 24, 37-40
Bruges p. 9
Bruyn, Captain A. de nr. 170
Buffa and Sons, Frans nrs. 240-243
Buiksloot ferry nr. 55
burgher yacht nr. 160
Burgundian or St. Andrew's Cross nrs. 1, 3
Busenval, de nr. 31
buss see herring buss

Cadart, Vve. nr. 246
Cadart et Chevalier nr. 244
Cadart et Luce nr. 247
Cadart et Luquet nrs. 248-50
Cambridge, Fitzwilliam Museum nr. 50
Cameleon nr. 183
Camerarius, Johannes nr. 58
Capelle aan de IJssel nr. 121
caravel nrs. 4, 5, 18
Cardinaal, Hendrik nr. 110
cargo kaag nr. 28
carrack p. 9, ill. 3, nrs. 2, 4
Casembrot, Abraham nrs. 102-06
cat p. 23, ill. 28, nr. 221
caulking nrs. 13, 94, 188
Changuion, D.J. nr. 166
Charles V nr. 12
Charles the Bold p. 9
Chassé, General nr. 228
Chicago, Art Institute nr. 248
China nrs. 21, 31
chisel barge nr. 47
Christ p. 14, nrs. 6, 59, 69, 110
Cleynhens, Bernardus nrs. 24, 90
Cock, Hieronymus p. 7, nrs. 1-5
cod nrs. 27, 71
cog nr. 25
Collaert, Hans nr. 9
Columbus nr. 9
compass nr. 9
Comte, Pieter le p. 10, nrs. 193, 196 219-29, 243
Conradi, P. and V. v.d. Plaats nrs. 174-76
Cornelisz., Lambert nr. 5, fig. 5a
corvette nrs. 223, 226
Crabbe, De see Krabbe, De
Crajenschot, T. nr. 164
Cuba nr. 57
Curaçao nr. 176
curling nr. 16
cutter nrs. 223, 226

Daedalus nr. 2
Daiwaille and van Veldhuijsen nrs. 228, 229
damloper nr. 25
damschuit nr. 157
damsout nr. 80
Danckerts, C. nrs. 75, 86

Danckerts, Danckert nrs. 71, 72, 75, 94
Daubigny, Charles-François nr. 244
Delâtre, A. nrs. 244, 245, 247-50
Delfshaven nrs. 120, 206
Delfshavense Schie nr. 206
Delft nrs. 30, 206
   ferry services nrs. 54, 86, 87, 231
Denmark nr. 119
Desguerrois & Co. nrs. 223, 227
dijnop pp. 20-21, ill. 19, nr. 84
dispatch vessel nrs. 173, 213
dogger nr. 27
Dogger Bank, Battle of p. 11, nrs. 169, 173
   fishing on the Dogger Bank nr. 27
dolphin nr. 4
Dordrecht ill. 12, nrs. 30, 184, 194, 216, 218
   Synod of p. 14
Dordtsche Kil nr. 184
Drenthe nrs. 171, 172
Dresden, Kupferstichkabinett nr. 45
drijver nr. 78
double shore boat nr. 162
Downs, Battle of the p. 10, nr. 95
Dungeness, Battle of nr. 97
Dunkirk nrs. 76, 168
Dusseldorf nrs. 193, 232
Dutch East India Company nrs. 11, 12, 85, 110, 120, 135, 181
Dutch flag nrs. 228, 229

East Indiaman p. 10, nr. 170
East Indies nrs. 5, 10, 62
East Voorn nr. 98
Eeghen, C. van nr. 166
eel boat nr. 238
Eighty Years' War p. 10, nrs. 18, 76
eiker nrs. 192, 197, 243
Elba, Battle of nr. 119
elements, the four p. 14, ill. 16
Elsheimer, Adam nr. 46
Elwe, Jan Barend nrs. 170-73
England p. 11, nrs. 76, 98, 119, 133, 134, 169, 176, 215
   Admiralty nr. 91
   shipping nrs. 40, 71, 113, 168, 183, 204, 214, 215, 220
Enkhuizen nrs. 1, 30, 34
   arms of nr. 1
   ferry serving nr. 53
Evertsen, Jan nr. 95

Fargue, Paulus Constantijn la p. 10, nr. 168
Fargue van Nieuwland, Isaac Lodewijk la nr. 167
Félicité, La p. 10, nr. 168
Feltz, Captain van der nr. 176
ferry kaag nr. 28
ferry services see under Amsterdam, Delft, Enkhuizen, Friesland, Gouda, The Hague, Hoorn, Leiden, Naarden, North Holland, Rotterdam, Schiedam, Utrecht, Weesp
First Company of Far Lands nr. 21
flags see under Amsterdam, 'bloody' flag, Flushing, Hoorn, Dutch flag, Porto, Portugal, Prince's flag, Rotterdam, States flag, Zeeland

Fleyn, Captain nr. 215
flogging nr. 170
floods p. 10, nrs. 164, 174
Florence p. 9
flush-decked corvette nr. 226
Flushing (Vlissingen) nrs. 107, 214, 223
   flag of nr. 12
   Nortier Shipping Co. nr. 214
flute ill. 4, nrs. 98, 100, 101, 112, 221
flyboat nr. 1
Fokke, Simon p. 13, nrs. 165, 166
Fortune, ship of nr. 63
Fouquet, Pierre pp. 8, 13, nrs. 166, 177
Four Days' Battle nr. 119
France nrs. 31, 81, 98, 110
   shipping nr. 168
Francq van Berkhey, le nrs. 165, 169
Frederick Henry nrs. 28, 31
Friesland nrs. 83, 84
   ferry serving nr. 53
   yacht of nr. 135
frigate p. 23, ill. 31, nrs. 76, 92-94, 96, 97, 168, 181, 183, 212, 227
Frisian pram nr. 200
Frisian kaag p. 17, ill. 18, nr. 83
Frisius, Simon pp. 8, 13, nrs. 17, 88

gaff kaag nr. 240
gaff ship nr. 240
gaff yacht nr. 201
Galilee, Sea of nrs. 59, 69
Galle, Philips p. 7, nrs. 9, 10
Galle, Theodoor nrs. 1-5, 9, 10, fig. 9a
galleon nr. 4
galley nrs. 5, 104, 105
galliot nrs. 58, 181
Geel, Joost van p. 12, nrs. 98-100, fig. 98a
Gelderland nrs. 83, 164
Gelderland kaag p. 17, ill. 18, nr. 83
Gerrits, Hessel p. 13, ill. 14
Gheyn, Jacob de ill. 13, fig. 31a
Gibraltar, Battle of nr. 62
Goede Hoop, De p. 22, ill. 26
Goede Verwachting, De nr. 215
Gole, Jacob nr. 110
Goltzius, Hendrick nrs. 7, 8
Goos, Abraham nr. 30, fig. 30a
Goos, Pieter nrs. 18, 52
Gouda nr. 30
   Donkere Lock nr. 53
   ferry serving nrs. 54, 86, 167, 197
   Mallegat Lock nr. 53
Goudt, Hendrick nr. 46
Granada nr. 2
Grave p. 10, nr. 18
's-Gravenmoer aak nr. 243
's-Gravenzand nr. 168
Great Elector nr. 119
Greenlander p. 22, ill. 26
Greive, Johan Conrad pp. 10, 13, nrs. 237-243, fig. 240a
Groenewegen, Gerrit pp. 8, 20-23, ills. 21-23, 25-30, nrs. 191-213
Groningen nr. 83
Groot Ammers nr. 128
Guicciardini, Francesco p. 12

gunboat nrs. 228, 229

Haarlem pp. 7, 13, nrs. 17, 28, 30, 88
   arms of nr. 13
   militia nr. 18
Haarlem Lake nrs. 17, 28
Hagen, Admiral Steven van der nr. 11
Hague, The nrs. 30, 168, 183, 197, 216, 232
   ferry serving nrs. 54, 86, 87
   National Shipping Company nr. 183
Harlinger, De nr. 171
Harrison, John nr. 9
Harwich nr. 215
Hasewint, De nr. 81
Hasselt, Overijssel nr. 18
Heemskerck, Jacob van nr. 62
Heerman, Leenders Symonsz. nr. 120
Hein, Piet nrs. 57, 95
hektjalk nrs. 200, 230, 232, 233, 244
Hellevoetsluis nrs. 133, 215
Hengst, P. den nr. 166
Herckmans, Elias nrs. 62, 63
Hercules nr. 171
Hering, J.H. nrs. 174, 175
Herodotus nr. 4
herring buss pp. 9, 10, nrs. 23, 36, 77, 99, 162, 163, 179
herring carrier nr. 179
herring fishing p. 10, nrs. 36, 77, 99, 161-63, 179
Hodges, Charles nr. 166
Hoeck van Klein Ammers nr. 125
Hogenberg, Frans p. 12, ill. 12
Holland nr. 173
Holland, county of nrs. 30, 31, 68
   arms of nrs. 19, 20
   States of nr. 98
Hollands Diep Channel nr. 68
Hollandsche Schilder en Letterkundig Album, Het nrs. 217, 233, 234
Hollandsche Schilderschool, De nrs. 217, 230, 235
Hollar, Wenzel p. 10, ill. 4
Hondius, Hendrik nrs. 11, 12
Honfleur p. 13, nrs. 248-50
Hooghe, Romeyn de p. 11, ill. 10
hooker p. 22, ill. 25, nrs. 71, 159, 161, 181, 204, 224
Hoorn, Jan ten nr. 120
Hoorn nr. 30
   coat of arms of nr. 1
   ferry serving nr. 53
   flag of nrs. 1, 21
horse-drawn barge p. 10, nrs. 118, 231, 246
Houtman, Cornelis de nr. 21
hoy nr. 29
hulk nrs. 1, 4
Huybrechts, Adriaen nr. 6
Huygen van Linschoten, Jan nrs. 5, 31, fig. 51
Huys, Frans pp. 7, 10, ill. 8, nrs. 1-5, 24, 37, 38
Huyssen, Johan, Lord of Cattendyke nr. 12

Icarus nr. 2
ice boat nrs. 32, 165

ice skating nrs. 13-16
IJ River nr. 182; see also under Amsterdam
L'Illustration Nouvelle nr. 247
India nrs. 21, 40
Ingram collection nr. 31
Italy p. 10

Jaarsveld nrs. 122, 164
James II, King of England nr. 133
Jansen, Willem nrs. 8, 22, 31
Janssonius, Johannes nrs. 12, 13
Jansz., Joost nr. 33, fig. 33a
Janus, temple of nr. 63
Japhetia nr. 21
Jarry, Captain Nicolas nr. 214
Java nr. 21
Jong, Dirk de nrs. 181-83
Jonge, Skipper Kees de nr. 71
Jonghe, Clement de nrs. 72, 73, 75, 86, 90
Jongkind, Johan Barthold pp. 8, 13, 16, 17, nrs. 244-250, ill. 244a

kaag p. 17, ill. 18, nrs. 28, 73, 74, 83, 112, 178, 240
Kaal, F. nrs. 228, 229
Kampen nr. 174
keen nr. 237
Keere, Pieter van den nr. 30
keulenaar nr. 193
Keyser, Hendrick de nr. 86
Keyzer, Harmanus nrs. 170-73
Kijkduin, Battle of nrs. 97, 119
Kinsbergen, Captain van nr. 169
Kleyne, David p. 10, ill. 5
Kobell, Hendrik p. 15, nrs. 178-80, 184-90
Kobell, Jan nrs. 214, 215
Koekoek, De nr. 174
koff nrs. 221, 222
kolf nr. 16
kop yacht nr. 158
Kostverloren nr. 17
kraak nr. 192
Krabbe, De nrs. 99, 100, 184
Krimpen nr. 124
Krul, J.M. ill. 17
Kunstkronijk nr. 234
kwak nr. 78

Laan, Adolf van der pp. 17-23, ills. 20, 24, 31, nrs. 157-63
land yacht nr. 31
Langendijk, Dirk nr. 185
Langerak nr. 123
Lapp nr. 20
Laurens, Hendrik nrs. 12, 17
Lazarus nr. 69
Leeghwater, Jan Adriaensz. nr. 28
Leickert, Charles nr. 230
Leiden p. 13, nrs. 17, 30, 33
  ferry serving nrs. 17, 28, 74, 167
  militia p. 10, nr. 18
Leghorn, Battle of nr. 119
Lek, River p. 13, nrs. 121-32
Lekkerkerk nr. 130
Leth, Hendrik de nr. 91
Leyden, Lucas van p. 7

Lexmond nr. 131
Liefrinck II, Cornelis p. 10, nr. 18
Lievens, Jan nr. 95
lighters nr. 19
Lodewycksz., Lodewyck nr. 95
Loenersloot Castle ill. 14
London, British Museum nrs. 110, 112, 114
longboat and small gig nrs. 173, 180
Lons, Dirck Eversen p. 10, nrs. 52-56, fig. 52a
Loosjes, Adriaen nr. 32
Loosjes, L. nr. 165
Lopik nr. 126
Loveringh and Allart nrs. 174, 175
Lowestoft, Battle of nrs. 97, 119
lugger nr. 220
Luther nr. 6
Luyken, Caspar nrs. 120, 135, fig. 135a
Luyken, Jan nrs. 119, 120

Maas, River nrs. 98-101, 184, 218; see also under Rotterdam
  Admiralty of nrs. 181, 208
  map of see Geel, Joost van
Maaskamp, Evert nrs. 166, 177, 181
Madrid, Palacio Real nr. 30, fig. 30a
mahona nr. 4
mail packet nrs. 98-101
Malaga nr. 171
Mallegat nr. 184
Mary, Virgin nr. 6
Mary Stuart, Princess of Orange p. 11, ill. 11, nr. 134
Matanzas Bay nr. 57
Maurice, Prince p. 14, ill. 15, nr. 18
  arms of nr. 20
  land yacht of nr. 31
Medea nr. 172
Medemblik nr. 226
  Royal Naval College nr. 226
Mediterranean Sea nrs. 119, 171, 172
Meer, Noach van der nrs. 174, 175
meersschip nr. 2
Mendosa, don Francisco de nr. 31
merchant caravel nr. 4
merchant hooker nr. 224
mermaid nr. 30
Méryon, Charles nr. 244
Messina ill. 8, nrs. 102-06
Meulen, Sieuwert van der pp. 8, 10, nrs. 138-53, 157-63
Meysens, Johannes nrs. 64, 68
Middelburg nr. 12
Mieling, C.W. nrs. 217, 218, 230, 233-36
Minorca nrs. 171, 172
mock sea battle p. 11, nr. 135
Monet, Claude, L'Impression nr. 247
Montaigne see Plattenberg
Mooker Heath nr. 18
Morin, Jean nrs. 60, 61
Moses nr. 21
Mousijn, Michiel nr. 95, fig. 95a
Muller, Frederik p. 10, nr. 11
Munich, Staatliche Graphische Sammlung nr. 50
Muscovite nrs. 21, 135

Naarden ferry nr. 74
nao nrs. 2-4
Navire Royale p. 10, ill. 6
Nederlandsche Etsclub nr. 232
nef nr. 4
nef de bande nrs. 1-3
nef de hautbord nr. 1
Neptune nrs. 63, 110
nereids nr. 110
New Maas River nr. 206
Nicolaas van Loon, Folkert nrs. 191, 194
Nieuwerkerk nr. 243
Nieuwpoort, Battle of nr. 31
night ferries nrs. 86, 87
Nijmegen nrs. 18, 164, 237
Nooms, Reinier pp. 8, 10, 14, 16, ills. 16-18, nrs. 28, 71-94, 137, fig. 137a
Noordholland nrs. 171, 172
North Holland, Province nrs. 33, 83
  ferries serving nr. 157
North Holland Canal nr. 182
North Sea nrs. 27, 33, 119, 198, 241; see also Dogger Bank

Octavian nr. 63
Öland, Battle of nr. 119
Oppijnen nr. 18
Orange, House of p. 11; see also Frederick Henry, Mary, Maurice, William the Silent and William III
Orlers, J. p. 13
Otto, E.J. nr. 33
Overijssel pot nr. 26
Overschie nrs. 206, 231

packet boat nr. 215
Palermo nr. 81
Pampus nr. 182
Paris, Fondation Custodia (Frits Lugt Collection) nr. 25
  Louvre nr. 249
  Petit Palais (Dutuit Collection) nr. 110
Parker, Sir Hyde nr. 169
passage boat p. 20, ill. 20, nrs. 199, 240
Passe II, Crispijn nr. 57
paviljoenjacht nrs. 181, 189, 201
paviljoenpoon nrs. 191, 199
peat boat pp. 9, 20, ill. 19, nrs. 26, 47, 192, 197, 242, 243
Peeters, Bonaventura nrs. 50, 64-68
Peeters, Jan nr. 50
pennant, Spanish nr. 5
Pepys, Samuel nr. 91
Pers, Dirck Pietersz. p. 16
Persian nr. 21
Peter, St. nr. 6
Peter the Great, Tsar p. 11, nr. 135
Petten nr. 31
Philip II nr. 12
Philips, Jan Caspar p. 11, nr. 164
pilot boat nrs. 101, 170, 220
pink p. 22, ill. 29, nrs. 27, 89, 115, 162, 216
piracy see privateer
plaice boat nr. 89
Plancius, Petrus nr. 9

Plantin, Christopher p. 7, nrs. 1-5
Plattenberg, Matthijs van nrs. 60, 61
pleasure craft nrs. 56, 135, 158, 166, fig. 52a
pont nrs. 84, 192
Poot, H.K. p. 15, ill. 17
Porcellis, Jan p. 10, nrs. 24-29
Porto, flag of nr. 3
Portugal, flag of nr. 3
Portuguese nao nr. 3
Postal Map see Geel, Joost van
pot nrs. 26, 84
pram nr. 200
Prince's flag nrs. 19, 110
Prins Willem nrs. 170, 171
privateer, piracy p. 10, nrs. 176, 183, 214 215
Provincial States nrs. 82, 160
Punt, Jan nr. 176
punter nr. 230
Purmer, Lake nrs. 30, 33

Quack, Jacob nr. 98

Rademaker, Abraham p. 13
Ram, Johannes de nrs. 72, 86, 116
Rammekens nr. 12
Reijnst, Vice-Admiral P.H. nrs. 171, 172
Reisz & Co. nr. 232
Rembrandt p. 8, nrs. 62, 63
Requesens nr. 33
Rhine, River nr. 193
Rijneveld, N.A. van nr. 172
Ringels, Klaas nr. 178
Ripa, Cesare p. 16
river gods nr. 164
Rochussen nr. 230
Roghman, Roelant fig. 17a
Roguié nr. 41
Romans nr. 21
Roos, Cornelis Sybille nr. 178
Rotterdam p. 13, nrs. 30, 98, 121-32, 181, 197, 205, 206, 208
  Admiralty depot nrs. 181, 205, 208
  arms of nr. 68
  Boompjes Wharf nr. 205
  Church of St. Lawrence nrs. 181, 205
  East India Company depot nr. 181
  East Oudehoofd Gate nrs. 181, 189
  Feijenoord nr. 208
  ferry serving nrs. 54, 86, 87, 181, 231
  flag of nr. 68
  Katendrecht nrs. 181, 205
  Leuvehaven Docks nrs. 181, 205
  Maas, River nrs. 113, 181, 205
  National or Naval Dockyard see Admiralty depot
  New Maas, River nrs. 189, 208
  Ooster Nieuwehoofd Gate nrs. 184, 205
  Oranjeboom windmill nr. 181
  Oude Haven Docks nrs. 181, 189
  Pelikaan windmill nrs. 181, 205
  Schiedam Gate nr. 181
  Stolk, Atlas van nr. 176
  Town Hall nr. 181
  Westzeedijk nr. 206
  White Gate nr. 181

Rotterdam (cont.)
    windmills on Boerengat and Buizengat nr. 189
Roy, H. le nrs. 41-44
royal yacht nr. 134
Ruyter, Michiel de p. 11, nrs. 81, 95, fig. 95a

Saftleven, Herman p. 13, nrs. 121-32
St. James's Day Battle nr. 119
Sallieth, Matthias de pp. 10, 13, nrs. 178-82
salmon nr. 49
samoreus nr. 193
San Domingo nr. 168
San Salvador nr. 57
Savery, Jacob ill. 17
Scheldt, River p. 7, nrs. 223, 247
Schelfhout, Andreas nrs. 217, 218, 230
Schenk, Petrus nrs. 138-53, 157, 161
Scheveningen nr. 31
Schey, Gillis nr. 135
Schiedam ill. 13
    ferry serving nr. 231
Schiedges, Petrus Paulus nrs. 233, 234
schietschuit nr. 73
Schillemans, Frans ill. 15
Schinkel nr. 17
schokker nrs. 28, 198, 233
Schokland nr. 198
Schoonderloo nr. 206
Schooneveld, Battle of nrs. 97, 119
Schoonhoven nr. 129
Schotel, G.D. nr. 232
Schotel, Johannes Christiaan p. 16, nr. 216
Schotel, Petrus Johannes nr. 232
Schoute(n), Hermanus p. 13, nr. 177
sea battles pp. 7, 10, nrs. 90, 150, 168; see also Actium, Barfleur, Dogger Bank, Downs, Dungeness, Elba, Gibraltar, Kijkduin, Leghorn, Lowestoft, Matanzas, Messina, Nieuwpoort, Öland, Schooneveld, Slaak, St. James's Day, Four Days', Willemstad
sea monsters nr. 10
seasons, the four pp. 13, 14, ill. 14, nrs. 13-16
Segers, Hercules nrs. 8, 45
Seine, River nr. 248
Senefelder, Aloys nr. 216
Serwouter, Pieter p. 11, nr. 21
Seven Provinces, personification of p. 14, ill. 15
Sextroh, Captain I.W. nr. 215
ship of the Church p. 14, nrs. 6, 59
ship of the line nrs. 112, 173, 227
ship compared to a lover p. 14, ill. 17
ship as a symbol of human life pp. 15-16, nr. 59
ship of state p. 14, ill. 15
shipwreck pp. 10-11, nrs. 61, 106, 151, 152, 156, 170-173, 178
shrimper p. 9, nr. 241
Siamese vessels nr. 120
Sibrantsz., Pieter nr. 21
Sichem, Cornelis van fig. 31a
Sicily nr. 4

Silo, Adam nrs. 154-56
Slaak, Battle on the nr. 63
sloop nr. 181
smack pp. 20, 21, ills. 21, 23, nrs. 204, 221, 222
smalschip nrs. 18, 53, 80, 83, 112, 157
snik nrs. 196, 242
snow p. 23, ill. 30
Société des Aquafortistes nrs. 244, 247-50
South American brig nr. 225
Southern Haaks sandbank nr. 170
South Holland, Province of nrs. 29, 83, 84, 86, 191, 194, 197, 243
Spaarndam nrs. 41, 74
    fishing boats nr. 78
Spakenburg p. 13, nrs. 238, 239
Spain p. 7, nrs. 62, 63, 76, 81, 95, 222
Spaniarder nr. 181
Spanish carracks nr. 4
Sperwer, De ill. 7
Speyk, J.C.J. van p. 11, nrs. 228, 229
Speyk, Van nrs. 228, 229
Spilman, Hendrik p. 13
Spinola, Ambrosio da nr. 18
Spion, De nr. 173
Sri Lanka nr. 21
States flag nr. 81
States-General nrs. 82, 111, 114, 134, 160, 171
States yacht nrs. 82, 111, 114, 134, 160
steigerschuit nrs. 55, 137, 158, fig. 137a
Steuerwald & Co., C.H.G. nr. 216
Stevin, Simon nr. 31
storm p. 15, nrs. 50, 60, 67, 106, 151, 152, 171, 172, 175, 178, 211
Stradanus, Johannes nrs. 9, 10, fig. 9a
Streefkerk nr. 132
Sunda, Strait nr. 21
Supreme Maritime Court Martial nr. 170
Swanenburgh, Willem Isaacsz. nr. 31, fig. 31a
Sweden nr. 119

Tartar nr. 21
Texel p. 13, nrs. 83, 171, 178, 182, 183, 240
    arms of nr. 182
Tiel nr. 18
Tienhoven nr. 127
timber carrier ill. 28
timber yard nr. 46
times of day p. 14, nr. 46
tjalk ill. 21
tochtschuit nr. 78
Todos los Sanctos, Battle in the Bay of nr. 57
Tooker, Arthur nrs. 91, 92
Toulon nr. 171
towbarge nrs. 73, 74, 86, 231
transom stern nrs. 2, 56, 82
transom yacht p. 21, ill. 22, nrs. 93, 111, 114, 190, 201
Tromp, Cornelis nrs. 95, 119
Tromp, Maarten Harpertsz. pp. 10, 11, nrs. 81, 95, 119
Turc, Pierre le nr. 214

Urania nr. 226
Utrecht, Province of nr. 242
    ferry serving nr. 73

Valck, Gerard nrs. 24, 25, 90
Vasco da Gama nr. 21
Veere nrs. 12, 107
Velde, Esaias van de p. 13, nr. 41
Velde, Jan van de pp. 8, 14, nrs. 8, 46-51
Velde, Willem van de p. 8
Venice p. 9, nr. 171
Verbaan, Captain Daniël nr. 183
Vianen nr. 121-32
Vinne, Isaak van de nr. 137
Virgins, Holy nr. 6
Visscher, Claes Jansz. pp. 8, 10, 12, nrs. 18-20, 22-36, 46-48, fig. 52a
Visscher, Nicolaas nr. 17
Visscher, Roemer p. 15, nrs. 22, 23
Vlieland nrs. 71, 83
Vlissinger, De nr. 214
Volendam kwak nr. 78
Voskuyl, Dirck Pietersz. nr. 21
Vries Jr., R. de nrs. 240-43
Vrijheid, De nr. 171
Vrijheijt, De nr. 81
Vroom, Hendrick nrs. 12, 50

WA, Monogrammist p. 9, ill. 3, nrs. 1-5
Waal, River nrs. 18, 237
Wadden Zee nrs. 198, 222
Wadden Zee convoy ship nr. 82
Wadden Zee Islands nr. 33
Waddinxveen nr. 243
Wagenaar, Jan nrs. 73, 168, 173, 176
Walcheren nr. 12
Waldberg collection, Wolfegg nr. 37
Waldorp, Antonie nrs. 230, 231
Walpot, Ad. nr. 184
Warmond nr. 196
Wassenaer, Nicolaes van nr. 13
waterschip nr. 19
Weesp, ferry serving nr. 167
well-deck corvette nr. 223

West India Company, yacht of nr. 135
West Indies nr. 176
westlander nr. 242
whales p. 16, nrs. 10, 58, 180
whaling p. 10, nrs. 161, 180
Wieringen, Cornelis Claesz. pp. 8, 14, 15, nrs. 7, 8, 13-16, 41-45, 49-51
Wierix brothers p. 7
wijdschip nrs. 18, 53, 83, 112
William the Silent nr. 68
William III, Stadholder-King p. 11, ill. 10, nrs. 133, 134
Willemstad nr. 68
    flag of nr. 68
Winschoten, W. à nr. 83
Winter, Antonie de nrs. 138-53
Wit, Cornelis de nr. 164
Wit, F. de nrs. 73, 90, 95
With, Witte de nr. 95
Witsen, Nicolaas pp. 10, 17, nrs. 78, 80, 82, 84, 157, 158, 193

yacht nrs. 56, 201, 207
Yk, Cornelis Jansz. van nrs. 120, 197
Yver, P., J. Smit and Son, and F.W. Greebe nrs. 181, 182

Zaandam nrs. 78, 165
Zeeburg Castle nr. 12
Zeeland, Province of nrs. 29, 68, 107, 191, 195, 196, 214, 215
    arms of nrs. 214, 215
    flag of nr. 12
Zeeland passage boat p. 20, ill. 20
Zeelandia nr. 97
Zeeman see Nooms
Zevenhuizen peat ponts nrs. 197, 243
Zierikzee nr. 1
zodiac nrs. 69, 70
Zoutman, Rear-Admiral nr. 169
Zuider Zee nrs. 1, 33, 78, 182, 198, 226, 238
Zwolle nr. 18